Contemporary Wales

Volume 24

CONTEMPORARY WALES

Volume 24

Edited by

Andrew Thompson (University of Glamorgan)
Elin Royles (Aberystwyth University)
Paul Chaney (Cardiff University)

Published on behalf of the University of Wales

Cardiff
University of Wales Press
2011

http://www.uwp.co.uk

British Library Cataloguing in Publication Data
A catalogue record for this book is available from the British Library.

ISBN 978-0-7083-2251-2
e-ISBN 978-0-7083-2252-9
ISSN 0951-4937

Original cover design by Marian Delyth
Cover photograph: © Keith Morris/Photo Library Wales
Printed in Wales by Dinefwr Press, Llandybïe

CONTENTS

FIGURES, MAPS AND TABLES

FIGURES

MAPS

TABLES

CONTRIBUTORS

Simon Brooks is Principal Lecturer in the Glamorgan Business School, University of Glamorgan.

Jane Bryan is based in the Welsh Economy Research Unit at Cardiff Business School, Cardiff University.

Christopher G. A. Bryant is Emeritus Professor of Sociology in the College of Arts and Social Sciences, University of Salford, and was the O'Donnell Lecturer, 2010.

Owen Evans is currently a DBA student at the University of Glamorgan and was formerly Director of Business in the Community, Wales.

Rhian Siân Hodges is a Lecturer in the School of Social Sciences, Bangor University.

Laura McAllister is Professor of Governance at the University of Liverpool and was a member of the Richard Commission (2002).

Marie Navarro is a Research Associate at Cardiff Law School and Chief Researcher to Wales Legislation Online.

Alison Parken is Senior Research Fellow in the School of Social Sciences, Cardiff University, for the EURODITE research programme and a freelance equalities research and policy consultant.

Corinna Patterson is a Lecturer in sociology, Bangor University.

Teresa Rees is a Professor in the School of Social Sciences, Cardiff University. She has recently completed a six-year term of office as Pro Vice Chancellor (Research).

Neil Roche is based in the Welsh Economy Research Unit at Cardiff Business School, Cardiff University.

Diana Stirbu is a Senior Lecturer in the Faculty of Law, Governance and International Relations at London Metropolitan University.

Gerald Taylor is a Senior Lecturer in the Department of Social Sciences at the University of Glamorgan.

1. WELSH-MEDIUM EDUCATION AND PARENTAL INCENTIVES AT THE START OF THE TWENTY-FIRST CENTURY: THE CASE OF THE RHYMNI VALLEY, CAERFFILI

Rhian Siân Hodges

ABSTRACT

Language transmission is at the centre of current language planning strategies in Wales. Indeed, Welsh-medium education, along with the family, community and the workplace, is one of four dominant language transmission spheres. Furthermore, education is currently seen as arguably the most effective language-planning tool for transmitting the Welsh language in Wales. This is especially evident within south east Wales, where there has been a substantial increase in the numbers of Welsh speakers five to fifteen years old according to the 2001 Census. This increase can be largely attributed to the success of Welsh-medium education. Subsequently, the aim of this paper is to decipher the multi-dimensional and complex field of parental education incentives by asking why parents (most non-Welsh-speaking) choose this educational path for their children in the Rhymni Valley, Caerffili. Qualitative in-depth interviews were administered amongst parents from the meithrin (Welsh-medium nursery), primary and secondary school sectors in the Rhymni Valley. The main reasons/ incentives for parents to choose this educational system for their children are cultural, educational, economic and personal. However, it is pertinent to note from the outset that integrative rather than instrumental incentives came to the forefront in this locality. Indeed, cultural reasons dominated the research findings, rather than economic reasons, which featured heavily in past studies such as research by Williams et al. (1978) in the Rhondda. This suggests parents in the Rhymni Valley study were what Watson (1964) calls 'burghers'– they seek Welsh-medium education for their children as they foresee their children's futures living and working in a bilingual Wales. This study is one of the first in a larger corpus of work and addresses the existing lacunae in the field of sociology of education through the medium of Welsh in Wales.

INTRODUCTION

The success of Welsh-medium education, especially within south east Wales, is a much debated topic. It is a matter of public debate and an area of concern for academics and policy makers in Wales alike. Welsh-medium education is seen as an effective language-planning tool for transmitting the Welsh language in Wales, especially within localities with a low social usage of the language. Baker (2004, p. i) emphatically noted that the education system is a 'a major plank in language revitalization and language reversal'. Furthermore, research by Lewis (2006, p. 23) also underlines the value of the Welsh-medium education system for those from a non-Welsh-speaking background, especially as 98 per cent of Welsh-medium pupils across south-east Wales are from this particular linguistic background (including the Rhymni Valley itself).[1] Additionally, research by C. H. Williams (2000, p. 25) describes Welsh-medium education as the main language transmission sphere, especially since the secularization of an increasingly urban and post-industrial society. Indeed, Gruffudd (2000, p. 195) further emphasizes the worth of Welsh-medium education as the only language transmission sphere on the increase in terms of language use amongst the youth of Wales today.

However, it is understood that the educational system is often singlehandedly shouldering the burden of sustaining and preserving the Welsh language in contemporary Wales because of a substantial lack of Welsh transmission in the family in Wales (Welsh Language Board, 1999, p. 2) and a low social usage of the language (Hodges, 2009). Such research in Wales also reflects seminal studies by Joshua Fishman (1991). Indeed, Fishman emotively referred to the education system as the sole 'language rescuer' of minority languages (Bourdieu, 1991, p. 23).

Certainly, a dominant thematic pattern amongst key language-planning academics in Wales is that the Welsh-medium education sector is increasing and developing rapidly across many post-industrial communities of south Wales (Williams and Morris, 2000; C. H. Williams, 2000). Consequently, Welsh-medium education, especially in the south Wales valleys, is a timely and contemporary field of sociological study. Currently, there is a resurgence in this educational system since its establishment over half a century ago. During its infancy, parents fought for Welsh-medium education in the south Wales valleys (Wyn Williams, 2003); the current situation is such that parents are fighting for places in these specific schools. However, a key language-planning dilemma in these Anglicized areas is the paradox between the formal language use of the educational system and the informal language use within the community, as stated by the Welsh Language Board's Youth Strategy (2006, pp. 9–10):

The demand for Welsh-medium education continues, especially in the more Anglicized areas of south Wales, such as Rhondda, Cynon and Rhymni Valleys and in Cardiff, where the community use of Welsh is relatively low.

The aim of this paper, therefore, is to attempt to decipher the complex and multi-dimensional field of parental education incentives and assess, specifically, why parents (mostly non-Welsh-speaking) choose the Welsh-medium education system for their children in the Rhymni Valley. Before turning to the study itself, it is pertinent to state that this is an exciting and challenging period of time for the Welsh language in Wales. The Welsh-medium education system is at the forefront of the current Welsh social policy agenda. Notable developments have been the establishment of the National Curriculum for Wales in 1988 (HMSO, 1988), the Welsh Language Act 1993 (HMSO, 1993) and a commitment to a 'truly bilingual Wales' by the National Assembly. The National Assembly has also stated a further commitment to Welsh-medium education in its publication of the following documents: *The Learning Country* (Welsh Assembly Government, 2001); *Everyone's Language* (Welsh Assembly Government, 2003); *Welsh-Medium Education Strategy* (Welsh Assembly Government, 2010); and the forthcoming Welsh-medium National College (R. Williams, 2009).

2001 Census figures state that there has been a 40.8 per cent increase in the number of children and young people aged five to fifteen years speaking Welsh in Wales in comparison with 1991 Census statistics.[2] Furthermore, there has been a substantial increase in the use of the Welsh language within English-speaking schools in Wales; this is a marked theme since the establishment of the National Curriculum for Wales in 1988. This is now an exciting time to study the Welsh language in Wales, and indeed the Welsh-medium education system in the Rhymni Valley. Aitchison and Carter (2004, p. 2) epitomize the irony of this resurgence: 'the paradox is that the greatest increases had been achieved in those areas where the language had traditionally been the weakest'.

A key thematic pattern is the linguistic decline of young people who have left the Welsh-medium education system (Hodges, 2006, 2009). Policy workers have expressed deep concern regarding the difference between the number of individuals who speak and use minority languages in Wales (Welsh Language Board, 2004) and Europe (Euromosaic Study 1996[3]). Such research raises key language-planning questions, such as that posed by Gruffudd (2000, p. 180): 'is language transmission through education likely to produce future parents who will transmit the language at home?'

The main aim of the Rhymni Valley study is to ask why parents, the majority of whom are non-Welsh-speaking, would choose the Welsh-medium education system within a largely Anglicized area. A plethora of research questions emerged. What was behind parental educational incentives? Had these reasons/ incentives developed and evolved since the establishment of Welsh-medium schools? Is Welsh-medium education, as a language-planning tool, strong enough to sustain the Welsh language within the south Wales valleys in the future? By now, the Welsh-medium education system is more prominent in the communities of the south Wales valleys. This educational choice is no longer considered a 'crusade', and the educational and cultural benefits of the system have been clearly documented (Packer and Campbell, 1997, 2000; Reynolds et al., 1998). With these questions in mind, the objective of this paper is to consider the parental incentives for choosing Welsh-medium education and is an attempt to fill the existing literature gap regarding the contribution of the Rhymni Valley to the research of Welsh-medium education.

STUDY LOCATION

The location of the study is the Rhymni Valley, Caerffili County. The Rhymni Valley is a valley spanning sixteen miles from Rhymni in the north, to Bargod in the centre, and, in the south, to Caerffili. Variable and diverse communities make up the Rhymni Valley and it is pertinent to state that it is not possible to discuss the valley as a uniform and homogeneous community. The Rhymni Valley is located north of Cardiff, with Caerffili only eight miles from Wales's capital city. The Rhymni Valley is only a stone's throw from nearby Rhondda, Taf, Cynon, Sirhywi and Ebwy Valleys and is located at the very centre of the south Wales valleys. Although the area is increasingly Anglicized, the Welsh language was historically prominent in this valley location (S. Rh. Williams, 1998, 2004)

The Rhymni Valley is a prominent part of Caerffili County Borough, formed during 1996 as a result of the reorganization of counties throughout Wales. Caerffili is the fifth largest local authority in Wales with seventy-three coun- cillors representing thirty-three wards (Caerffili County, 2009, p. 9). Caerffili is amongst the counties with the highest numbers of Welsh speakers in south Wales. Table 1.1, compiled by Aitchison and Carter (2004, pp. 38–9) from 2001 Census Data (*http://www.nationalstatistics.co.uk*), states that 27,228 people have an understanding of the Welsh language, but more importantly 13,916 are competent in all three linguistic skills of speaking, reading and writing in Welsh.

Data from the above table clearly show the area has great potential to influ- ence national language policy decisions and Welsh language-planning strategies of the future. The numbers of Welsh speakers in Caerffili have increased since

Table 1.1
Results of Welsh speakers in Caerffili County according to the 2001 Census

Caerffili inhabitants who: (Caerffili population 169,519):	Percentage	Number
Understand oral Welsh only	2.8	4,617
Speak but do not read/write Welsh	1.7	2,814
Speak and read Welsh, but do not write Welsh	0.7	1,095
Speak, read and write Welsh	8.5	13,916
Have other linguistic combinations	2.9	4,786
Understand Welsh (at least one linguistic skill)	16.7	27,228

Source: Aitchison and Carter (2004, pp. 38–9).

the 1991 Census, when approximately 6 per cent, or a little over 9,700 people, spoke Welsh. However, these percentages are relatively low compared with the wider context of Welsh speakers in Wales. What is not mentioned, however, are the numbers of Welsh speakers *using* the Welsh language, which has key language-planning implications for the future of the Welsh language in south Wales.

In line with the increase of Welsh speakers, there has been a significant increase in the numbers of Welsh-medium schools in Caerffili. When Caerffili was officially formed in 1996 there were eight Welsh-medium primary schools and one Welsh-medium comprehensive school in the vicinity. By 2010, there were eleven Welsh-medium primary schools (including Ysgol Gymraeg Penalltau, which opened in September 2009) and one Welsh-medium comprehensive school, with proposed plans for a second located in Caerffili town itself.

The increase in Welsh speakers in the Rhymni Valley can largely be attributed to the success of Welsh-medium education, which reflects the increase in young Welsh speakers in post-industrial south Wales valleys (C. H. Williams, 2000, p. 24). According to the 2001 Census, the highest increases amongst Welsh-speakers were within the five to fifteen years old category. Caerffili experienced a 20.8 per cent increase amongst this age category since the 1991 Census.[4] There has also been a notable increase in the numbers of second-language Welsh speakers in English-medium schools in the area.[5] Table 1.2 notes the increase in the numbers of pupils receiving their education through the medium of Welsh in Caerffili since the establishment of Welsh-medium schools.

The above figures could, however, be misleading, as the numbers in several schools have decreased on account of the opening of new Welsh-medium schools in the valley. According to Caerffili County Borough's Welsh-Medium Education Scheme 2009–2014, during January 2008 there were 29,551 children aged three to eighteen years who received education in Caerffili. Of those,

Table 1.2
Chronology of Welsh-medium education in the Rhymni Valley

Name of school	Opening date	Number on register on opening date	Number on register January 1997	Number on register January 2008
Ysgol y Lawnt	1955	15	148	150
Ysgol Ifor Bach	1961	11	291	166
Ysgol Gilfach Fargod	1963	62	170	158
Ysgol Gymraeg Caerffili	1970	97	324	276
Ysgol Gyfun Cwm Rhymni	1981	156	884	1,195
Ysgol Gymraeg Trelyn	1991	112	164	188
Ysgol Gymraeg Cwm Gwyddon	1992	112	146	157
Ysgol Gymraeg Bro Allta	1993	150	210	284
Ysgol y Castell	1995	120	134	281
Ysgol Bro Sannan	2004	18	Irrelevant	103
Ysgol Gymraeg Cwm Derwen	September 2008	34	Irrelevant	Irrelevant

Source: Caerffili County Borough Council (2009).

16,915 were educated in the primary sector, 12,513 in the secondary sector and 123 within the special educational needs sector. In Caerffili County Borough, 12.7 per cent of primary school pupils and 10.6 per cent of secondary school pupils received their education through the medium of Welsh whilst 3.3 per cent of pupils who had special educational needs also received their education though the medium of Welsh (Caerffili County Borough Council, 2009).

AIMS AND OBJECTIVES OF THE STUDY

The aim of this research is to collect, assess and interpret the main educational incentives of non-Welsh speaking parents choosing Welsh-medium education for their children in the Rhymni Valley. The objective of the study is to assess opinions and perceptions of a sample of parents in relation to the local Welsh-medium education system – a system they have chosen for their children. In order to successfully achieve these aims and objectives, the target group are parents from the *meithrin* (Welsh-medium nursery), primary and secondary Welsh-medium sectors. This research uses parents as the target group as they have been instrumental to the establishment of Welsh-medium education in south east Wales.

Furthermore, it is hoped that the study can re-asses and re-evaluate parental incentives for Welsh-medium education three decades on from Williams et al.'s

(1978) seminal research on bilingual education in the Rhondda. Indeed, it is pertinent to decipher whether a clear attitudinal shift has established during this period of time or whether parents still value the same incentives as previous generations. The importance of this research in the Rhymni Valley is evident as a clear literature gap emerged in the field of parental incentives and Welsh-medium education in the Rhymni Valley. The aim of the research is to fill an existing literature gap and inform future language-planning and policy decisions.

THEORETICAL UNDERPINNING

The main theoretical underpinning of the Rhymni Valley study was based on research by Williams et al. (1978) in the Rhondda, where Watson's (1964) concept of parents as 'burghers' and 'spiralists' was adapted to bilingual education in the locality. The focus of the research was the status and prestige of bilingual education and how it offered its pupils higher social mobility and key resources to succeed within their specific language-based communities, possibly reminiscent of Bourdieu's 'class habitus' (1987).

Williams et al. (1978) distinguished between parents as 'burghers' or 'spiralists' depending on their preferred language of education for their children. 'Burghers' were parents who valued learning the Welsh language because they envisaged their children's futures in Wales and thought they would benefit occupationally from speaking Welsh. However, 'spiralists' were parents with largely European perspectives who valued learning what they deemed 'useful' European languages such as French, Spanish and German. Their children's futures would most definitely involve a life outside Wales and its language was therefore deemed unnecessary. Williams et al. suggest that parents' economic aspirations for their children, such as entry to the 'minority language economy' (C. H. Williams 2000, p. 120), are the most important factors in selecting Welsh-medium education. This seminal study is used to compare the development and evolvement of parental educational incentives over the last quarter of a century in the south Wales valleys.

Bourdieu's concept of 'cultural capital' (Bourdieu and Passeron, 1974) was also drawn on when discussing parental incentives and Welsh-medium education in the Rhymni Valley. According to Bourdieu (1987), 'cultural capital' can be defined as the skills, knowledge and information, education and essential advantages that individuals possess in order to gain a higher hierarchical and cultural status within society. Bourdieu distinguishes three distinctive forms of cultural capital. The first involves a state of incorporation which includes the forming and shaping of an individual, including the way in which they process thoughts (through the process of socialization). The second form involves the possession of specific possessions or artefacts owned by the individual, such as musical instruments or works of art. Indeed, it could be argued that these assets originate from an individual's 'habitus', a set of 'dispositions' according to Bourdieu (1990, p. 13). The third type of cultural capital is linked to specific institutions focused on academic educational attainment (Bourdieu, 1986), which could be useful when discussing parents' education motivations.

Parents transmit 'cultural capital' to their children by providing the essential cultural information needed to succeed in the educational system and within the larger society. It could be argued that parents who choose Welsh-medium education in the Rhymni Valley are in fact recreating and reproducing this 'cultural capital' for their children. Parents transmitted a unique Welsh-language 'cultural capital' to their children in order for them to succeed in the system and to gain access to a wider culturally and linguistically orientated community. Parents wanted their children to possess higher social and cultural mobility and placed a value and prestige on the educational system in order to achieve this. However, this is possibly less evident today.

It could be said that these specific forms of cultural capital are closely associated with the individual's relationship with the labour market, which could possibly highlight the significant number of Welsh-speaking professionals from higher social classes in society who chose Welsh-medium education in the Rhymni Valley during its establishment (Khleif, 1974, 1980; Bush, 1979; Bush et al., 1981). Moreover, Bourdieu (1991) states that education is indeed classed as a tool to drive the norms, values and power of the higher classes in society. It is pertinent to note here, however, that this was not the case for all communities in the Rhymni Valley during the establishment of Welsh-medium education.

A more worthwhile use of 'cultural capital' in relation to the Rhymni Valley study is that 'cultural capital' is also heavily associated with cultural and social prestige (Baker and Brown, 2009). Bourdieu himself (1986, p. 248) claims that education is defined as a 'certificate of cultural competence'. Essentially, pupils require educational success in order to gain a prominent status within the cultural hierarchy of society. This could possibly explain parents' motives for choosing Welsh-medium education in the Rhymni Valley. Their children were granted access to specific cultural practices and social networks of language communities not available unless they possessed knowledge of the Welsh language gained through education. Parents' identity-based motives were closely linked with the idea of Welsh-medium education providing 'cultural competence' for their children, especially for non-Welsh-speaking families within a largely non-Welsh-speaking locality.

Indeed, it could be argued that Welsh-medium education in the Rhymni Valley afforded like-minded parents membership of a common interest group or community where shared norms and values in relation to Welsh-medium education were upheld. This particular Welsh-medium education community could be likened to any minority language community as it valued similar cultural practices and unique behavioural patterns. According to Fishman (1991, p. 26):

> To really know a language well, one must know its associated culture (indeed even the history of that culture) ... as well as the cultural specifics and behavioural goals ... every bit as much as it is necessary to know the associated language if one wants to know a culture well.

Furthermore, Walliman (2006, p. 15) recognizes that these united and symbolic meanings divulge some deep and rich social data. A key example is local parents protesting for the establishment of Welsh-medium schools through staging 'sit-ins' in disused English-medium schools and lobbying petitions to the local authority (Jones and Richards, 2003).

METHODOLOGY

The Rhymni Valley study draws upon the interpretative perspective epitomized by Max Weber. The purpose and function of sociological research according to this perspective is to understand individuals within society in order to understand society at large rather than researching the society in order to understand the individuals within it. Roth and Wittich (1968, p. 14) emphasize this very point: 'for sociological purposes, there is no such thing as a collective personality which "acts"'. According to Weber (1964), we should understand social acts by studying the deep and complex meanings and incentives behind social behaviour. This philosophical standpoint is used effectively to gain insights into the incentives of parents choosing Welsh-medium education in the Rhymni Valley.

This qualitative study drew on rich social data gathered from fifty in-depth interviews with parents of the Welsh-medium *meithrin* (Welsh-medium nursery), primary and secondary school sectors in the Rhymni Valley. A sample of parents was successfully gathered from communities throughout the Rhymni Valley based on differing linguistic and socio-economic backgrounds. Consequently, linguistic background distinctions were made: 'non-Welsh-speaking' (families where neither parent spoke Welsh); 'mixed-language families' (families where one parent spoke Welsh and the other spoke English or another language); and 'Welsh-language families' (families where both parents spoke Welsh). Owing to the linguistic composition of this particular location, the vast majority of parents belonged were non-Welsh-speaking. This qualitative research strategy is significant in order to reflect the passion, enthusiasm and strong viewpoints of parents in relation to Welsh-medium education in the Rhymni Valley. Participants were afforded opportunities to elaborate upon their views in a dynamic style which adequately reflected the nature of the research field whilst adhering to strict ethical guidelines of the Data Protection Act (1998), The British Sociological Association and Bangor University Ethics Committee.

PRIMARY DATA RESULTS

The main focal point of this research is to assess parents' reasons/incentives for choosing Welsh-medium education for their children in the Rhymni Valley. NVivo 2 was used to code the main primary research patterns. Four main categories of reasons/incentives emerged from the primary research; these were cultural, educational, economic and personal reasons. A diverse set of complicated and interesting reasons emerged and the main primary data results are collated in the tables below.

As Table 1.3 indicates, parents from the Rhymni Valley chose Welsh-medium education for their children mainly for cultural reasons. Half the sample chose cultural reasons as their main Welsh-medium education incentive. The second reason, discussed by a little over a third of the parents, was educational reasons, whereas only 8 per cent chose economic and personal reasons. As well as their main reasons, participants were asked to state their top three reasons. The second and third reasons appear in Tables 1.4 and 1.5.

Table 1.4 shows that almost half the sample chose educational reasons as their second reason for choosing the Welsh-medium education system whilst a little under a third of parents chose cultural reasons. Of the sample, 12 per cent did not have a second reason whilst only 8 per cent and 4 per cent chose economic and personal reasons, respectively.

Furthermore, the research participants in the Rhymni Valley study were also asked to state their third reasons for choosing Welsh-medium education and data from Table 1.5 state that their third most prominent reason was economic; however, a fifth of participants did not have a third reason, 16 per cent chose

Table 1.3
Main reasons/incentives for Welsh-medium education in the Rhymni Valley

Main reason/incentive	Percentage	Number
Cultural	50	25
Educational	34	17
Economic	8	4
Personal	8	4

Table 1.4
Second main reasons/incentives for Welsh-medium education in the Rhymni Valley

Second reason	Percentage	Number
Educational	46	23
Cultural	30	15
None	12	5
Economic	8	4
Personal	4	2

Table 1.5
Third main reasons/incentives for Welsh-medium education in the Rhymni Valley

Third reason	Percentage	Number
Economic	56	28
None	20	10
Educational	16	8
Cultural	8	4

educational reasons and 8 per cent chose cultural reasons. These data highlight the complex and multi-layered nature of the Rhymni Valley primary research data. The main parental reasons and incentives are discussed in more detail below.

CULTURAL REASONS

The main reasons parents chose Welsh-medium education for their children in the Rhymni Valley were cultural, which reflects research conducted by Lyon (1996) on Anglesey and Thomas (2007) in south east Wales. Moreover, 50 per cent ($n = 25$) of the sample chose cultural reasons, which disproves the hypothesis based on research by Williams et al. (1978) which noted economic reasons. Participants emphasized cultural themes such as the 'lost generation', the intrinsic value of speaking Welsh, the importance of roots and belonging, culture and nationhood, and integrating to the valleys communities as described below.

Cultural identity
Welsh cultural identity emerged as a key primary research theme. This was mostly prominent amongst non-Welsh-speaking parents (40 per cent of the parents who chose cultural reasons as a main incentive). This result suggests patriotism towards Wales and its cultural identity, as stated by a non-Welsh-speaking mother with children in the secondary sector:[6]

I just wanted it, I'm Welsh, they are Welsh and I just wanted them to speak Welsh ... my children didn't have to wear a tall black hat, a woollen shawl and a pleated skirt to prove they are Welsh ... all they have to do is to open their mouths. (Interview 32, ll. 237–42)

This unique culture, identity and idea of nationhood was stipulated further by participants because Welsh-medium education, according to parents, promoted a specifically Welsh identity rather than a global, generic identity. The following statement from a non-Welsh-speaking mother[7] emphasizes the importance of sustaining a truly Welsh identity:

They go to the Urdd and there's Santes Dwynwen, other people have never heard of it, but our children have been brought up with the Welsh feel to their lives. With Sky TV, they are brought up as little Americans so I think it's lovely that they've got the Welsh culture when they go to school. (Interview 56, ll. 142–9)

Proud to be Welsh: belonging and heritage
A significant number of research participants upheld patriotic tendencies. Indeed, this could be a useful tool in defining and interpreting what it means to be a south Walian non-Welsh-speaking individual. According to a non-Welsh-speaking father with children in the secondary sector:

You get a sense of being proud when you hear them speaking Welsh, you feel immensely proud that they can do it and I love to hear them speak it. (Interview 36, ll. 322–3)

A number of parents thought their children should learn, use and appreciate their mother tongue and they emphasized Welsh roots and belonging. 'Welsh' and 'living in Wales' were clear identity markers here. Welsh-medium education was a natural choice for some, as stated by a non-Welsh-speaking mother with children in the secondary sector:

It is important for our children to learn their own language, they are born in Wales, they are Welsh, and have the opportunity to learn, speak and use Welsh. (Interview 4, ll. 99–101)

Intrinsic value of speaking Welsh
The intrinsic value of the ability to speak Welsh was a clear cultural reason for many; 35 per cent of the sample chose this as their main reason). Parents spoke about how the 'language itself is good for them to learn' (Interview 34, ll. 36–7), which reflects research by Bush et al. (1981) and Thomas (2007) but diverges

from research by Williams et al. (1978) that notes the economic value of Welsh. The majority of participants did not feel the need to justify their educational choice. According to a father[8] from a mixed-language background:[9]

> I would have chosen Welsh education for them anyway. It was always my first choice. I believe it's worth speaking Welsh in itself (Interview 2, ll. 314–15)

Certain parents, such as the following 'mixed-language' father with children in the secondary sector,[10] wanted their families to be first-language Welsh-speaking families and therefore hoped Welsh-medium education would help create this:

> I would like us to be a Welsh-speaking family. I'm a proud nationalist and I would like my children to be nationalists ... I think Welsh people should, whenever possible, learn and speak Welsh, and anyone who comes here should do the same. (Interview 49, ll. 86–90)

The 'lost generation'

The majority of non-Welsh-speaking parents in the Rhymni Valley study were not afforded the choice to learn Welsh; theirs was a lost generation. A quarter of the sample stated this as their main cultural reason for choosing Welsh-medium education. A non-Welsh-speaking mother[11] from the secondary education sector noted that her childhood embarrassment ultimately influenced her educational choice for her children:

> When I was about ten I remember meeting all these people on holidays and I couldn't speak any Welsh. I just felt that was so wrong. I felt, how can I say that I'm from Wales and I can't speak my own language? (Interview 21, ll. 7–10)

As a part of the lost generation, a number of parents were inspired to give their children the chance to learn Welsh, a chance that clearly eluded themselves as children, as noted by a Welsh learner with children in the secondary sector:[12]

> I wanted them to have the opportunities I missed out on – that they could speak Welsh naturally as children. (Interview 7, ll. 169–70)

The lost generation was also a powerful tool, inciting parents, especially those from mixed-language households, to learn Welsh themselves. A multitude of adult learners were aware of the close-knit Welsh-speaking community and social networks that had eluded them as children. The following comment by an adult Welsh learner, who is now head teacher at a local Welsh-medium school in the valley,[13] epitomizes this deep sense of regret:

I wanted them to have what I missed out on, the culture, the commitment, the intense feeling of belonging to a close Welsh-speaking community ... and also to give them the opportunity that Mum and Dad weren't brave enough to give me. (Interview14, ll. 72–5)

An equal opportunity for Welsh and English in Wales

A significant proportion of the parents referred to the importance of learning to speak Welsh, 'the mother tongue' or *mam iaith* (Interview 3, l. 13) in Wales. They strived for equality between Welsh and English and did not consider Welsh a 'minority language' compared with English. This viewpoint was emphasized by a non-Welsh-speaking mother with children in the secondary sector:

> we believe it is important for our children to learn their own language, they are born in Wales, they are Welsh, and have the opportunity to learn, speak Welsh and use it, not as a backup language, but as a language side by side to English ... we don't want the language to die out. (Interview 4, ll. 99–102)

It is possible such comments suggest a subconscious reference to principles of the 1993 Welsh Language Act, which called for an equal treatment of the Welsh and English languages within the public sector in Wales (HMSO, 1993). A case in point is that a significant number of the sample stated that Wales had received unfair treatment from England in the past and that speaking Welsh was in fact a way of showing ownership of unique aspects of the Welsh culture and traditions (Interview 13, ll. 266–9).

A natural choice for Welsh-speaking parents

100 per cent (*n* = 2) of Welsh-speaking parents within the sample stated that Welsh-medium education in the Rhymni Valley was a natural choice for their children (however, we need to recognize the small sample size). One of the main reasons mixed-language parents chose the system for their children was that the Welsh language is an integral part of their personality; this emphasizes thematic patterns from research by Packer and Campbell (1997). A Welsh-speaking mother with children in the secondary sector elaborates upon this point:[14]

> This was the natural choice for us. I received my education through the medium of Welsh ... both of us taught through the medium of Welsh, Welsh is our first language ... it would have been totally unnatural for us to even contemplate English-medium education. (Interview 11, ll. 218–24)

Welsh language learners also valued Welsh-medium education highly. A significant proportion wanted to transmit the Welsh language to their children. As one learner (who is now a Welsh-medium teacher) noted: 'I didn't think for a second about sending them through the English-medium sector, I can speak Welsh' (Interview 24, ll. 88–9). Fundamentally, a number of past pupils wanted to be able to speak Welsh with their children (often something their own parents could never do), and therefore this educational choice was a natural one for them (Interview 12, ll. 38–49). Interestingly, a pattern emerged amongst non-Welsh-speaking parents as they chose Welsh-medium education as a 'natural *cultural* choice', rather than a 'natural *linguistic* choice'.

EDUCATIONAL REASONS

Educational reasons were the second most popular incentive for parents to choose Welsh-medium education in the Rhymni Valley research sample. A little over a third (34 per cent, $n = 17$) of parents stated that educational reasons were the most important incentive when choosing an appropriate educational system for their children. Parents' incentives can be grouped accordingly, academic standards, good reputation, a better education, pastoral care, discipline, bilingual advantages, lower class sizes, and commitment of parents and teachers respectively. These are discussed in further detail below.

Educational standards and academic excellence

Educational and academic excellence was the main featured educational incentive in the Rhymni Valley study. Moreover, 60 per cent of those who chose educational reasons stated educational standards as the main component of the reason. A mixed-language father with children in the secondary sector stated that a 'better standard of education is the main reason' (Interview 49, ll. 85), a finding which consolidates research by Reynolds et al. (1998) that highlights the academic excellence of Welsh-medium schools. According to some parents, the success of Welsh-medium education was unparalleled within the Rhymni Valley, which further emphasizes research by Reynolds et al. (1998) and by Packer and Campbell (1997, 2000) respectively. This was especially true of non-Welsh-speaking parents within the Rhymni Valley study. Non-Welsh-speaking parents prioritized educational reasons/incentives, whilst Welsh-speaking parents prioritized cultural reasons/incentives for choosing this particular educational system. Linguistic background, to an extent, was a contributory factor. Contrary to belief, academic excellence was the main incentive according to a number of parents who showed nationalistic tendencies:

> If the education at Welsh-medium schools was not up to scratch, she would have gone to an English-medium school. She would have learnt Welsh in another way, like I did. (Interview 47, ll. 255–7)

Estyn Inspection reports were also a consideration factor when choosing Welsh-medium education (Interview 17, l. 83). It was almost as if impressive inspection reports justified this educational choice for non-Welsh-speaking parents.

Good reputation of Welsh-medium schools and their teachers
Traditionally, Welsh-medium schools have received a good reputation as schools providing an all-round education for their pupils. Certainly, there was staunch evidence of the good reputation of Welsh-medium schools in the Rhymni Valley and this good reputation spread by word of mouth amongst the research participants. A comment by a non-Welsh-speaking mother from the *meithrin* (Welsh-medium nursery) sector emphasizes this: 'I haven't heard a bad thing about it!' (Interview 47, ll. 55–6). A number of participants referred to the positive reputation of the local Welsh-medium comprehensive school as noted by a non-Welsh-speaking father with children in the primary sector:[15]

> The feedback about the Welsh-medium comprehensive school is very positive. In terms of the quality of education, what we've heard and what we've seen is a good standard. We are looking forward to him attending this school. (Interview 55, ll. 78–80)

A significant proportion of the research sample referred to the influence of specific nursery assistants, teachers and head teachers in choosing Welsh-medium education for their children (Interview 19, ll. 29–31). Furthermore, the value and influence of 'Mudiad Ysgolion Meithrin' and the 'Ti a Fi' ('You and Me') playgroups were evident amongst the sample of parents. A non-Welsh-speaking mother with children in the primary sector describes the following:

> One of the main reasons really was the Welsh-medium playgroup, 'Ti a Fi'. She made a good group of friends up there and I made a good group of friends there too so it just really progressed from there. (Interview 59, ll. 70–3)

'A better education'
There was a consensus amongst the research sample that Welsh-medium education in the Rhymni Valley offered a better education than English-medium education, which confirms research by Thomas (2007). However, this was the opinion of individuals within the research sample and it is important to state that this research was not a comparative study. It is mainly non-Welsh-speaking and certain mixed-language parents who expressed these views, which runs counter to research by Khleif (1974, 1980) which stated parents from Welsh-language backgrounds held this view. It was possible that Welsh-medium education offered higher social mobility for its pupils, a finding which reflects research on bilingual education in the Rhondda by Williams et al. (1978).

Moreover, parents defined 'Mudiad Ysgolion Meithrin' as a 'better education' in relation to offering a bilingual education for their children. It is possible that language policy drives within education by bodies such as the Welsh Language Board and their specific programmes such as TWF (Transfer of Welsh in Families) have entered the subconscious of some of parents from the *meithrin* sector. This is confirmed by a non-Welsh-speaking mother with children in that sector, who said that it offered 'a better start, at the end of the day. What do we want for our children, but the best?' (Interview 46, l. 90). Furthermore, a number of Welsh-medium education past pupils stated that Welsh-medium education offered 'a better education, it is a family-orientated education' (Interview 1, ll. 281–4). Elitist tendencies were also evident amongst a minority of parents. Such parents stated they chose the Welsh-medium education system simply because it was a better education system. Such beliefs echo similar comments made in research by Williams et al. (1978, p. 201) in the Rhondda, where certain parents demonstrated 'a belief in the superiority of bilingual education'.

Further evidence of elitist attitudes was found. Research participants drew comparisons between Welsh-medium education and the private education system, which confirms research by Packer and Campbell (1997) in Cardiff. A non-Welsh-speaking mother with children in the secondary sector elaborates upon this:[16]

> It's almost like having a public school education in the national system ... the teachers' discipline and expectations are immense, they strive for only the best results. (Interview 30, ll. 56–8)

Claimed failings of local English-medium schools

The purpose of this extended study was not to compare the Welsh-medium education sector with the English-medium education sector, therefore the following claims were made purely as comments from the research participants during primary data collection. However, as local schools are mainly English-medium it was somewhat natural for the research participants to make the comparison between the two education systems.

A certain proportion viewed English-medium schools as impersonal institutions compared with the close-knit environment of Welsh-medium education. A clear theme amongst participants was that Welsh-medium education offered a broad spectrum of extracurricular activities not offered by English-medium education. A mother from a mixed-language background stated that Welsh-medium schools:

> offer more activities during school time and after, there are more school concerts, cultural activities like Eisteddfodau, well more of everything really. (Interview

1, ll. 285–7)

However, according to non-Welsh-speaking parents, the main reason they chose Welsh-medium education was to give their children the chance to learn Welsh. Fundamentally, they did not think this would be possible if they sent their children through the English-medium system. Indeed, such parents wanted their children to learn Welsh as a language on an equal footing with English, rather than as an 'extra' second language. Moreover, parents wanted their children to learn more than 'a second-language smattering of Welsh' (Interview 42, l. 23) within an English-medium school. Some parents (mainly non-Welsh-speaking) viewed learning the Welsh language as a 'qualification in its own right' (Interview 34, ll. 29–30) and stated this as a benefit not associated with English-medium education.

Bilingual advantages
The bilingual advantages of Welsh-medium education and speaking Welsh were an evident primary research pattern. This finding is similar to research conducted by Thomas (2007), who states that the main reason why parents choose Welsh-medium education in south east Wales is the desire for their children to become bilingual.

A percentage of research participants stated that bilingualism was a respected addition to any CV and held prestige within the workplace (Interview 32, ll. 262–5). Furthermore, parents thought the ability to speak Welsh would benefit their children's language skills in English too – encouraging a wider occupation and language flexibility. Parents believed that bilingual transferable skills would be advantageous for learning other languages, which reinforces research by Baker and Prys Jones (1998). According to a mixed-language mother with children in the secondary sector:

> the advantage they then have in learning other languages is quite marked. That moving on from a second language to a third and a fourth seems a lot more natural than moving on from being a monolingual English speaker. (Interview 6, ll. 37–40)

Pastoral care and discipline
Parents stated that 'pastoral care' and an 'expected level of discipline and structure' were key incentives in choosing the Welsh-medium education system (Interview 17, ll. 123–4). Pastoral care was of paramount importance, especially as the majority of parents were non-Welsh-speaking themselves. According to a mixed language mother with children in the primary sector, 'there's a personal

and family-orientated vibe in Welsh-medium schools' (Interview 1, ll. 279–89). The strong community and social Welsh-medium networks were an increasing influence and parents wanted their children to be a part of a strong, culturally driven local network. Increasingly evident amongst non-Welsh-speaking parents was the 'welcoming nature' of Welsh-medium schools (Interview 47, ll. 42–3). The favourable treatment of non-Welsh-speaking parents was an area especially commented upon by the research sample. This viewpoint was emphasized by a non-Welsh-speaking mother with children in the Welsh-medium primary education:

> We were very worried because neither of us could speak Welsh and nobody in the family spoke Welsh but they explained the situation to us non-Welsh speakers and they took the fear out of the situation. Teachers showed us simple ways we could help our children practise Welsh phrases at home and they also helped us tackle homework in Welsh too. (Interview 47, ll. 44–5).

Discipline was also a key factor in making the choice. Parents in the research sample stated they believed Welsh-medium education had a clear structure and emphasized discipline not too dissimilar to old local grammar schools. Discipline was closely associated with the unique ethos that belonged to Welsh-medium schools and how they successfully transmitted the Welsh-language to children from non-Welsh-speaking homes. The following comment from a non-Welsh-speaking father with children in the primary sector accentuates these feelings:[17]

> there seemed to be a nice feeling like an old grammar school and they seemed to still have all the old values and traditions there; you could tell there was good discipline in the school. (Interview 59, ll. 82–5)

ECONOMIC REASONS

The third most popular reason parents chose Welsh-medium education in the Rhymni Valley was economic. The third most popular reason parents chose Welsh-medium education in the Rhymni Valley was economic as 8 per cent (*n* = 4) stated this as their main reason. However, parents placed varied importance and significance on economic reasons. The majority mentioned economic reasons as a benefit and a bonus of the Welsh-medium education system rather than the main incentive for choosing the system. Moreover, economic benefits of the system were often used to justify non-Welsh-speaking parents' educational choice (mainly if there was animosity regarding the decision). Ultimately, economic reasons were not the main educational incentive amongst research participants, which disproves the original hypothesis based on research by Williams et al. (1978). The parents who prioritized economic benefits thought Welsh-medium education would provide better future labour market opportunities for their children. Their educational choices were far-reaching ones on an individual level as they wanted to invest in their children's future. It is pertinent here to draw upon research by Williams et al. (1978) that uses the term 'burghers' for parents choosing bilingual education for their children; they value the Welsh language, as they see their children's future as living and working in Wales. Bilingual education is therefore used as a tool to improve social mobility.

Indeed, economic reasons included the following themes: 'better employment', 'work anywhere in Wales', 'bilingual advantages in the workplace', 'better opportunities', 'National Assembly for Wales' vision of creating a truly bilingual Wales'. Themes concerning economic incentives will now be discussed in further detail.

A truly bilingual Wales: better occupations and chances

The main economic reasons were for better and more varied occupations for their children in the future. A non-Welsh-speaking mother with children in the primary sector stated Welsh-medium education gave her children a clear advantage:

> The main reason was to give them an advantage in life ... I wanted better for my children ... I think they'll benefit in job prospects. (Interview 13, ll. 171, 172–3, 75)

Moreover, a mixed-language mother described the bilingual benefits of Welsh-medium higher education:

> The main reason for me is that my children will have further and extended opportunities when they're older if they speak two languages ... the Welsh language has opened so many doors for so many people in this area. I would not have got my job had I not been able to speak Welsh; it gives you that edge in the labour market. (Interview 3, ll. 310–13, 325–30)

The economic advantages of bilingualism

The research sample also referred to the economic advantages associated with bilingualism. A significant proportion of parents were of the opinion that bilingual children had clear and marked advantages over monolingual children. A non-Welsh-speaking mother stated that the ability to speak Welsh was highly valued within workplaces in Wales and that Welsh was an excellent addition to her children's CVs (Interview 7, ll. 183–5). Parents also discussed the present poor economic climate and stressed the importance of the Welsh language as a vital advantage during these difficult times. According to a non-Welsh-speaking mother with children in the secondary sector:

> I always felt that if they came out of school with the same qualifications as a person from the English school, because they were bilingual they'd have a better chance of getting employment, especially during these difficult times. (Interview 21, ll. 64–7)

PERSONAL REASONS

The fourth main incentive for choosing Welsh-medium education in the Rhymni Valley was personal reasons or reasons best described as wanting to belong to Welsh-medium family/community/social network. Some 8 per cent (*n* = 4) chose these particular reasons. As the primary data results show, only a small number of parents noted this reason; however, this discovery has a wider significance. Indeed, along with integrative (the desire to assimilate to a particular linguistic community) and instrumental (the desire to possess social mobility such as by passing an examination) incentives for learning a language (Gardner and Lambert, 1972) it can be argued that learning could also mean expressing a personal identity (Crookes and Schmidt, 1991). These particular reasons are discussed below.

Partner/extended family are Welsh-speaking

Certain parents chose Welsh-medium education for their children because their extended families were Welsh speakers (Interview 43, ll. 31–2). Welsh-medium education was indeed a natural choice for Welsh speakers, which reflects research by Packer and Campbell (1997). According to a non-Welsh-speaking father with children in the primary and secondary sector:

> My wife has been educated through Welsh-medium education. She was the driving force behind sending the children through Welsh-medium education, I supported that, and I'm a passionate Welsh man. (Interview 20, ll. 12–14)

Interestingly, a number of parents reported that their siblings had attended Welsh-medium education even though they themselves did not. Following this, they seemed even more determined to send their own children to local Welsh-medium schools.

Influence of friends

The influence of friends was evident within the primary data results. Friends were a huge influence on other parents opting to send their children to Welsh-medium schools in the Rhymni Valley. This influence was at its strongest amongst non-Welsh-speaking parents in the target group. A number of such parents turned to friends for advice and support when choosing an educational system for their children, as noted by a non-Welsh-speaking father from the centre of the Rhymni Valley:

> My very good friends went to the Welsh school; I spoke to them about it and sought advice. My one friend who works at the BBC said he had carved out a very good career for himself due to Welsh-medium education. (Interview 55, ll. 105–8)

Friends' children attending Welsh-medium schools was clearly a strong influence on parents, especially those within the local *meithrin* sector (Interview 15, ll. 17–18). The 'Ti a Fi' groups also proved very influential as they created well-established parent social networks and certain parents chose Welsh-medium education for their children en masse as a group of committed friends who created a clear support network for each other. According to a non-Welsh-speaking mother from the secondary sector:, 'we all decided to send our children to the Welsh school together at the same time' (Interview 60, ll. 56–8). 'Ti a Fi' groups were also influential as these introduced parents to the Welsh-medium sector in an informal yet enthusiastic manner (Interview 47, ll. 42–6).

CONCLUSION

Primary data findings from the Rhymni Valley study state that parents' motives for choosing Welsh-medium education form a plethora of complex and varied reasons. What can be gleaned from the evidence is that Welsh-medium education in the Rhymni Valley is largely a well-respected and supported educational system. It could also be said that the system is hoped to be a successful language-planning tool for the future development of the Welsh language in south Wales. This study corroborates the success of this educational system, largely due to the faith and commitment of non-Welsh-speakers in the valley.

Cultural reasons (rather than educational, economic and personal reasons) were the main incentives for choosing Welsh-medium education in the Rhymni Valley. This result has a positive effect on the development of the Welsh language on a micro level (Rhymni Valley) and on a macro level (Wales). This finding could also possibly impact upon reversing Welsh language shift (Fishman, 1991) in the locality.

This primary data finding contradicts research by Williams et al. (1978) which alludes to economic reasons as the primary incentives for parents choosing bilingual education for their children in the Rhondda. However, the emphasis on culture, identity and nationhood in the Rhymni Valley study (Hodges, 2010) suggests parents are increasingly aware that their educational choices could have far-reaching cultural implications for the Welsh language itself. Interestingly, simply because both sets of incentives were present during both studies, this could be viewed as a shift from economic to culture-based incentives, rather than a reversal. In the case of the Rhymni Valley this shift is particularly pertinent as integrative incentives were strongest within these communities. In discussing the varied incentives for learning a language, it could be argued that an integrative incentive of choosing a language can be more effective than an instrumental incentive in the long term (Crookes and Schmidt, 1991; Ellis, 1997)).

To conclude, it is perhaps pertinent to offer an explanation for the shift from economic reasons, so prominent in Williams et al.'s seminal research in the Rhondda in 1978, to the focus on culture and identity-based incentives within the Rhymni Valley study (Hodges, 2010). There are many factors which could have contributed to this prominent shift in attitude during the last thirty years and, whilst it impossible to provide definitive answers, we can suggest some reasons. The development of the National Curriculum following the Education Reform Act (HMSO, 1988) and indeed more specifically the development of 'Y Cwricwlwm Cymreig' (the Welsh dimension of the curriculum; Estyn, 2006) could also offer an insight into this heightened awareness of Welsh identity and respect for the Welsh language with the education system in Wales. The Welsh Language Act (1993) also called for equality between Welsh and English within the public sector in Wales, securing a higher status for the Welsh language. Undoubtedly, the political landscape today in Wales is rather different from that of the late 1970s when Wales said 'no' to devolution. Wales is now a country with devolved powers since the establishment of the National Assembly for Wales in 1999 and it could be argued that there is a heighted sense of Welsh identity since this development. This could reflect the shift in the attitudes and perceptions of the Welsh language amongst parents in the Rhymni Valley at the start of the twenty-first century. Certainly, looking to the future, this could be an important result when planning the growth and development of Welsh-medium education in Wales.

NOTES

1   HMI Ysgol Gyfun Cwm Rhymni 2004, *http://www.cwmrhymni.com/newyddion/ Hanes%20yr%20arolwg.htm* (accessed 1 May 2010): 'Although 99% of the pupils come from a non-Welsh-speaking background, the success of the school is notable in securing to a large degree a strong feeling of Welshness amongst pupils of the school'.

2   2001 Census: The Main Statistics about the Welsh Language, *http://www.byig-wlb. org.uk/english/publications/pages/publicationitem.aspx?puburl=%2fenglish%2fpu blications%2fpublication 332.doc (accessed 4 May 2010).*

3   *http://www.uoc.edu/euromosaic/web/homean/index1.html* (accessed 10 September 2008).

4   Since 1991 Census, there has been an increase of 20.8 per cent of Welsh speakers three to fifteen years old in Caerffili county (source: 2001 Census Report on the Welsh Language, http://www.statistics.gov.uk/downloads/census2001/Report_on_ the_Welsh_language.pdf, accessed 7 July 2011].).

5   According to The Welsh Language Scheme (2010–2014) (Caerffili County Borough Council, 2009, p. 17) the numbers of pupils learning Welsh as a second language during Key Stage 3 in English-medium schools increased from 3,851 in 1996 to 6,604 in 2008.

6   A non-Welsh-speaking mother, forty-two years old, higher professional occupation (NS-SEC 1), headteacher of an English-medium primary school, living in the northern region of the valley.

7   A non-Welsh-speaking mother, thirty-eight years old, intermediate-level occupation (NS-SEC 3), civil servant, living in the centre of the valley.

8   A father from a mixed-language background, forty-three years of age, a Welsh speaker, higher professional occupation (NS-SEC 1) managing a government department; originates from west Wales, now living in the centre of the valley.

9   Mixed-language background means one parent who could speak Welsh and another who could not speak Welsh.

10 A father from a mixed-language background, forty-seven years old, who has learnt Welsh as an adult learner, had nationalistic tendencies, has a repetitive occupation (NS-SEC 7) working as a factory worker and lives in the southern region of the valley.

11 A non-Welsh-speaking mother, thirty-eight years old, living in the northern region of the valley and unemployed (NS-SEC 8).

12 A mother who has learnt Welsh, fifty years old, living in the centre of the valley and working as a teaching assistant (NS-SEC 5).

13 A mother from a mixed-language family, forty-one years old, a Welsh language learner, higher professional occupation (NS-SEC 1), a head teacher of a local Welsh-medium primary school, living in the south of the valley.

14 Welsh-speaking mother, forty-seven years of age, lower professional occupation (NS-SEC 2), Welsh-medium primary school teacher, originating from a neighbouring valley and living in the southern region of the valley.

15 A non-Welsh-speaking father, twenty-five years old, repetitive occupation (NS-SEC 7) collecting rubbish, living in Bargoed in the centre of the valley.

16 A non-Welsh-speaking mother, forty-three years old, higher professional job (NS-SEC 1) managing a local authority policy department, originating from England,

having spent her childhood mainly in Africa, has lived in south Wales for fifteen years.

[17] Non-Welsh-speaking father, thirty-seven years old, higher professional (NS-SEC 1), civil engineer, originating from the northern region of the valley but now resident in its central region.

REFERENCES

Aitchison, J. and Carter, H. (2004). *Spreading the Word: The Welsh Language 2001.* Talybont: Y Lolfa.

Baker, C. (2004). golygyddol, *Cylchgrawn Addysg Cymru*, 13, 1, 1–7.

Baker, C. and Prys Jones, S. (eds) (1998). *Encyclopaedia of Bilingualism and Bilingual Education*, Clevedon: Multilingual Matters.

Baker, S. and Brown B. (2009). 'Harbingers of feminism? Gender, cultural capital and education in mid-twentieth century rural Wales', *Gender and Education*, 21, 1, 63–79.

Bourdieu, P. and Passeron, J. C. (1974). 'Cultural reproduction and social reproduction', in R. K. Brown (ed.), *Knowledge, Education and Cultural Change*, London: Tavistock.

Bourdieu, P. (1986). 'The forms of capital', in J. Richardson (ed.), *Handbook for Theory and Research for the Sociology of Education*, London: Greenwood Press.

Bourdieu, P. (1987). 'What makes a social class? On the theoretical and practical existence of groups', *Berkeley Journal of Sociology*, 32, 1–18.

Bourdieu, P. (1991). *Language and Symbolic Power*, Cambridge: Polity Press.

Bush, E. (1979). 'Bilingual education in Gwent: parental attitudes and aspirations', unpublished MEd thesis, University of Wales, Cardiff.

Bush, E., Atkinson, P. and Read, M. (1981). *A Minority Choice: Welsh-Medium Education in an Anglicized Area – Parents' Characteristics and Motives*, Cardiff: Sociological Research Unit, Department of Sociology, University College, Cardiff

Caerffili County Borough Council (2009). *Advisory Draft Welsh-Medium Education 2010–2014*, Tredomen: Caerffili County Borough Council.

Crookes, G. and Schmidt, R. (1991). 'Motivation: reopening the research agenda', *Language Learning*, 41, 469–512.

Ellis, R. (1997). *The Study of Second Language Acquisition*, Oxford: Oxford University Press.

Estyn (2006). 'Cwricwlwm Cymreig Phase 2', *http://www.estyn.gov.uk/uploads/publications/6447.pdf* (accessed 13 March 2011).

Fishman, J. (1991). *Reversing Language Shift*. Clevedon: Multilingual Matters

Gardner, R. C. and Lambert, W. E. (1972). *Attitudes and Motivation Second Language Learning*, Rowley, MA: Newbury House.

Gruffudd, H. (2000). 'Planning for the use of Welsh by young people', in C. H. Williams (ed.), *Language Revitalisation and Language Planning*, Cardiff: University of Wales Press.

HMSO (1988). *Education Reform Act 1988*, London: HMSO.

HMSO (1993). *Welsh Language Act 1993*, London: HMSO.

Hodges, Rh. (2009). 'Welsh language use among young people in the Rhymni Valley', *Contemporary Wales*, 22, 16–35.

Hodges, Rh. (2010). 'Tua'r Goleuni: Addysg Gymraeg yng Nghwm Rhymni – rhesymau rhieni dros ddewis addysg Gymraeg i'w plant', PhD heb ei gyhoeddi, Ysgol Gwyddorau Cymdeithas Prifysgol Bangor, Bangor.

Jones, B. and Richards, L. (2003). 'Welsh restored in the Rhymney Valley' in I. Wyn Williams (ed.), *Our Children's Language: The Welsh-Medium Schools of Wales*, Talybont: Y Lolfa.

Khleif, B. (1974). 'Cultural regeneration and the school: an anthropological study of Welsh-medium schools in Wales', *International Review of Education*, 22, 2, 176–89.

Khleif, B. (1980). *Language, Ethnicity, and Education in Wales*, The Hague: Mouton.

Lewis, W. G. (2006). 'Addysg gynradd Gymraeg: her a chyfle yr unfed ganrif ar hugain', yn C. Redknap, W. G. Lewis, S. Rh. Williams a J. Laugharne (gol.), *Addysg Cyfrwng Cymraeg a Dwyieithog*, Bangor: Ysgol Addysg Prifysgol Cymru, Bangor.

Lyon, J. (1996). *Becoming Bilingual: Language Acquisition in a Bilingual Community*, Clevedon: Multilingual Matters.

Packer, A. and Campbell, C. (1997). *Pam for Rhieni yn dewis Addysg Gymraeg i'w Plant? Astudiaeth Ansoddol o Agweddau Rhieni, wedi ei chynnal o fewn Dalgylch Ysgol Gymraeg ei Chyfrwng, mewn Ardal Seisnigedig*, Aberystwyth: Undeb Cenedlaethol Athrawon Cymru.

Packer, A. and Campbell, C. (2000) 'Parental choice in the selection of Welsh-medium education', in P. T. Thomas and J. Mathias (eds), *Developing Minority Languages: The Proceedings of the Fifth International Conference on Minority Languages July 1993, Cardiff, Wales*, Llandysul: Gwasg Gomer.

Reynolds, D., Bellin, W. and ab Ieuan, R. (1998). *Mantais Gystadleuol: Pam Fod Ysgolion Cyfrwng Cymraeg yn Perfformio'n Well?*, Caerdydd: Y Sefydliad Materion Cymreig.

Roth, G. and Wittich, C. (eds) (1968). *Max Weber: Economy and Society*, New York: Bedminister Press.

Thomas, H. (2007). 'Brwydr i Baradwys? Y Dylanwadau ar dwf Ysgolion Cymraeg De-Ddwyrain Cymru', traethawd PhD heb ei gyhoeddi, Ysgol y Gymraeg, Prifysgol Caerdydd, Caerdydd.

Walliman, N. (2006). *Social Research Methods*, London: Sage Publications.

Watson, W. (1964). 'Social mobility and social class in industrial communities', in M. Gluckman and E. Devons (eds), *Closed Systems and Open Minds*, London: Oliver and Boyd.

Weber, M. (1964). *The Theory of Social and Economic Organization*, Glencoe, IL: Free Press.

Welsh Assembly Government (2001). *The Learning Country: A Comprehensive Education and Lifelong Learning Programme to 2010 in Wales*, Cardiff: Welsh Assembly Government.

Welsh Assembly Government (2003). *Iaith Pawb: A National Action Plan for a Bilingual Wales*, Cardiff: Welsh Assembly Government.

Welsh Assembly Government (2010). *Welsh-Medium Education Strategy*, Cardiff: Welsh Assembly Government.

Welsh Language Board (1999). *Continuity in Welsh Language Education*, Cardiff: Welsh Language Board.

Welsh Language Board (2004). *Strategy for Welsh-Medium and Bilingual Education and Training*, Cardiff: Welsh Language Board.

Williams, C. H. (ed.) (2000). *Language Revitalization*, Cardiff: University of Wales Press.

Williams, G. and Morris, D. (2000). *Language Planning and Language Use: Welsh in a Global Age*, Cardiff: University of Wales Press.

Williams, G., Roberts, E. and Isaac, R. (1978). 'Language and aspirations for upward social mobility', in G. Williams (ed.), *Social and Cultural Change in Contemporary Wales*, London: Routledge and Kegan Paul.

Williams, R. (2009). 'Y Coleg Ffederal: report to the Minister for Children, Education, Lifelong Learning and Skills', *http://wales.gov.uk/docs/dcells/publications/090622C olegFfederalReporten.pdf* (accessed 26 November 2010).

Williams, S. Rh. (1998). 'Y Gymraeg yn y Sir Fynwy Ddiwydiannol c. 1800–1901', yn G. H. Jenkins (gol.), *Iaith Carreg fy Aelwyd: Iaith a Chymuned yn y Bedwaredd Ganrif ar Bumtheg*, Caerdydd: Gwasg Prifysgol Cymru.

Williams, S. Rh. (2004). 'Pentref mwyaf Cymreig Sir Fynwy: Rhymni a Chyfrifiad Iaith 1891', yn H. T. Edwards (gol.), *Cyfres y Cymoedd: Ebwy, Rhymni a Sirhywi*, Llandysul: Gwasg Gomer.

Wyn Williams, I. (ed.) (2003). *Our Children's Language: The Welsh-Medium Schools of Wales 1939–2000*, Talybont: Y Lolfa.

2. RECONFIGURING BRITAIN: THE 2010 O'DONNELL LECTURE*

Christopher G. A. Bryant

ABSTRACT

The break-up of Britain has been touted since the 1970s but continues to elude those who favour it. Following devolution, however, fewer people consider themselves British than before. People and the political parties who represent them are reconfiguring Britain. Where that it is taking Britain tomorrow no one can say for sure. However, it is possible to say the following about Britain today provided attention is paid to Scotland, to Wales and to England, as well as to Britain itself. (1) Britain is an asymmetrical union state on the threshold of a quasi-federation. (2) Some of its citizens do not consider it a nation at all but for those that do it amounts to a nation of nations, and is thus also not so much a nation-state as a nation-of-nations state. (3) Britain as a social union or a mutual community of citizens is under threat. Failure to reform or replace the Barnett formula makes desired welfare benefits affordable in some parts of the union but not in others. (4) There are three different national conversations in Scotland, Wales and England, but no conversation of comparable weight among all the people of Britain about Britain itself. A union at ease with diversity would nevertheless be a good political structure with which to meet the challenges of the future.

INTRODUCTION

I was honoured and delighted to be asked to give the 2010 O'Donnell lecture in the University of Wales – but also surprised. Celtic studies is not my field and British studies by the O'Donnell definition seemed too much of a stretch. Then I

---

* Text as given at Swansea (27 April, 2010) and Bangor (4 May, 2010) before the general election of 6 May 2010, and at Aberystwyth (11 May, 2010). Some notes were written after the election.

saw that James Mitchell gave the 2006 lecture on a contemporary topic – social citizenship in a union state – and concluded that latterly 'British' has come to be interpreted more broadly than before (Mitchell, 2007). My next worry was that the university had really meant to invite my namesake, the Labour MP for Rhondda and commentator on constitutional affairs, but apparently there was no mistake. So you have as your lecturer a sociologist from Greater Manchester. I hope that is not a let-down.

In *The Nations of Britain*, published in 2006, I discussed separately, and at some length, the national communities of Scotland, Wales and England as currently imagined and represented, before turning to comment on the future of Britain in the context of devolution. Few social scientists are bold, or rash, enough to address Scotland *and* Wales *and* England *and* Britain, and I can only assume that it is this that caught the attention of the university. This evening I will be talking about Britain. But I will also be indicating how and why it is often necessary to take account of particular developments in Scotland, Wales and England if one is to reach persuasive conclusions about Britain. I will not be saying anything about Northern Ireland. In my view the unionists in Northern Ireland are a self-defined British population beyond Britain itself and thus beyond the scope of this lecture. And I will often refer to the British government and state, just as ministers mostly do, rather than the United Kingdom government and state.

As far back as 1977 Tom Nairn, the Scottish academic and journalist, famously published *The Break-Up of Britain*. The break-up had still eluded him in 2000 when he published *After Britain*, though, following devolution to Scotland a year earlier, it would have seemed nearer. A decade on it still eludes him. A YouGov poll for the *Scotsman* in February this year [2010] found that only 29 per cent of Scots would support independence in a referendum compared with 55 per cent opposed.[1] The combination of a Conservative government in London with next to no MPs in Scotland and an SNP (Scottish National Party) government in Edinburgh, would, however, test the union. In addition to the 13 per cent who said they would vote for independence regardless of the 2010 General Election result, 30 per cent said they would be more likely to support independence if the Conservatives were to win. In Wales Plaid Cymru finally declared for independence in 2003 and it launched its WalesCan independence website in March 2009.[2] But given a range of constitutional options only 11 per cent opted for independence in an ICM poll for BBC Wales in February this year [2010].[3] In England, there have been occasional figures in favour of English independence but no more than that. An interesting one to watch now is Mark Perryman. He is a guiding light in an association of England football fans intent on consigning hooliganism to the past. Inspired by the likes of Albert Camus, existentialist and goalkeeper, he is also a joint owner of Philosophy Football: Sporting Outfitters of Intellectual Distinction, an online purveyor of football tee-shirts. More seriously, he is that rarity among academics, an English nationalist left-wing activist. You will not be surprised to hear that Perryman's inspiration is Nairn. He assumes that devolution has set the break-up of Britain going, that it is unstoppable and that the English are slowly coming to realize this. He identifies a new Englishness in popular culture (perhaps best exemplified by the singer Billy Bragg (2006)), he admires what progressives have already achieved in Scotland, Wales and Ireland, and he seeks an England similarly confident about its future and responsive to a regenerated left. His *Imagined Nation: England after Britain* (2008) has been quickly followed by another edited collection, *Breaking Up Britain: Four Nations after a Union* (2009). Contrary to Perryman, however, there is scant evidence that the English do believe that the break-up of Britain is under way. There is not even an English independence party as such. There is a new party, the English Democrats, dedicated to establishment of an English parliament, preferably within a federal Britain, but they remain at the political margins.

Whether or not Britain is breaking up, fewer people consider themselves British than before devolution. There are different ways social scientists can ask survey questions about 'national' identities in Britain but however they do it a consistent picture emerges. Fewer people in Scotland identify themselves as British than in Wales, and fewer people in Wales than in England. The most sophisticated way, the Moreno or weighted choice question, asks residents in Scotland whether they consider themselves British only, more British than Scottish, equally British and Scottish, more Scottish than British, or Scottish only. In Wales the weighted question choice substitutes Welsh for Scottish, and in England English.

According to the British Social Attitudes survey and its Scottish and Welsh counterparts, by 2005 only two fifths of the people of Scotland considered them-selves at a minimum equally British, and a third considered themselves Scottish only.[4] And by 2007 only half of the people of Wales regarded themselves as at least equally British, and a quarter regarded themselves Welsh only. Even in England only three fifths of the people by 2007 considered themselves at least equally British, and a fifth opted for English only – possibly a reaction to devolution to Scotland and Wales.

BRITAIN: UNITARY STATE, UNION STATE OR A FEDERATION IN THE MAKING?

So what is this Britain that may or may not be breaking up, and some of whose citizens do not even consider themselves British? That Britain is a state is incontestable, but what sort of state is it? Is it a unitary state, a union state or a federation in the making?

Britain has often been characterized as a unitary state. A unitary state is one with a single centre of government, a uniform public administration and a single jurisdiction. The idea of such a state has appealed to celebrants of the sovereignty of the Westminster parliament. But the depiction of Britain prior to devolution as a unitary state was an exaggeration. Government and parliament were in London but, far from administrative standardization, there was large-scale administrative devolution to Scotland and a separate legal system there, and significant administrative devolution to Wales. And after political devolution in 1999, Holyrood and Cardiff Bay have made it patently clear that there is no longer 'one unambiguous political centre' (Rokkan and Urwin, 1982, p. 11).

So if Britain is not a unitary state, what else might it be? The favoured candidate is a union state. A union state is one that has incorporated at least part of its territory by means other than conquest – such as by treaty. In union states, we are told, there survive 'in some areas ... pre-union rights and institutional infrastructures which preserve some degree of regional autonomy and serve as agencies of indigenous elite recruitment' (ibid.). Great Britain as formed by the union of England and Scotland in 1707 clearly meets this definition of the union state. The annexation of Wales by England in 1536 only partly does. Wales was annexed following conquest. The Scots were partners to union in 1707. The Welsh in 1536 were not. English parliamentary, legal and fiscal systems were extended to Wales, and subsequently much else was common to England and Wales. But Wales was never turned into a region of England. There were always some ways in which it was administratively, and even politically, different and from Victorian times onwards these grew.

Back in 2006 when he gave his O'Donnell lecture, James Mitchell was well-known for his characterization of Britain as a union state. In his latest book, *Devolution in the UK* (2009), he argues that a more accurate conceptualization is a 'state of unions'. Union is most often discussed in terms of England and Scotland since 1707. It is also discussed in terms of Britain and Ireland between 1801 and 1922 (the union that gave us the United Kingdom), and Britain and Northern Ireland since. Mitchell now adds England and Wales since 1536. His new-found attention to Wales is welcome. But annexation led to a status for Wales inferior to a full partner in a union, as a glance at the union flag or the royal standard, each devoid of Welsh motifs, confirms. Nevertheless the proposition that the United Kingdom of Great Britain and Northern Ireland today is a union state is supported by the presence of parliaments or assemblies and of governments in London, Edinburgh, Cardiff and Belfast, albeit ones with different powers. It is also complicated by the doubling up of the British government and parliament in London as a government and parliament for England. What we currently have in Britain is perhaps best described as an asymmetrical union state.

Changes to what we currently have are likely. In Scotland it is not possible to read off support for independence from support for the SNP. In recent times about a third of SNP voters have not supported independence, and about a fifth of the Labour vote has.[5] These have cancelled each other out. And it certainly cannot be read off from the number of Scots defining themselves primarily as Scots, rather than British, as most Scots do that. For some Scots the SNP may serve as a social democratic alternative to a discredited Labour Party. Almost all Scots put Scotland first in the sense that their prime objective is not what's best for Britain but what's best for Scotland. The argument in Scotland is about the pros and cons of independence versus the pros and cons of union, and for those who remain in favour of union it is about whether more matters should be devolved, including more fiscal powers.

Until recently, the SNP offered the prospect of an independent Scotland joining the 'arc of prosperity' that stretched from the Irish Republic, through Iceland, to Norway, Sweden and Finland. The Irish and Icelandic examples now point more to the pit of insolvency, and the time has long gone when an independent Scotland could have used oil revenues to establish a sovereign wealth fund on the Norwegian scale. Following expansion of the European Union (EU) to the east in 2004, there is also not the remotest prospect of Scotland benefiting from a net inflow of EU funding on the scale Ireland enjoyed. Support for independence normally falls when the Scottish economy weakens. With the Royal Bank of Scotland and HBOS at the heart of the 2008 banking crisis, pride in the Scottish banks has taken a hard knock, and confidence that financial services could be a mainstay of a successful economy in an independent Scotland has diminished. Support for independence is currently at its lowest since devolution.

The greatest support in Scotland is for more devolution. The SNP has dubbed this 'devolution max' – the devolution of the maximum possible range of responsibilities while still remaining in the UK. It is not clear whether max really means max – everything except defence, foreign and macroeconomic affairs, including full fiscal responsibility and the determination of all pension and welfare benefit levels and their full funding – so I would say what most supporters of devolution currently seek is 'devolution maxish'.

As you all well know, the 1979 devolution referendum in Wales delivered a decisive 'no' vote. By contrast the 1997 referendum delivered a 'yes' vote, but only by a hair's breadth and with Cardiff voting 'no'. The National Assembly for Wales was set up with a large budget but no primary legislative powers, and it had to transform itself from something akin to a glorified county council into the generator of the Welsh Assembly Government. The Richard Report in 2004 recommended that the assembly acquire more powers and the Government of Wales Act 2006 provided for the supersedence of the assembly by a parliament with primary legislative powers following a referendum. Following the recommendation of the All-Wales Convention in 2009, the assembly voted in March this year in favour of a referendum next year. Polls have suggested general support for each of these moves.[6] Given the different provenance of a Welsh parliament and the absence of an equivalent to Scottish law, the powers and practices of a Welsh parliament would not be identical to those of the Scottish parliament. I would characterize the course of devolution in Wales as devolution-gradual.

Concluding his book on *The Independence of Scotland* (2009), Michael Keating argues that the pros and cons of independence versus those of union are all about shades of grey and that Scotland is unlikely to secede so long as it has other options. The bigger threat to the union comes, he says, from an England still wedded to a unitary conception of the state and resistant to federalism 'in the interest of retaining its notional supremacy' (2009, p. 178). I think this misconstrues the limited demand in England for an English parliament (see Bryant 2008, 2010). I do not think it has anything to do with a deluded attachment to a unitary state or a smug belief in English supremacy. What the majority of the people of England want is English votes on English laws (EVoEL), without saddling themselves with hundreds more politicians in an English parliament and the extra civil servants to go with them. The 2007 British Social Attitudes survey asked respondents in England whether Scottish MPs should no longer be allowed to vote on English legislation. Sixty-one per cent agreed they should not (Curtice 2009, p. 14). In April that year YouGov asked respondents to choose between the Westminster status quo, an English parliament or EVoEL.[7] 51 per cent chose EVoEL. There is little doubt that the people of England, who make up around 84 per cent of the people of the UK, simply have not wanted an English parliament in addition to 500-plus MPs at Westminster and I do not expect that to change in the short term. Following the parliamentary expenses scandal, 'Let's have more politicians' is about as unpopular as any cause could be.

The simple demand that English MPs alone vote on matters which pertain only to England has horrified parliamentarians, civil servants and commentators fixated on how Westminster currently operates, and it has wrong-footed those social scientists whose only alternative to the status quo for England, devolution to the regions, was decisively rejected in the North East regional referendum in 2004.

Only the Conservative Party has been prepared to accommodate EVoEL. It has been Conservative policy since 2000. Opponents have argued that the English should put up with the anomaly or inequity represented by the West

Lothian question – Scottish MPs voting on English matters when English MPs cannot voting on equivalent Scottish matters because responsibility for them has been devolved – until such distant time as a remedy could be found which did not threaten the union. Shortly after becoming Conservative leader in 2005, David Cameron established a Democracy Task Force chaired by the former cabinet minister Ken Clarke to consider governance issues including the West Lothian question. It published its proposed answer in July 2008.

The task force's proposal is very simple:

> Bills certified as English would pass through the normal Commons processes as far as and including Second Reading. The whole House would vote on Second Reading.
>
> The Committee Stage, however, would be undertaken by English MPs only, in proportion to English party strengths.
>
> At Report Stage, the Bill would similarly be voted on by English members only.
>
> However, at Third Reading the Bill would be voted on again by the whole House. Since no amendments are possible at this stage, the government party would have to accept any amendments made in Committee or at Report or have the Bill voted down and lost. (Conservative Democracy Task Force, 2008, p. 1)

The standard objection to EVoEL, much repeated by Gordon Brown, is that it would create two classes of MPs, those English members who could debate and vote on everything and those Scottish, Welsh and Northern Irish members excluded from votes on England-only matters, and that in so doing it would run counter to the sovereignty of parliament exercised equally by all who are elected to it and thereby threaten the union. This overlooks the fact that we already have two classes of MPs: English members who can debate and vote on all matters concerning their constituents and Scottish, Welsh and Northern Irish members who cannot. Of more concern to the task force were the two classes of constituents we have now: Scottish, Welsh and Northern Irish constituents who, following devolution, are assured of Scottish, Welsh and Northern Irish determination of matters pertaining only to their respective home countries, and English constituents who have no such assurance. The task force's compromise does not ensure that a majority of English members get what they want (the vote of the whole house on the third reading may stop it), but it does ensure that they do not get what they do not want (the vote of the whole house on the third reading cannot overturn the all-English committee's amendments). It also ensures that, thanks to the third reading provision, a British government is not faced with the enactment of English laws it opposes. But it is obliged to ensure that its England-only measures are acceptable to a majority of English MPs if it is to legislate at all. This prospect alarms some, but the bargaining and compromise it may sometimes necessitate ought to be familiar. It is called politics.

It is also argued that parliamentary bills are often drafted with different territorial remits for different parts or clauses and it would be hard for parliamentary draftsmen and women to do otherwise and hard for the Speaker to rule on who was eligible to vote on what. Labour government practice, however, has been to move away from bills with mixed territorial remits and the task force was confident they could be avoided if there were a will to do so. To claim it is impossible is surely a nonsense. If Scottish-only, and by extension Welsh-only, matters can be identified so can English-only matters. Finally it is correctly argued that the funding of measures that pertain only to England has, via the Barnett formula (of which more in a moment), knock-on consequences for the level of funding received by the devolved administrations. But funding is dealt with in finance bills, finance bills always have an all-UK remit and MPs from all parts of the UK would continue to vote on them.

David Cameron has said that 'For English-only legislation, we would have a sort of English grand committee'.[8] The Conservative manifesto for the 2010 General Election includes a commitment to EVoEL, but says nothing about the mechanics.[9] It would represent a kind of 'devolution mini, but by any other name'. The Labour and Liberal Democrat parties have long fought shy of addressing the West Lothian question and the government of England and now propose in their 2010 manifestos to leave it to a UK constitutional convention to come up with proposals. Do not hold your breath.[10]

Let us suppose that more powers are devolved to the Holyrood parliament, that the national assembly in Cardiff Bay is transformed into a parliament, and that the parliament at Westminster adopts English votes on English laws. Would what we have then still be a union state or would it be a federation in the making?

Micheal Keating (2009) anticipates 'ever looser union'. That could mean a continuing cession of powers from Westminster and increasing constitutional differences between Scotland, Wales and England, or it could mean sovereignty for Scotland within a British Union, possibly one hardly more consequential than the Nordic Union is for Scandinavian countries. It could even mean something as exotic as the sovereignty-association proposed by Quebec before the 1995 referendum on secession from Canada, i.e. first demonstrate your sovereignty by seceding then exercise it by partially re-attaching on terms acceptable to you and also revocable by you. Charlie Jeffery (2010) very recently suggested that there might not be much difference between devolution-max and independence-lite.

Loosening union would seem more apt than ever looser union. But when does looser union turn a union state into a federation? One point of difference must surely be that a federation has a legislature and a government with similar powers in each of its constituent parts as well as a central government and legislature for reserved matters. This is the future sought by David Melding, the Conservative member for South Wales Central in the National Assembly for Wales, in his *Will Britain Survive beyond 2020?* (2009). Melding would like the development of Wales from a cultural to a political nation to culminate in a fully federal Britain in which parliaments in Holyrood, Cardiff Bay, Stormont and wherever the English choose to locate one, have equal powers of home rule, and the UK parliament at Westminster deals with macroeconomic affairs, foreign affairs and defence. John Osmond (2010), former director of the Institute of Welsh Affairs, has replied, correctly in my view, that whatever being English and British means for the English it does not mean readiness to embrace the Celtic periphery in a federal constitution in the near future. Perhaps the Liberal Democrats think differently. They use the f word in their 2010 manifesto – but without making clear what they mean by it.

If federation is not possible, independence for Wales could succeed, Melding argues, but not without difficulty. As a second best to full federation, he prefers a partial or quasi-federation in which England contents itself with English votes on English matters in the UK parliament at Westminster and the British government continues to serve as the government of England. He is well aware of the objections to EVoEL but does not think them insurmountable for reasons similar to those I have already outlined.

A quasi-federation is what in practice I think we are heading towards, but without articulating it as such.[11] It would be a typical British compromise consistent with the make-it-up-as-you-go-along character of Britain's unwritten constitution. Whether it would prove refinable enough to endure for the long term, a stepping stone to federation, or a path to the break-up of Britain, only time would tell. Perhaps the constitutional conventions mooted by the Labour and Liberal Democratic parties in their manifestos would clarify this, or perhaps not.

BRITAIN: A NATION, A NATION OF NATIONS, OR NOT A NATION AT ALL?

Britain is incontrovertibly a state, but is it only a state? Is it also a nation, or a nation of nations, or not a nation at all? There is in Scotland a common view that Scotland is the nation, so therefore Britain must be something else. Reflecting this David McCrone (2002; also Bechhofer and McCrone, 2009a, ch. 1), co-director of the Institute of Governance in the University of Edinburgh, distinguishes between English and Scottish national identities and British state identity. This is hard to justify.

Britain meets most definitions of a nation. Anthony Smith (1991, p. 21), for example, argues that nations have five attributes:

1   an historical territory, or homeland
2   common myths and historical memories
3   a common, mass culture
4   common legal rights and duties for all members
5   a common economy with territorial mobility for members.

Britain has all of these. It is also, as Benedict Anderson (1982) says nations are, an imagined community. The older thinking of Max Weber (1948 [1912], 1978 [1922]), however, gives pause for thought. Weber itemized his own attributes of nations but he also discussed nations relationally. We may speak of a nation where a people makes a claim to be a nation and has that claim accepted by others. Given the frequency of references to, for example, the British national interest, it is counterintuitive to argue Britain is not a nation and the claim that it is not one has met with fierce criticism (e.g. Uberoi and McLean, 2009). Nevertheless we do have in Britain today some citizens who no longer make the claim that Britain is a nation.

What Weber did not consider is the possibility of a nation of nations. The idea of Britain as a nation of nations acknowledges that national identifications are not necessarily exclusive and it allows that layered and dual identities are possible, even common (see Bryant, 2006, ch. 1; Kenny, English and Hayton, 2008). According to Stuart Hall (2000: para. 6) 'Britain always was and really is now a nation of nations'. That it always was runs contrary to Linda Colley's famous thesis in *Britons: The Forging of a Nation 1707–1837* (1992) that Britain was not a nation at the time of the union of England and Scotland in 1707 but had been forged as one by the time of Victoria's accession in 1837. That it really is a nation of nations now is a claim most of those who (still) consider Britain a nation would have to accept unless they demote England, Scotland and Wales to regions.

Those who consider Britain a nation must also consider it a nation-state – though, mindful of the nations that compose it, they might also think it a multi-national state. By this reasoning Britain is both a nation-state and a multi-national state, indeed a nation-of-nations state – not the easiest notion for a citizenry to grasp.

BRITAIN: A MUTUAL COMMUNITY OF CITIZENS, A SOCIAL UNION

Weber characterized the nation as a community of sentiment. Community of sentiment calls to mind solidarity, and shades into the idea of a mutual community of citizens, a social union. One can set aside argument about whether Britain still is, or ever was, a nation, and still acknowledge that the notion that Britain is a single mutual community is a very important one. Scottish and Welsh respondents have indicated to pollsters that decisions about their welfare benefits and pensions should be taken in Edinburgh and Cardiff, not Westminster.[12] Mitchell argued in his O'Donnell lecture that devolution can only lead to policy divergence, including social policy divergence, between different parts of the UK. What, after all, is the point of devolution if it does not allow devolved political bodies to do things differently? But can Britain remain a mutual community of citizens, a social union, if welfare entitlements are no longer common to all its citizens? It is significant that the 'Calman Commission', the Commission on Scottish Devolution established by the majority unionist parties in the Scottish parliament, indicated from the start its commitment to Britain as a social union in which welfare benefits are broadly comparable throughout.

Currently, free personal care for the elderly is provided in Scotland for all who need it. This has been ruled out in England, and in Wales, as unaffordable. There is hardly a more sensitive issue in an ageing society such as Britain's. Can Scotland afford what the English and Welsh cannot afford, but would like, because it has forgone something else the English and Welsh do have – in other words because it has accepted the opportunity cost? Or can it afford it (so far at least) because, as of 2007–8, the Barnett formula provides for per capita public spending in Scotland at a level 25 per cent higher than in England and 12 per cent higher than in Wales (calculated from figures in McLean et al., 2008, Table 4.1)? It is hard to imagine an issue more potentially rancorous than reform or replacement of the Barnett formula and it is easy to understand why Gordon Brown ducked it in all his years at the Treasury. But if Britain is to remain a mutual community of citizens it will, I suggest, only be able to accommodate different welfare provisions made by devolved political bodies if they are made following an equitable division of public funding. In other words reform or replacement of the Barnett formula and other fiscal reform will have to be faced if Britain is to remain a mutual community of citizens.

The June 2009 final report of the Calman Commission, endorsed by the Labour, Liberal Democrat and Conservative parties in Scotland, proposes that two thirds of current devolved spending in Scotland should continue to be funded by a block grant calculated according to the Barnett formula until such time as the formula is reformed or replaced. The other third should be funded mostly by a Scottish rate of income tax, but also by the Scottish proceeds of four minor taxes. To make way for the Scottish rate of income tax, the basic and higher rates of UK income tax would be levied at ten pence less in Scotland and the block grant to Scotland would be reduced by the sum forgone. The Scottish parliament would then set the additional Scottish rate at more or less than ten pence in line with Scottish priorities. This would give Scotland greater fiscal responsibility. In so doing it would also open the way to eventual reduction or removal of the advantage bestowed by the Barnett formula. The British Labour and Liberal Democrat Parties accepted Calman and have confirmed this in their 2010 manifestos. The British Conservatives did not.[13]

When I saw Ieuan Wyn Jones and Alex Salmond jointly launch the Plaid Cymru and SNP General Election campaigns on television and announce a Celtic alliance, I had to smile. With respect to reform or replacement of the Barnett formula, at least, Welsh and Scottish interests are not the same. It is often supposed that the Barnett formula took account of relative need. It did not. Relative per capita GVA [gross value added] and income suggest that in any change that took account of need and current population Wales would indeed win but Scotland just as surely would lose. The July 2009 first report of the 'Holtham Commission', the Independent Commission on Funding and Finance for Wales established by the National Assembly for Wales, proposes the replacement of Barnett by a needs-based formula. Were a needs-based formula to mimic the criteria used in England to allocate funding to local authorities, Holtham calculated Wales would secure both a small gain and a release from the Barnett squeeze that is slowly bringing Wales's per capita funding down to the English level. Scotland by contrast would lose heavily, which is why none of the Scottish parties is seeking replacement of Barnett by a needs-based formula (McLean, 2010).

Surveys and polls have long shown a majority of English respondents believe higher per capita public spending in Scotland to be unfair.[14] And when he launched the SNP manifesto on television, what did Alex Salmond give as a prime example of the financial concessions he hoped the SNP could obtain in bargaining following a hung parliament? A guarantee of continued free personal care for the elderly in Scotland.

NATIONAL CONVERSATIONS IN BRITAIN

Whether Britain itself is (still) a nation is disputed. That it is made up of nations is not. The management of any union becomes difficult when the preoccupations of the constituent nations overshadow those of the union itself. In Britain today the main preoccupation everywhere is the state of the economy. But there are also different national conversations in Scotland, Wales and England. The SNP minority government introduced the term 'national conversation' to refer to debate about the future governance of Scotland. I want to use it differently to refer to current debates about nation in Scotland, Wales and England.

In Scotland, Michael Keating (2009) speaks of a 'nation-building' project. In some ways talk of nation building is surprising. Who ever doubted that Scotland was a nation? Well, perhaps some Scots did. After all, 'Flower of Scotland', the 'national anthem' unofficially adopted in the early 1990s, assures Scots that 'we can still rise now, and be the nation again'. The implication is that the union of Scotland and England had developed into an Anglo-Britain that diminished Scotland and too often ignored the sensibilities of its people. This was not all Margaret Thatcher's fault, but she came to symbolize Scottish grievance. 'Rise now and be the nation again' is a demand for Scottish self-respect, for care for Scottish institutions, culture and traditions, and for home rule if not independence. There is near-universal assent to that today. Collective self-doubt has given way to renewed confidence.[15]

The SNP minority Scottish government has launched initiatives on citizenship which make no mention of Britain and it has set out policies which treat links with the rest of Britain and with the British government as scarcely more significant than with anywhere else in Western Europe (Leith, 2010). Claims that Britain is a nation are rejected by many Scots or simply ignored. British government ministers may still talk of Britain's *national* interest but that is a misnomer. Britain is being denationalized. Britain for Scots of this persuasion is a state but one that no longer best serves Scottish interests. Other Scots may not go that far but for almost all Scots the priority is national regeneration.

The challenge in Wales is to transform Wales from being a cultural nation only to being both a cultural and a political nation. At the heart of Wales the cultural nation is the Welsh language, but six times as many people do not speak it at all as speak it fluently and changing that can only be a long-term goal.[16] It is therefore essential to win support for the language, particularly its use as a public language, from all the people of Wales, including the English in Wales. It is also necessary to acknowledge fully the contributions to Wales made by those who do not speak Welsh and to assure them that theirs is not a secondary Welsh identity. It is necessary, too, to secure contributions from the English in Wales that make Wales a better place for all its citizens. But this still is not enough. Scotland has shown since 1707 how a civil society different from England's can underpin nationhood (McCrone, 1992; Paterson, 1994). There is a comparable need to transform civil society in Wales into a distinctively Welsh civil society

(Day, 2002; Day et al., 2006). A Welsh civil society relevant to all the people of Wales is a necessary complement to the Welsh language in the making of Welsh national identity. It also an important constituent in the making of Wales as a political nation (Royles, 2007). But its development can only take a long time. I have listened to Adam Price, the Plaid Cymru MP for Carmarthen East and Dinefwr, argue that among the Welsh, *especially* the Welsh-speaking Welsh, there is still a collective lack of self-confidence that has held Wales back and that only independence for Wales can overcome it.[17] Plaid Cymru's WalesCan independence website, with Adam Price to the fore, makes the same point. I just observe that collective self-doubt has been an issue in Scotland, but is so no more, or at least is much less so nowadays, and that (re-)establishment of a Scottish parliament has had a lot to do with that.

Susan Condor's qualitative research in Scotland and England indicates that Scots, especially young Scots, regard Scottish nationalism as a progressive force, and there is reason to believe something similar applies in Wales (Condor and Faulkner, 2002; Condor and Abell, 2006a,b). By contrast there is also evidence that people in England, perhaps especially young people in England, are more inclined to treat *all* nationalism warily including English and/or British nationalism (Condor, 1996; Fenton, 2007). McCrone (2006) has referred to England as 'a nation that dare not speak its name'. Peter Mandler (2006), in his history of the idea of English national character from Edmund Burke to Tony Blair, claims writers in the last half-century have largely given up on that idea. More pertinently, there has also been limited interest in the successor concept of an English national identity in the absence of any particular English cultural or political project to which to attach it. Where once England was the heart of Empire, or the vanguard of civilization, or a beacon of liberty, the argument goes, there is now a void, and thus no persuasive reason to embrace English identity. 'Looser common values upheld by large sections of the English population such as freedom, tolerance, fairness, diversity are associated as much with Britain as with England, or indeed with no particular national identity at all' (Mandler, 2006, pp. 240–1). Instead, for today's English 'a looser British citizenship would suffice ... without the stronger common culture or common project apparently possessed additionally by the Scots' (2006, p. 241).

Contrary to Mandler, there is a conversation in England about who we the people are. It centres on multiculturalism, although I think it is better conceived in terms of cosmopolitanization (Bryant, 2006, pp. 191–200; Bryant, forthcoming). People who are not white British made up 14.7 per cent of the population of England and a remarkable 41.6 per cent of the population of London in 2004. In that year multiculturalism was questioned from the left and from the Commission for Racial Equality as never before. David Goodhart (2004, n.p.), the editor of *Prospect* magazine, argued that progressives want 'plenty of both solidarity (high social cohesion and generous welfare paid out of a progressive tax system) and diversity (equal respect for a wide range of peoples, values and ways of life)' but there comes a point beyond which these are inversely related. The volume of asylum seekers, he thought, threatened to take us beyond that point. Trevor Phillips, the co-author of *Windrush* (Phillips and Phillips, 1998) and the then head of the Commission for Racial Equality, agreed, arguing that multiculturalism was out of date. It encouraged separateness when the need now was to re-emphasize 'common values ... the common currency of the English language, honouring the culture of these islands, like Shakespeare and Dickens'.[18] The view seemed to prevail that multiculturalism could issue in a dangerous separateness though it need not, that all responsible citizens should guard against this, that more attention to common values and practices was overdue, that the problem of the radicalized minority of young Muslims who rejected Britishness could no longer be ignored, that the ceremonies to mark the award of British citizenship introduced by the then Home Secretary, David Blunkett, were a good idea, and that it was time to take forward a Britain of which all citizens would be proud. A rebalancing was called for.

This has not settled the debate about multiculturalism. In a speech shortly after the London bombings, Phillips (2005) gave voice to the fear that there are 'districts on the way to becoming fully fledged ghettoes' and that 'we are sleepwalking our way to segregation'. Subsequent research suggests that the incidence of residential segregation has been exaggerated and the dynamics of such segregation as there is are more complex than the mythmakers would have us believe (Finney and Simpson, 2009). Even so there is a general view that multiculturalism without interaction between bearers of the different cultures is undesirable. Responses to this include the articulation of more sophisticated versions of multiculturalism (Modood, 2007), the switch in emphasis to interculturalism (James, 2008), and government support for 'community cohesion' understood as respect for cultural differences within a community, that of the majority as well as minorities, allied to the generation of shared experiences and values (Cantle, 2005). This all has an air of making the best of the diversity we have found ourselves with.

There is an argument that London points to something better. In a world city such as London, the spontaneous interaction of diverse people and peoples generates ever new cultural and economic possibilities (Massey, 2007). And according to Paul Gilroy (2004), there increasingly prevails there a 'convivial cosmopolitanism'. Londoners agree. The Greater London annual survey in 2007 found that 81 per cent agreed with the statement 'London may not be perfect but I enjoy living here', and 76 per cent agreed with the statement 'I enjoy the cultural diversity of London' (Greater London Authority, 2008, p. 18). And asked 'Which of the following [two] statements would you say comes closest to your view?', 68 per cent of respondents opted for 'London's diverse communities make London a better place to live', compared with 25 per cent opting for 'London's diversity threatens the way of life in London' (2008, p. 27).[19]

London's diversity is recognized as a huge asset and not just something to be accommodated, but the world-in-one-city character of London is untypical of England as a whole. One could say that it is uneven cosmopolitanization that better characterizes England. There are, however, many cities and regions with a conspicuous mix of people whose families have come from many parts of the world. It is a cosmopolitan England that increasingly prevails. Attitudes to these ethnic, cultural and religious differences vary. There is a cosmopolitan continuum with the bitterly resented cosmopolitanism fanned by the British National Party at one pole and the convivial cosmopolitanism lauded by Gilroy at the other. Certainly the reality of life is often far short of a convivial cosmopolitanism, but arguably it is the latter which offers England the greatest benefit (Bryant, forthcoming). There is then a progressive 'nationalism' available to the English even if it is not always cast in national terms. It values England's cultural diversity.

The national conversation taking place in England is crucially different from those in Scotland and Wales in that it is as often framed in terms of Britain as England. In particular black and Asian immigrants to post-war England have mostly chosen to identify themselves as British rather than English, albeit often Black-British, Asian-British or British Muslim, for two good reasons.[20] First, it is as a consequence of the British Empire that most of them find themselves here. Second, Britain is in origin a territorial community that has formally accommodated more than one way of being British at least since the Treaty of Union between Scotland and England in 1707. It is easier in the short term for immigrants to relate to Britain while maintaining elements of the culture of their families' countries of origin than to embrace Englishness and buy in to England's national story – which is not to deny that in the longer term very many will. In Scotland, by contrast, the balance between assimilation and integration is tilted more towards assimilation. Immigrants, the English apart, are officially encouraged to become 'new Scots' although there is research evidence that ordinary Scots are often disinclined to see them as such. Immigrant self-definitions with British in them are an impediment to acceptance in Scotland, whilst anti-Englishness can facilitate it. Where Scottish (and Welsh) separatists see Britain in terms of English hegemony, English 'multiculturalists' and cosmopolitans see it in terms of diversity. For the former Britain invites rejection; for the latter it deserves renewal.

If I am right about what constitutes the national conversation in Scotland and in Wales, it has to be said that it does not focus on Britain. And if I am right about what constitutes a national conversation in England, whether labelled national or not, the focus is blurred. The conversation shifts, unsure whether to refer to England or Britain, indeed unsure sometimes whether talk of the nation should be happening at all. What is missing altogether is a conversation about Britain itself. To call it a national conversation would put many Britons off, especially in Scotland. Arthur Aughey's (2008) call for a 'shared conversation' might be more acceptable. Of course, Gordon Brown (2004, 2006) tried to start one, but he failed (Lee, 2006, ch. 5; Bryant, 2010). Instead of proclaiming British values, he would have done better to ask what citizens value about Britain. Instead of trying to pin down Britishness, he would have done better to discuss attachments to Britain, practical as well as sentimental, and how they might be strengthened. Instead of celebrating a British past that was sometimes – Runnymede and Magna Carta for instance – English not British, he would have done better to invite discussion of the place a truly post-imperial Britain, one that had abandoned great power pretensions, could have in a globalizing age. But at least he tried.

Does it really matter that Brown failed? Is civic education or political orchestration really necessary? Are not the surest attachments to Britain those that citizens form untutored in the course of their ordinary lives? (see Crick, 2009). Bechhofer and McCrone (2009b) argue that asking Scots, in particular, to sign up to British values is counterproductive given the strength of their primary attachment to Scotland. They also say it is unnecessary. 'Attempts by politicians to impose a common sense of being British assume erroneously that it is a moral–cultural identity rather than a political–institutional one' (2009b, p. 92). If Britain should cease to be a social union, a mutual community of citizens, being British would indeed be less of a moral–cultural identity than before. If Britain is to remain a social union, a moral community requiring solidarity – the position that Gordon Brown, also a Scot, took – Bechhofer and McCrone are, I think, wrong to dismiss the moral dimension to being British. In their assessment of the *State of the Union* (2005), Iain McLean and Alistair McMillan conclude that a union without unionism could lumber on for some decades yet. Well may be for some dimensions of union, but a social union without solidarity seems to me unsustainable beyond the short term.

CONCLUSIONS

People and the political parties who represent them are reconfiguring Britain, but where that is taking us no one can be sure. I have argued that Britain today is an asymmetrical union state on the threshold of a quasi-federation – a hard notion to grasp and therefore an awkward place for a citizenry to be. I have also acknowledged that some of Britain's citizens do not consider it a nation at all. And for those that do it amounts to a nation of nations, and is thus not so much a nation-state as a nation-of-nations state – another hard notion to grasp. I have suggested, too, that Britain as a social union or a mutual community of citizens will be compromised if a failure to effect fiscal reform, including reform or replacement of the Barnett formula, makes desired welfare benefits affordable in some parts of the union but not in others. Finally, I have pointed to the different national conversations in the nations that compose Britain but have claimed that there is no conversation of comparable weight among all Britons about Britain itself.

In the twentieth century Britain succeeded in generating the solidarity a social union requires, and it could do so again in the twenty-first century. In the short to medium term, Britain has to reduce its public borrowing very substantially. There will be funding cuts and tax rises, and there will be attempts by governments in Scotland and Wales to wring financial concessions from the British government. The union would surely be best served by a fiscal reform that treated all its constituent parts equitably.

In the medium to long term Britain has also to support an ageing society. This is likely to necessitate further immigration both to provide care for the elderly and to sustain an economy large enough to yield the tax revenues to pay for care of the elderly. Further immigration means more diversity. Whatever the difficulties, Britain has historically not just accommodated, but also benefited from, a very great deal of diversity. We need to learn from this record and acknowledge that a union at ease with diversity within would be a good political structure with which to meet the challenges of the future. That is why I think Britain's potential is far from exhausted.

NOTES

[1] All YouGov polls were accessible via the YouGov website (*http://www.yougov.com*) on 25 April 2010.
[2] *http://www.walescan.com* (accessed 25 April 2010).
[3] All ICM polls were accessible via the ICM website (*http://www.icmresearch.co.uk*) on 25 April 2010.
[4] For precise percentages see Table 2.1.
[5] Given the fluctuations in support for Labour and the SNP this is a rough guess. Using Scottish Social Attitudes data, Bond and Rosie (2002, Table 9) indicate that 25 per cent of Labour identifiers supported independence in 2001 and 38 per cent of SNP identifiers did not.
[6] For example, an ICM poll for BBC Wales in February 2010 found 56 per cent 'In

Table 2.1
National identity by nation in 1997 and 2005/7 (%)

	England		Wales		Scotland	
	1997	2007	1997	2007	1997	2005
British not X	9	12	15	9	4	5
More British than X	14	14	10	9	4	5
Equally British and X	45	31	26	32	27	22
More X than British	17	14	29	20	38	32
X not British	7	19	13	24	23	32
Other/none	7	10	6	5	4	5

X = English, Welsh, Scottish.

Sources: All 1997, British Election Survey; England 2007, British Social Attitudes; Wales 2007, Wales Life and Times; Scotland Social Attitudes.

favour of giving the national Assembly full law making powers in the areas for which it has responsibility'.

[7]   This is a very rare – indeed possibly the first – case of a survey or poll offering EVoEL as a constitutional option alongside the status quo and an English parliament. British Social Attitudes' failure to do so is particularly regrettable.

[8]   In an interview with the Scottish *Mail on Sunday*, 14 February 2009.

[9]   The Conservative, Labour and Liberal Democratic manifestos for the May 2010 General Election were accessed via the three parties' websites on 25 April 2010.

[10] The Conservative and Liberal Democrat coalition government formed after the May 2010 General Election (which does not depend on Scottish and Welsh MPs for its majority) has referred the West Lothian question to another committee.

[11] McLean (2010, p. 4) refers to a 'not-quite-federation'.

[12] An ICM poll for the BBC in June 2009 asked 'Who do you think should make the most important decisions about old age pensions, the Scottish Government in Edinburgh or the UK Government at Westminster?' 65 per cent said the Scottish Government, and 35 per cent the UK Government. Scottish Social Attitudes (accessed at info@natcen.ac.uk, 20 January 2010) asked Scots in 2009 'Which do you think should make the most important decisions about levels of welfare benefits?' 60 per cent said the Scottish parliament compared with 19 per cent who said the UK government and 16 per cent local councils in Scotland.

[13] David Cameron, the new Prime Minister, quickly signalled broad acceptance of Calman, though revisions would be necessary to take into account intended changes in UK income tax personal allowances.

[14] For example, ICM's Britishness Survey for the *Sunday Telegraph* in December 2007 told respondents that 'Government spending per head of population is higher in Scotland than it is in England' and asked whether this is justified or unjustified. Sixty-three per cent of respondents in England replied 'unjustified'. Even when not told that spending in Scotland is higher, the percentage of English respondents saying that Scotland gets more than its fair share of government spending has,

according to British Social Attitudes surveys, doubled from 21 per cent in 2000 to 40 per cent in 2009 (Curtice, 2010, Table 4).

[15] Still unconvinced, Nairn (2008) argues that only independence can work the trick.

[16] ICM's February 2010 poll for BBC Wales found that 11 per cent 'speak Welsh fluently' and 22 per cent speak it 'enough to get by'.

[17] At an Academy for the Study of Britishness seminar in the University of Huddersfield, 27 January 2010.

[18] In an interview in *The Times*, 3 April 2004.

[19] All Ipsos MORI polls were accessible via the Ipsos MORI website (*http://www.ipsos-mori.com*) on 25 April 2010.

[20] Using data from the 2007 British Social Attitudes survey, Curtice and Heath (2009, p. 57) found that, forced to choose between English and British, 44 per cent of white residents in England opted for English as their national identity (compared with 47 per cent British) but only 5 per cent of non-white residents chose English (compared with 58 per cent British).

REFERENCES

Anderson, B. (1983). *Imagined Communities: Reflections on the Origin and Spread of Nationalism*,   London: Verso.

Aughey, A. (2008). 'The wager of devolution and the challenge to Britishness', in A. Gamble and T. Wright (eds), *Britishness: Perspectives on the British Question*, London: Political Quarterly.

Bechhofer, F., and McCrone, D. (eds) (2009a). *National Identity, Nationalism and Constitutional Change*, Basingstoke: Palgrave Macmillan.

Bechhofer, F. and McCrone, D. (2009b). 'Being Scottish', in F. Bechhofer and D. McCrone (eds), *National Identity, Nationalism and Constitutional Change*, Basingstoke: Palgrave Macmillan.

Bond, R. and Rosie, M. (2002). 'National minorities in post-devolution Scotland', University of Edinburgh Institute of Governance working paper, *http://www.institute-of-governance.org/onlinepub/bondrosie.html* (accessed 28 September 2008).

Bragg, B. (2006). *The Progressive Patriot: A Search for Belonging*, London: Bantom Press.

Brown, G. (2004). Annual British Council lecture, London, 8 July.

Brown, G. (2006). Speech to the Fabian Society, 'Future of Britishness' Conference, 14 January.

Bryant, C. G. A. (2006). *The Nations of Britain*, Oxford: Oxford University Press.

Bryant, C. G. A. (2008). 'Devolution, equity and the English question', *Nations and Nationalism*, 14, 4, 644–83.

Bryant, C. G. A. (2010). 'English identities and interests and the governance of Britain', *Parliamentary Affairs*, 63, 2, 250–65.

Bryant, C. G. A. (forthcoming). 'Towards a cosmopolitan England?', in A. Aughey and C. Berberich (eds), *These Englands: A Conversation on National Identity*, Manchester: Manchester University Press.

Cantle, T. (2005). *Community Cohesion: A New Framework for Race and Diversity*, Basingstoke: Palgrave Macmillan.

Colley, L. (1992). *Britons: The Forging of the Nation 1707–1837*, Hew Haven, CT: Yale University Press.

Commission on Scottish Devolution (2009). *Serving Scotland Better: Scotland and the United Kingdom*. Final report, http://www.commissiononscottishdevolution.org.uk/contact.php (accessed 10 August 2009).

Condor, S. (1996). 'Unimagined community? Some psychological issues concerning English national identity', in G. M. Breakwell and E. Lyons (eds), *Changing European Identities: Social Psychological Analyses of Social Change*, Oxford: Butterworth Heinemann.

Condor, S. and Abell, J. (2006a). 'Romantic Scotland: tragic England, ambiguous Britain: constructions of "the empire" in post-devolution national accounting', *Nations and Nationalism*, 12, 3, 453–72.

Condor, S. and Abell, J. (2006b). 'Vernacular constructions of "national identity" in post-devolution Scotland and England', in J. Wilson and K. Stapleton (eds), *Devolution and Identity*, Aldershot: Ashgate.

Condor, S. and Faulkner, M. (2002). 'Discourses of national identity and integration in England and Scotland', in D. Meyer-Dinkgrafe (ed.), *European Culture in a Changing World: Between Nationalism and Globalism*. Proceedings of the 8th International Society for the Study of Ideas Conference, Aberystwyth.

Conservative Democracy Task Force (2008). 'Answering the question: devolution, the West Lothian question and the future of the union', *http://www.toque.co.uk/witan/docs/DTF_Answering_the_Question.pdf* (accessed 16 May 2010).

Crick, B. (2009). 'Do we really need Britannia?', in A. Gamble and T. Wright (eds), *Britishness: Perspectives on the British Question*, London: Political Quarterly.

Curtice, J. (2009). 'Is there an English backlash? Reactions to devolution', in A. Park, J. Curtice, K. Thomson, M. Philips and E. Cleary (eds), *British Social Attitudes: 25th Report*, London: Sage.

Curtice, J. (2010). *Is an English Backlash Emerging? Reactions to Devolution Ten Years On*, London: IPPR.

Curtice, J. and Heath, A. (2009). 'England awakes? Trends in national identity in England', in F. Bechhofer and D. McCrone (eds), *National Identity, Nationalism and Constitutional Change*, Basingstoke: Palgrave Macmillan.

Day, G. (2002). *Making Sense of Wales: A Sociological Perspective*, Cardiff: University of Wales Press.

Day, G., Dunkerley, D. and Thompson, A. (eds) (2006). *Civil Society in Wales: Policy, Politics and People*, Cardiff: University of Wales Press.

Fenton, S. (2007). 'Indifference towards national identity: what young adults think about being British', *Nations and Nationalism*, 13, 2, 321–39.

Finney, N. and Simpson, L. (2009). *'Sleepwalking to Segregation': Challenging Myths about Race and Integration*, Bristol: Policy Press.

Gilroy, P. (2004). *After Empire: Melancholia or Convivial Culture*, London: Routledge.

Goodhart, D. (2004). 'Too diverse?', *Prospect Magazine*, 95, February, *http://www.prospect-magazine.co.uk/article_details.php?id=5835* (accessed 10 April 2009).

Greater London Authority (2008). 'Focus on London 2008', *http://www.london.gov.uk/gla/publications/factandfigures/fo12008* (accessed 18 May 2009).

Hall, S. (2000). Contribution to 'A question of identity (II). Special report: What is Britain?', *The Observer*, 15 October, *http://www.guardian.co.uk/uk/2000/oct/15/britishidentity.comment1/print* (accessed 31 October 2008).

Independent Commission on Funding and Finance for Wales (2009). *Funding Devolved Government in Wales: Barnett & Beyond*. First report, *http://wales.gov.uk/icffw/home* (accessed 10 August 2009).

James, M. (2008). *Interculturalism: Theory and Policy*, London: Baring Foundation, *http://www.baringfoundation.org.uk* (accessed 16 February 2009).

Jeffery, C. (2010). 'An outbreak of consensus: Scottish politics after devolution', *Political Insight*, 1, 1, 32–5.

Keating, M. (2009). *The Independence of Scotland: Self-Government and the Shifting Politics of Union*, Oxford: Oxford University Press.

Kenny, M., English, R. and Hayton, R. (2008). *Beyond the Constitution: Englishness in a Post-Devolved Britain*, London: IPPR.

Lee, S. (2006). 'Gordon Brown and the "British Way"', *Political Quarterly*, 77, 369–77.

Leith, M. S. (2010). 'Governance and identity in a devolved Scotland', *Parliamentary Affairs*, 61, 286–301.

McCrone, D. (1992). *Understanding Scotland: The Sociology of a Stateless Nation*, London: Routledge.

McCrone, D. (2002). 'Who do you say you are? Making sense of identities in modern Britain', *Ethnicities*, 2, 3, 301–20.

McCrone, D. (2006). 'A nation that dares not speak its name? The English question', *Ethnicities*, 6, 2, 267–78.

McLean, I. (2010). 'Calman and Holtham: the public finance of devolution', paper presented at the PSA: Territorial Politics Conference, Oxford, January.

McLean, I., Lodge, G. and Schmuecker, K. (2008). *Fair Shares? Barnett and the Politics of Public Expenditure*, London: IPPR.

McLean, I. and McMillan, A. (2005). *State of the Union: Unionism and the Alternatives in the United Kingdom since 1707*, Oxford: Oxford University Press.

Mandler, P. (2006). *The English National Character: The History of an Idea from Edmund Burke to Tony Blair*, New Haven CT: Yale University Press.

Massey, D. (2007). *World City*, Cambridge: Polity.

Melding, D. (2009). *Will Britain Survive beyond 2020?*, Cardiff: Institute of Welsh Affairs.

Mitchell, J. (2007) 'Citizens and nations: the rise of nationalism and decline of the British Keynesian welfare state (The 2006 O'Donnell lecture)', *Contemporary Wales*, 20, 1–20.

Mitchell, J. (2009). *Devolution in the UK*, Manchester: Manchester University Press.

Modood, T. (2007). *Multiculturalism*, Cambridge: Polity.

Nairn, T. (1977). *The Break-Up of Britain: Crisis and Neo-Nationalism*, London: New Left Books.

Nairn, T. (2000). *After Britain: New Labour and the Return of Scotland*, London: Granta.

Nairn, T. (2008). 'Globalization and nationalism: the new deal?' An Edinburgh Lecture delivered on 4 March 2008, *http://www.scotland.gov.uk/News/News-Extras/edlecture08* (accessed 2 April 2010).

Osmond, J. (2010). Review of *Will Britain Survive Beyond 2020* by David Melding (2009), *Scottish Affairs*, 70 (Autumn), 142–7.

Paterson, L. (1994). *The Autonomy of Modern Scotland*, Edinburgh: Edinburgh University Press.

Perryman, M. (ed.) (2008). *Imagined Nation: England after Britain*, London: Lawrence and Wishart.

Perryman, M. (ed.) (2009). *Breaking Up Britain: Four Nations after a Union*, London and Wishart.

Phillips, M. and Phillips, T. (1998). *Windrush: The Irresistible Rise of Multi-Racial Britain*, London: HarperCollins.

Phillips, T. (2005). 'Sleepwalking to segregation', speech to Manchester Council for Community Relations, 22nd September, http://83.137.212.42/sitearchive/cre/Defaulta866.html?LocID=0hgnew07s&RefLocID=0hg009c002.Lnag-ENhtm (accessed 18 May 2009).

Rokkan, S., and Urwin, D. W. (eds) (1982). *The Politics of Territorial Identity: Studies in European Regionalism*, London: Sage.

Royles, E. (2007). *Revitalizing Democracy? Devolution and Civil Society in Wales*, Cardiff: University of Wales Press.

Smith, A. D. (1991). *National Identity*, London: Penguin.

Uberoi, V. and McLean, I. (2009). 'Britishness: a role for the state?', in A. Gamble and T. Wright (eds), *Britishness: Perspectives on the British Question*, London: Political Quarterly.

Weber, M. (1948 [1912]). 'The nation', in H. H. Gerth and C. Wright Mills (eds), *From Max Weber: Essays in Sociology*, London: Routledge and Kegan Paul.

Weber, M. (1978 [1922]). *Economy and Society*, trans. G. Roth and C. Wittich, Berkeley, CA: University of California Press.

3. LABOUR AFTER POWER: WELSH LABOUR IN THE AGE OF COALITION

Gerald Taylor

ABSTRACT

The defeat of the Labour Party and the creation of a new coalition government at Westminster has led to a questioning of the New Labour project and a review of the Labour Party. This articles uses a critique of the 'renewal' of the Labour Party developed in 1997 to reassess the position of Welsh Labour now. It argues that the three issues facing the party then – ideological confusion, a lack of direct contact with potential support and a lack of a theory of the state – continue to face the party now and are, in some ways, more marked in Wales than in the UK as a whole. The article suggests that Welsh Labour needs to create new channels to contact its potential support if it is to address the continuing erosion of this support.

INTRODUCTION

The first decade of the twenty-first century has been an exciting, historic, even revolutionary one for Welsh politics. The creation of the National Assembly for Wales provided a new arena for the development of Welsh politics which proved the Welsh capacity for drama in the removal of the original First Secretary, Alun Michael; surprise in the failure of the expected Labour Party dominance of the body to materialize; and change in the continual development of Assembly powers, which demonstrated that Welsh devolution was indeed a process and not an event (Davies, 1999).

Preceding these changes, in 1997 at Westminster Labour had emerged from eighteen years of Conservative government with the brash New Labour project under the charismatic Tony Blair. Earlier that year I had provided my own damning critique of the Labour Party and its electoral chances (Taylor, 1997), just in time to herald thirteen years of Labour government and an unprecedented three consecutive majority Labour governments. In the last few years the New Labour project, which had appeared to deliver these successes, has become increasingly questioned and with the end of Labour government at Westminster the Labour Party itself, under its newly elected leader, Ed Miliband, has come to question its recent history and suggest a revision of policy and approach. It therefore seems an apt time to revisit such arguments and assess their significance considering the changes in the intervening period.

This has a particular salience in Wales given the supposed dominance of Labour in Wales and the fact that Welsh Labour now finds itself with a Westminster government composed of non-Labour parties. Why has the New Labour project failed? Why has Labour's supposed Welsh dominance not been reflected in dominance of the National Assembly? Has the last decade strengthened Labour in Wales?

LABOUR RENEWED?

In 1997 I argued that New Labour was rather a myth creating a straw man by revising Labour's history and presenting itself in opposition to it. I suggested that Blair's leadership was, in fact, a continuation of past Labour leaderships stretching back to Ramsey MacDonald and beyond. Centrally, I had stated that there were three major obstacles to Labour's renewal and that Labour would never be renewed as a left-of-centre democratic party unless these were dealt with (Taylor, 1997).

The first of these problems was Labour's ideological identity. Throughout its history Labour has sought to manage an effective compromise between holding a principled position, not necessarily socialist as such but at least leftward leaning and intellectually coherent, with the need to obtain power in the centralized, top-down British political system. No one has expressed these issues better than Aneurin Bevan, who argued that, whilst power was necessary to implement principles (Foot, 1975, p. 146), Labour had no hope of obtaining power if it did not hold to its principles (Bevan, 1978, p. 126). By 1997, 'the pragmatic basis of Labour's ideology, and its identification with Labour in government, and therefore Labour's parliamentary leadership' (Taylor, 1997, p. 10) had formed part of a gulf between Labour's leadership and party activists; exacerbated by the stance of New Labour this added to an ideological confusion amongst Labour's support about the party's core principles and beliefs.

As indicated, this had contributed to a second problem for the Labour Party: the relationship between the central party, particularly the party's parliamentary leadership, and its activists. Many commentators had observed the problem (see Tatchell, 1983; Wainwright, 1987; Whitley, 1983; Seyd and Whiteley, 1992), and Labour's attempts to avoid using the party and working through the media to contact members and supporters had provided a new dimension to this problem. For Labour's renewal the issue was twofold: 'Firstly, by attempting to reach potential supporters through non-party means Labour has separated out opinion forming and opinion receiving ... Secondly, in bypassing party channels crucial aspects of Labour's attempt to reach potential support are outside of its control' (Taylor, 1997, p. 12). So, Labour's attempts to marginalize 'extremist' activists left it in the hands of the media for communicating with its support, and public opinion researchers in determining reactions from that support. In the process, the leadership became more isolated and distanced from Labour's supporters, actual and potential, unable either to understand their concerns or to persuade them directly.

My third concern about Labour's renewal was essentially a development and restatement of the view put forward by Jones and Keating (1985), that: 'Labour's problem is not that it embraces state power as such, but that it uncritically embraces the British state as the form of state power' (Taylor, 1997, p. 13). This was particularly inconvenient in the 1980s, when a cocksure and confident Thatcherism had a very clear idea of the legitimate role of the state and to what the state should be restricted; in contrast Labour had little to offer in the way of a critique or theory of the state, and even the Blair government's constitutional reforms were based more on pragmatic political expediency than on any clear developed idea of the relationship between state and citizen (see, for example, Catterall, 2000, pp. 30–1). Faced with the New Thatcherism of David Cameron based on the presumption, amongst others, that that 'public services should be open to a range of providers competing to offer a better service', based on 'a clear rationale that the best way to raise quality and value for money is to allow different providers to offer services in an open and accountable way' (Cameron, 2011), Labour can only offer the belief that they are a better management team of the state, not that they have a developed and clear idea of the way the state might be improved.

I would argue that New Labour in fact addressed none of these issues and, indeed, exacerbated some aspects of them. I will consider this only tangentially with respect to the UK party because my focus will now be on Wales and the performance of Welsh Labour and to see how these issues have played out in Wales and what effect they may have on Labour's retention of power in the National Assembly.

CLEAR RED WATER?

In December 2002, in a speech to the National Centre for Public Policy, the then First Minister, Rhodri Morgan, set out what he saw as the distinctiveness or, as he termed it in a phrase borrowed from *The Guardian*, 'the so-called "clear red water" ... which has emerged over the lifetime of my administration between the way in which things are being shaped in Wales and the direction being followed at Westminster for equivalent services' (Morgan, 2002). Moreover, Morgan promised to reveal 'the ideological underpinnings which link these programmes together'. His argument put forward a commitment to 'citizenship rights' based on services free at the point of use, universal and unconditional, with an emphasis on equality seen as the marker of citizenship-based services, as opposed to the choice associated with consumer-based services. All of this is little more than a restatement of 'traditional' UK Labour perspectives from 1945 to 1975.

This is not to belittle this commitment; it certainly was a marked difference from the New Labour policies then being pursued by the Blair government. This was demonstrated by the criticism the Assembly government drew from Welsh Labour MPs over health policies and the failure to promote private finance initiative projects in Wales (Laffin *et al.*, 2004, pp. 69–70). However, it also followed the pragmatic approach of historic UK Labour values with no clear underlying ideological approach. Moreover, other pragmatic concerns were also an important aspect here, notably the need to maintain a coalition government in Wales, first with the Liberal Democrats from 2000 to 2003, and then with Plaid Cymru from 2007 to 2011, meaning that for more than half of the twelve years of the Assembly's existence Labour has maintained coalition government. Whilst the claims of both of Labour's coalition partners to have had a significant role in designing policy are unsurprising, this situation has not encouraged an alternative, identifiably Labour, ideological position to emerge.

One further restriction on Labour's 'clear red water' has been its relationship with the Westminster government, particularly those of Tony Blair. These restrictions have come in two forms, funding and policy-making. With respect to funding, as Jon Shortridge has pointed out:

> Wales remains on most measures one of the poorest parts of the UK. The Barnett formula is designed to make the Assembly's expenditure per head converge with that of comparable English departments over time. This in itself represents a huge challenge. (Shortridge, 2010, p. 90)

Given the emphasis of the current Cameron–Clegg coalition on reducing the public deficit, it seems unlikely that this challenge will diminish any time soon. With respect to policy-making, the tensions between Labour AMs and their MP colleagues in the Blair years have been noted above; these were exacerbated by the idiosyncratic division of policy responsibilities between Cardiff Bay and Westminster, the relationship between the Welsh Labour Party and the UK party and the design of the Assembly. Again, to quote Shortridge: 'The founding legislation – the Government of Wales Act 1998 – simply took a snapshot of the Welsh Office's powers at the point of devolution and transferred them to the Assembly. This meant that the powers had some jagged edges' (2010, p 87).

Ideological divisions between Labour in Wales and the Blair governments were also perceived by many in the election of Alun Michael as Labour's Welsh leader, following the departure of Ron Davies, and the attempt to broaden the process for the selection of candidates which notably focused on the selection of women candidates for winnable seats (Taylor, 2003a: 165–8). However, this was more perception than reality, particularly in the case of Michael's election, as at least some of the Welsh Executive Committee were themselves opposed to Michael's opponent, Rhodri Morgan, seeing him as Cardiff-based and unrepresentative of the wider Welsh party. Once Morgan was installed as First Minister and Blair had won his second electoral term at Westminster, relations became more relaxed and even supportive; as Morgan himself pointed out, it was in the interests of neither Welsh Labour nor UK Labour to scupper the electoral chances of the other (Laffin *et al.*, 2007, p. 209).

There was another factor which was affecting Labour policy in Wales, and this had become clear in the management of Assembly–local government relations. Whilst the initial structure of the Assembly had set up a range of institutional policy influences, through subject committees, regional committees and connections with business and the voluntary sector, it was the relationship with local government which proved one of the most significant in the early years. In particular, a new relationship grew up which was more supportive than had been the case with the Welsh Office, and was then the case with the relationship between English local authorities and the UK government, and one key factor in this was size. The fact was that the Welsh policy environment was simply too intimate to allow a hectoring approach; the major players within the local authorities and at the Assembly knew each other and worked with each other on a much closer basis than was true in the UK. This required a more cooperative and sympathetic approach which meant that the atmosphere and working relationship between the Assembly and local government was subtly, but profoundly, different in nature from that between the UK government and English local authorities (Laffin *et al.*, 2002). In other words, a structural rather than an ideological factor was crucial to the more supportive and cooperative policy processes which developed in Wales, and this is true both within the Assembly and in the Assembly's relations with other key actors.

The much vaunted 'clear red water' is less clear than it first appeared. It is bounded by the restrictions faced by Welsh Labour in their activities in the Assembly, and existed in a relaxed relationship with the Blair governments. In effect, the Blair government was prepared to ignore the distinctive policies of Wales at least to the extent that they did not incite adverse comparison with UK policy. Whilst this distinctiveness may be seen as providing a Welsh dimension to policy, this is not obviously ideological unless Welsh Labour is intrinsically seen as representing the values of Wales in some intellectually coherent sense. Moreover, part, at least, of the distinctiveness emerged as a result of the structural issue of the size of Wales's policy-making system and the closeness of those who inhabit it rather than as a result of any ideological difference.

LABOUR AND ITS SUPPORTERS

So what about the second area of concern: has Welsh Labour fared any better with respect to its relationship with its supporters? To some extent, the whole claim of a creation of policy difference, on a putative ideological basis, between the Labour governments at Westminster and Welsh Labour, or Labour-led, governments in Cardiff Bay was a tacit acknowledgement, at least in a Welsh context, of the idea of an ideological gulf between the elected leadership and the wider party, or in this case the Welsh party. In addition, there was also the context of Welsh political culture, which shaped Welsh Labour's organization and management. Before the creation of the Assembly and devolution, Welsh Labour was dominated by the idea of the 'unity of the working class', which 'questions of territorial management merely served to undermine' (Bevan quoted in McAllister, 1981, p. 84). This meant that, historically, Labour MPs had tended to focus on their constituencies and the House of Commons, seeing Welsh organization as little more than a distraction; changing social and economic conditions of the 1970s and 1980s had eroded Trade Union influence; and the electoral dominance of the party had not served to encourage a sizeable or active membership base (McAllister, 1981, pp. 79–83). This had contributed to a sense of parochialism and paternalism in the Welsh Labour Party, especially in its 'heartlands' such as the South Wales valleys.

Devolution and the creation of the National Assembly radically altered this political landscape. The arrival of sixty more elected professional politicians, their various staffs and associates, the burgeoning civil service in Cathays Park and Cardiff Bay, all created a new and vibrant political class. Moreover: 'The emergence of a strong central authority represent[ed] a profound innovation in Welsh political life ... The notion of Wales having a civic culture is novel to a society with such little experience of its own institutions' (Osmond, 2002, p. xx). Nor was this the only pressure towards a professionalization of the Welsh Labour Party; the impact of New Labour was also being felt, if perhaps less profoundly (Taylor, 2003b).

Whilst such changes altered the structure and nature of the Welsh Labour elite they essentially created a new focus around the elected Assembly members at the expense of power in the party hierarchy, let alone the wider party. Far from creating new avenues of communication between the elected leadership and the party's membership and supporters, a Welsh elected elite has developed alongside the UK elected elite. Given the centralized, UK, nature of the party Welsh Labour has shared in the Labour Party's membership decline and financial concerns during the Blair years (BBC News, 2006), which have been partially reversed since Labour's loss of UK office (*The Independent*, 2010). This has done little to revitalize a party which was never a model of grassroots activism, except in the sense of trade unionism activism before the 1980s.

The linkage between Welsh Labour and the UK party has been clear in the party's electoral fortunes as well. In fact the traditional advantage of the Welsh Labour Party in terms of differential turnout and Labour voting have both diminished, with turnout advantage disappearing altogether. Table 3.1 shows turnout in UK and Welsh elections since 1997. The table shows the drop in turnout in UK General Elections since 1997, but also that Wales's traditional higher turnout than the UK average, 2.1 per cent in 1997 and 2.0 per cent in 2001, had actually reversed by 2010. In fact, this underplays the situation as the Welsh differential had been well over 3 per cent in the 1980s (Taylor, 2005). Of course, the loss of Margaret Thatcher to mobilize the Welsh vote is a factor here, but this decline does not suggest a great performance by the Welsh Labour party in mobilizing its own vote following the demise of the union presence in Wales.

Table 3.2 shows the share of vote, in which Labour has declined since 1997 but maintained a Welsh advantage, though this too has declined, by about a half, since the 1980s (Taylor, 2005). It also shows Labour's share vote in the Assembly holding at roughly UK Labour Party levels, though interestingly below Welsh Labour Party levels in General Elections. Finally Table 3.3 takes

Table 3.1
Turn-out in general, European and Assembly elections 1997–2010 (%)

	1997	1999	2001	2003	2004	2005	2007	2009	2010
General elections (UK)	71.5	n/a	59.4	n/a	n/a	61.3	n/a	n/a	65.1
General elections (Wales)	73.6	n/a	61.4	n/a	n/a	62.4	n/a	n/a	64.9
European elections (UK)	n/a	24.1	n/a	n/a	38.2	n/a	n/a	34.5	n/a
European elections (Wales)	n/a	28.1	n/a	n/a	41.4	n/a	n/a	30.4	n/a
National Assembly elections	n/a	46.3	n/a	38.2	n/a	n/a	43.7	n/a	n/a
UK–Wales difference	2.1	4	2	n/a	3.2	1.1	n/a	-4.1	-0.2

Sources: Balsom (2003); BBC elections website (Last accessed 26th February 2011); author's calculations.

Table 3.2
Labour share of vote in general, European and Assembly elections 1997–2010 (%)

	1997	1999	2001	2003	2004	2005	2007	2009	2010
General elections (UK)	43.2	n/a	40.7	n/a	n/a	35.3	n/a	n/a	29
General elections (Wales)	54.7	n/a	48.6	n/a	n/a	42.7	n/a	n/a	36.2
European elections (UK)	n/a	29	n/a	n/a	22.6	n/a	n/a	15.7	n/a
European elections (Wales)	n/a	31.9	n/a	n/a	32.5	n/a	n/a	20.3	n/a
National Assembly elections	n/a	37.6	n/a	40	n/a	n/a	32.2	n/a	n/a
UK–Wales difference	11.5	2.9	7.9	n/a	9.9	7.4	n/a	4.6	7.2

Sources: Balsom (2003); Butler and Kavanagh (2002); BBC election website (Last accessed 26th February 2011); author's calculations.

Table 3.3
Proportion of electorate voting Labour in general, European and Assembly elections 1997–2010 (%)

	1997	1999	2001	2003	2004	2005	2007	2009	2010
General elections (UK)	30.9	n/a	24.2	n/a	n/a	21.6	n/a	n/a	18.9
General elections (Wales)	40.3	n/a	29.8	n/a	n/a	26.6	n/a	n/a	23.5
European elections (UK)	n/a	6.5	n/a	n/a	8.6	n/a	n/a	5.4	n/a
European elections (Wales)	n/a	9	n/a	n/a	13.5	n/a	n/a	6.2	n/a
National Assembly elections	n/a	17.3	n/a	15.3	n/a	n/a	13.11	n/a	n/a
UK–Wales difference	9.4	2.5	5.6	n/a	4.9	5	n/a	0.8	4.6

Sources: Balsom (2003); Butler and Kavanagh (2002); BBC election website (Last accessed 26th February 2011); author's calculations.

account of turnout and shows the proportion of those eligible to vote in the UK and Wales who actually bothered to go out and cast their votes for Labour. This is even less happy reading for the Labour Party in the UK or Wales. It shows that in 2010 only 18.9 per cent of UK voters were prepared to actually vote Labour, and 23.5 per cent in Wales, figures which compare poorly with Labour's electoral disaster year, 1983, when it achieved 20.1 per cent and 28.6 per cent respectively (Taylor, 2005). In fact in 2005 as well Welsh Labour did worse than in 1983. In other words, in 2010 fewer than one in four of Welsh voters who were eligible to do so bothered to actually vote Labour; in the 2007 Assembly election the figure was just over one in every eight. This seems a less than convincing result for a party styling itself *the* party of Wales.

The fact is that, despite the 'clear red water' and its attempts to identify itself with a set of distinctive Welsh values, the Welsh Labour Party is fail-ing to maintain and to mobilize its grassroots support. This situation is exac-erbated by the fact that it is thrown back on the Welsh media in attempting to contact and address its supporters as a regional part of a UK party focused on UK media. Take the case of Policy Development Grants. In 2000 the Political Parties, Elections and Referendums Act was passed. This provided for funds, currently standing at £2 million, to be provided for eligible political parties to develop policy (Electoral Commission, 2011). This means that we now have in the UK parties which are partly publicly funded, at least for this specific purpose. What was interesting was the way the parties dealt with this money. As part of our research on the Labour party and intergovernmental relations in the UK at that time, Martin Laffin and I asked the UK and Welsh Labour parties who got the Policy Development Grants. The UK party, then based at Millbank, made it clear to us that it received the grant and that it was used for UK policy-making purposes. In contrast, the Welsh Labour party figures we spoke to were unaware the funding even existed, let alone that the UK party was benefiting from it. Meanwhile Plaid Cymru used the money it received from the Electoral Commission to fund and support the development of its policies in the run-up to the 2003 and 2007 Assembly elections.

Nor can Welsh Labour take solace in its relationship with the Welsh media. Broadcast media (television and radio) have been driven by a UK agenda and a degree of standardization which has eroded the specifically Welsh content of the media (Barlow, 2006; Williams, 2006). Newspapers have been seen as culturally important in Wales, but even with their perceived importance 'there has never been an all-Wales national daily' (O'Malley, 2006, p. 205), which does not help an all-Wales National Assembly get its message across. Even the new media such as the Internet suffer from the same UK policy focus and lack of identifiable Welshness, or at least all-Welshness, as other media (Mitchell, 2006). Welsh media has tended to have a sub-national and regional focus, or a UK focus, just as Welsh MPs have tended to focus on their constituencies and Westminster. Whilst the creation of the Assembly provided a new focus for media attention, much to the chagrin of many MPs (Laffin *et al.*, 2004, p. 65), the broadcast media at least have tended to be seen as hostile to devolution and the Assembly (Williams, 2006, p. 216). The lack of a clear all-Wales focus and the problems of managing media coverage this creates merely add to the problem Welsh Labour faces in utilizing the media as a means to contact supporters compared with the UK party.

LABOUR, DEVOLUTION AND THE STATE

The significance of the consideration given to the constitutional role of the National Assembly and the relationship between the 'citizens' and the state in Wales can perhaps be seen by the fact that the work of the National Assembly

Advisory Group (NAAG), whose job was 'effectively to fill in the details of the new Welsh constitution' (Laffin and Thomas, 2000, p. 561), has been virtually ignored in the discussions of the Assembly's creation (Morgan and Mungham, 2000; Shipton, 2011). Indeed NAAG was itself the product of a practical need and its initiation as much to do with political expediency as constitutional design; moreover throughout its work it was the political balance of Wales and the practical need to deliver support for the Assembly which drove discussion, not a principled debate about the nature of the Welsh constitution (Laffin and Thomas, 2000).

The result was to create the necessity for devolution in Wales to be a process through the hop, skip and jump approach to a full law-making body. So the Assembly set up by the Government of Wales Act 1998 was then subject to new debate about its proper role and powers with the Richard Commission created in 2002 and reporting in 2004. The Commission's Terms of Reference asked it to consider the Assembly's powers and electoral arrangements. Along with the Assembly's nature as a corporate body, and its committee system, these had been seen as key to assuaging existing political power centres in Wales, notably local government, who were fearful of the impact of the new Assembly.

The Commission's report advocated three main changes: that primary law-making powers be legislated for the Assembly; that the corporate status of the Assembly be modified to include an executive and legislature, which had essentially already occurred in practice; and the increasing of Assembly Member numbers from sixty to eighty to cope with the management of primary legislation (Richard Commission, 2004). The UK Government response, in the 2005 White Paper *Better Governance for Wales* (Welsh Office, 2005), allowed for enhanced law-making powers, with a possible referendum for full powers; the creation of a legislative and executive in the Assembly; and disallowing individuals standing as both constituency and regional list candidates in Wales's hybrid electoral system. The changes were clearly pragmatic and to do with short-term political advantage. Full primary powers were not granted because of the opposition of some Labour MPs (see Richard Commission, 2004, p. 305), although enhanced powers were provided in order to avoid the problems of managing Welsh legislation in a packed Westminster legislative timetable. Meanwhile, an increase in Assembly Member numbers was seen as a hard sell in an era when the cost of politics was a focus of the electorate, whilst disallowing joint candidacies for constituency and regional list Assembly Members provided a political problem for Labour's opponents in the Assembly, as Labour was most likely to win the constituency seats outright. The Government of Wales Act 2006 followed the White Paper and included the possibility of a referendum on full law-making powers.

The final jump into full law-making powers is now well on its way with the referendum having been triggered and won, in fairly emphatic fashion, in March 2011. However, the point is that the current constitution of the Assembly has been arrived at as a result of a series of pragmatic moves rather than a clear set of constitutional principles and perspectives. This is not to suggest that the form of the Assembly is either unsustainable or indefensible, though its original form proved to be so; rather it is to emphasize that in the context of Welsh devolution Labour has again demonstrated that it has no clear, overarching view of the proper role between the state and the citizen.

CONCLUSION

So what is the point of this debate? The Labour Party is in the midst of a policy review unlike anything since that of the 1980s. The Labour leader, Ed Miliband, has called on party activists to make Labour the 'people's party' again (BBC News, 2010). In 1997, I set out three areas Labour would need to address to achieve just this aim. Failure to tackle these areas would not mean that Labour would never be elected again, It is perfectly possible that Labour could regain power because of the unpopularity of the current coalition government, and, indeed, it is part of the premise of this argument, implied but unexplored here, that that is what happened from 1997 until 2010, leading to Labour's historical electoral victories achieved with a declining proportion of the UK and Welsh electorate in support. It is even possible, as Eric Deakins (1988) postulated, that a Labour Party could once again form a government but share no more than its name with the historical Labour Party. It might be argued that this is close to what happened under 'New' Labour and Tony Blair.

I have argued here that those same three issues, a lack of ideological clarity, a lack of direct connection with potential supporters, and a lack of any theory of the role of the state, also hamper the party in Wales. Indeed, when applied to Wales the problems take on a particular and, in some ways, more worrying perspective. As I have shown, the idea of 'clear red water' in ideological terms between the Welsh party and the UK party, and the changes to the constitution of the National Assembly have followed entirely pragmatic paths. However, where the Welsh party looks particularly vulnerable is in its connections with its activists and supporters. It is, to say the least, debatable whether Labour was ever the kind of 'people's party' which Miliband suggests, but in Wales a history of poor engagement by the party with the Welsh people, reliance on the trade unions to mobilize and organize support, and a fragmented, sub-national and UK-dependent media has exacerbated Labour's problems. In the UK the major problem for Labour in relying on the media to contact its core or potential support is that the media are not neutral and certainly not supportive of Labour; indeed it is difficult to imagine the circumstances under which a media business in a capitalist society might support the putative socialist aims of an organization such as the Labour Party. In Wales the additional problem of having a fragmented media makes the use of the media as a vehicle extremely difficult; add in Welsh Labour's own dependence on the UK party and the problem seems insurmountable.

These issues are, of course, interrelated, not isolated. As a result, particularly in the Welsh context, Labour needs to find new channels to link itself with its support. One means would be the old means of party activists and activism, but to achieve this would require a considerable culture change within the party itself.

REFERENCES

Balsom, D. (ed.) (2003). *The Wales Yearbook 2003*, Aberystwyth: Francis Balsom Associates.
Barlow, D. M. (2006). 'Reassessing radio: role, scope and accountability', *Contemporary Wales*, 18, 140–55.
BBC News (2006). 'Labour "facing membership crisis"', http://news.bbc.co.uk/1/hi/6209399.stm (accessed 15 February 2011).
BBC News (2010). 'Ed Miliband: Labour must reclaim "big society" concept', http://www.bbc.co.uk/news/uk-politics-11851318 (accessed 15 February 2011).
Bevan, A. (1978). *In Place of Fear*, London: Quartet.
Butler, D. and Kavanagh, D. (2002). *The British General Election of 2001*, Basingstoke: Palgrave.
Cameron, D. (2011). 'How we will release the grip of state control', *Daily Telegraph*, 20 February, http://www.telegraph.co.uk/comment/8337239/How-we-will-release-the-grip-of-state-control.html (accessed 3 March 2011).
Catterall, P. (2000). '"Efficiency with freedom"? Debates about the British constitution in the twentieth century', in P. Catterall, W. Kaiser and U. Walton-Jordan (eds), *Reforming the Constitution: Debates in Twentieth-Century Britain*, London: Frank Cass.
Davies, R. (1999). *Devolution: A Process Not an Event*, Cardiff: IWA.
Deakins, E. (1988). *What Future for Labour?*, London: Hilary Shipman.
Electoral Commission (2011). 'Public funding for parties', http://www.electoralcommission.org.uk/party-finance/public_funding (accessed 3 March 2011).
Foot, M. (1975). *Aneurin Bevan, 1897–1945*, St Albans: Granada.
The Independent (2010). '32,000 "surge" in Labour party membership', 13 September, http://www.independent.co.uk/news/uk/politics/32000-surge-in-labour-party-membership-2078249.html (accessed 15 December 2010).
Jones, B. and Keating, M. (1985). *Labour and the British State*, Oxford: Clarendon Press.

Laffin, M. and Thomas, A. (2000). 'Designing the National Assembly for Wales', *Parliamentary Affairs*, 53, 3, 557–76.

Laffin, M., Taylor, G. and Thomas, A. (2002). *A New Partnership? The National Assembly for Wales and Local Government*, York: Joseph Rowntree Foundation.

Laffin, M., Taylor, G. and Thomas, A. (2004). 'Devolution and party organization: the case of the Wales Labour Party', *Contemporary Wales*, 16, 53–74.

Laffin, M., E. Shaw and G. Taylor (2007). 'The parties and intergovernmental relations', in A. Trench (ed.), *Devolution and Power in the United Kingdom*, Manchester: Manchester University Press.

McAllister, I. (1981). 'The Labour Party in Wales: the dynamics of one-partyism', *Llafur: The Journal of Welsh Labour History*, 3, 2, 79–89.

Mitchell, P. (2006). 'Constructing the e-nation: the internet in Wales', *Contemporary Wales*, 18, 191–201.

Morgan, K. and Mungham, G. (2000). *Redesigning Democracy: The Making of the Welsh Assembly*, Bridgend: Seren.

Morgan, R. (2002). 'Clear red water', speech available at http://www.sochealth.co.uk/ Regions/Wales/redwater.htm (accessed 20 December 2010).

O'Malley, T. (2006). 'The newspaper press in Wales', *Contemporary Wales*, 18, 202–13.

Osmond, J. (2002). 'Introduction: emergence of the Assembly Government', in J. B. Jones and J. Osmond (eds), *Building a Civic Culture: Institutional Change, Policy Development and Political Dynamics in the National Assembly for Wales*, Cardiff: IWA/WGC.

Richard Commission (2004). *Report of the Richard Commission*, Cardiff: NAW. http:// www.richardcommission.gov.uk/content/finalreport/report-e.pdf (accessed date).

Seyd, P. and P. Whiteley (1992). *Labour's Grass Roots: The Politics of Party Membership*, Oxford: Clarendon Press.

Shipton, M. (2011). *Poor Man's Parliament: Ten Years of the Welsh Assembly*, Bridgend: Seren.

Shortridge, J. (2010). 'New development: the evolution of Welsh devolution', *Public Money & Management*, 30, 2, 87–90.

Tatchell, P. (1983). *The Battle for Bermondsey*, London: Heretic.

Taylor, G. (1997). *Labour's Renewal? The Policy Review and Beyond*, Basingstoke: Macmillan.

Taylor, G. (2003a). 'Labour', in J. Osmond and J. Barry Jones (eds), *Birth of Welsh Democracy: The First Term of the National Assembly for Wales*, Cardiff: IWA/WGC.

Taylor, G. (2003b). 'Can New Labour save Wales from itself', *Planet*, 158, 32–6.

Taylor, G. (2005). 'Disaster, whose Disaster? The National Assembly election 2003', *Contemporary Wales*, 17, 113–27.

Wainwright, H. (1987). *Labour: A Tale of Two Parties*, London: Hogarth Press.

Welsh Office (2005). *Better Governance for Wales* (Cm 6582), Norwich: HMSO.

Whitley, P. (1983). *The Labour Party in Crisis*, London: Methuen.

Williams, K. (2006). 'An uncertain era: Welsh television, broadcasting policy and the National Assembly in a multimedia world', *Contemporary Wales*, 18, 214–35.

4. AN EXERCISE IN DEMOCRATIC DELIBERATION: THE ALL WALES CONVENTION'S CONTRIBUTION TO CONSTITUTIONAL CHANGE

Diana Stirbu and Laura McAllister

ABSTRACT

This article assesses the work of the All Wales Convention, which met between July 2008 and November 2009, against the background of Wales's developing politics and constitution. It examines the establishment and operation of the Convention, its terms of reference and its guiding principles. It also explores the role and significance of independent inquiries similar to the Convention in promoting and enhancing participation in political processes, as well as augmenting constitutional debates and becoming an important mechanism for informing government decision-making. The article uses documentary research alongside elite interviews with the chair of the Convention, the former First Minister, the Rt Hon. Rhodri Morgan AM (whose One Wales coalition government had established the Convention), Convention members, and political commentators and academics.

INTRODUCTION

The All Wales Convention (the Convention) was established by the Welsh Assembly Government with the stated objective of gauging the public's views on a move towards primary law-making powers, as stipulated in Part IV of the Government of Wales Act 2006 (the 2006 Act). The Convention emerged late in the negotiations between Labour and Plaid Cymru which resulted in the *One Wales* coalition agreement, following the Assembly elections in May 2007 that produced no overall party majority (Labour won twenty-six of the sixty seats, Plaid Cymru fifteen, the Welsh Conservatives twelve, the Welsh Liberal

Democrats six and an independent candidate one). The One Wales agreement incorporated a pledge to:

> proceed to a successful outcome of a referendum for full law-making powers under Part IV [of the 2006 Act] as soon as practicable, at or before the end of the Assembly term. (One Wales, 2007)

There was some debate as to the value and validity of a referendum on what might be construed as a technical or constitutional shift that had already been provided for through the original devolution referendum held in 1997 (House of Lords, 2010, Institute of Welsh Affairs submission). Nevertheless, the 2006 Act was drafted in a political context that required the setting out of the steps necessary for a move to a different mechanism for drawing down powers, which it was deemed required support in a national referendum (GWA, 2006, §§ 103–4).

Although the Chair of the Convention, Sir Emyr Jones-Parry (the former British Permanent Representative to the UN and former UK Permanent Representative to NATO), was nominated in October 2007 by the First and the Deputy First Ministers of the Welsh Assembly Government, it was not until July 2008 that the rest of the Convention's membership was appointed (WalesOnline, 2008). The Convention's terms of reference were debated and agreed by an Establishing Committee comprising Labour and Plaid Assembly Members and MPs, as well as the Convention Chair (AWC, 2009). These included raising awareness and improving understanding of the current constitutional arrangements in Wales; facilitating a wide-ranging participatory consultation on the Assembly's law-making powers; and informing and advising the Welsh Assembly Government on people's views and the levels of support for a referendum proposing primary law-making powers to the National Assembly (AWC, 2009, pp. 9–10). It is against these core terms of reference that we base our evaluation of the Convention's role and impact.

The Convention undertook a wide consultation process between January and July 2009,[1] not only testing Welsh people's views in the light of the forthcoming referendum, but also seeking to raise awareness about existing constitutional arrangements in Wales. It reported to the government on 18 November 2009. Its findings highlighted increased support for devolution (with 72 per cent of the public favouring the present devolution or more), as well as the limited understanding of devolution arrangements in Wales (AWC, 2009, p. 7). The report also made the case for the substantial advantages presented by moving to Part IV of the 2006 Act (AWC, 2009, p. 6).

In response to the specific task set out in the Convention's terms of reference, the report suggested that a referendum on primary law-making powers was winnable, but with no guarantees of a 'yes' vote (AWC, 2009). The report was positively received in most circles, being praised by both the then First Minister, Rhodri Morgan, and the Deputy First Minister, Ieuan Wyn Jones. It is significant for what follows that they focused specifically on its success in engaging with the general public and its efforts to raise awareness about constitutional matters in Wales (WAG, 2009).

Subsequently, in February 2010, the Assembly unanimously passed a referendum motion proposed by the First Minister under Part IV of the 2006 Act (NAfW Record of Proceedings, 2010a). With an ensuing UK General Election and a subsequent change in government, it was not until June 2010 that the newly appointed Secretary of State for Wales, the Rt Hon. Cheryl Gillan, presented a draft referendum question for consultation (Wales Office, 2010). The Electoral Commission, as the UK's official body for setting the standards for running elections and referendums, reported in September 2010, after public consultation, with recommendations for the wording of the referendum question and of its preamble (Electoral Commission, 2010). Draft Orders in relation to the National Assembly for Wales referendum – setting the date as 3 March 2011 – were laid before Parliament by the Secretary of State for Wales on 21 October 2010, and the National Assembly unanimously agreed on the Draft Referendum Order on 9 November 2010 (NAfW Record of Proceedings, 2010b).

For fairly obvious reasons, the Convention has, to date, been subjected to little academic analysis. This article offers a first contribution through a contextualized evaluation of its work. We assess its contribution to a more evidence-based policy process, to the nature of participation engendered, and to its role in promoting greater civic self-governance. In examining the operation of the Convention, we locate it within the wider process of constitution building in Wales since the advent of devolution. The article's aims are threefold. First, we provide a narrative of the Convention's operation, exploring its terms of reference, membership and modus operandi. Second, we offer an early-stage evaluation of its main contribution to advancing a wider and more mature debate on constitutional arrangements through examination of its participatory nature. Third, we evaluate the Convention's impact on, and its contribution to, debates on framing the next stages of constitutional change through the staging of the 2011 referendum (in particular, considerations of the precise wording of the question and matters of timing).

In terms of theoretical perspectives, the evaluation is conducted against a backdrop of understandings of participatory democracy. We start with the assumption that this type of independent review or commission inquiry represents an important component of deliberative democracy, since it might potentially contribute to rational legislation (through evidence-based policy-making), a more participatory politics, and enhancing civic self-governance (Bohman and Rehg, 1997). Despite a possible confusion in the terminology, the Convention can, in fact, be regarded as the equivalent of a commission, understood in the broadest sense as a semi-independent body with an advisory role set up by government or parliament to examine certain issues of public and political concern (Rowe and McAllister, 2006). Constitutional conventions, on the other hand, may, in practice, differ from commissions on the grounds of their usual bottom-up approach as well as their methodology; they are usually purposeful associations established with a view to writing or revising constitutions (Dahl, 2002) (e.g. the Scottish Constitutional Convention).

Within the fluid context of devolution in Wales, independent commissions have been used informally to validate constitutional and institutional arrangements. In this context, the Convention is significant for three reasons. As indicated, these mirror the main tenets of its terms of reference: to raise awareness and improve understanding about the current arrangements (which we interpret as an educator role); to facilitate and stimulate a widespread, thorough and participative consultation at all levels of Welsh society (as public engagement facilitator); to prepare and analyse views expressed, assessing the levels of support for primary legislative powers, and to report its findings to the Welsh Assembly Government (as contributing to evidence-based policy-making). Its role in extending debate on constitutional matters beyond the 'usual suspects' and the consultation approaches used make it an interesting and important case study of approaches to deliberation and promoting wider participation.

METHODOLOGY

This article draws from several research projects on devolution, alongside some new research into preparations for the March 2011 referendum. We used semi-structured, elite interviews with former members of the All Wales Convention, and with government and parliamentary officials. Among our interviewees were the Convention's Chair, Sir Emyr Jones Parry, and the former First Minister, the Rt Hon. Rhodri Morgan AM. For ethical and confidentiality reasons we have chosen to use general references to interviews conducted in order to protect our interviewees' identity. The small size of the Convention makes its members easily identifiable, whereas the nature of some of its work, to which we had access through these in-depth interviews, raises confidentiality issues.

We assess the Convention's contribution to the broader constitutional process by looking at its deliberative and engaging operation within the context of an emergent participatory democracy in Wales, and ask whether, through its operation and dissemination, the Convention reached beyond the 'usual suspects', thus expanding the constitutional debate in Wales. In terms of its educator role, it is methodologically almost impossible to offer a hard empirical assessment of its success in closing the knowledge gap in Welsh society with regards to politics and constitutional arrangements. The two social research surveys commissioned by the Convention in November/December 2008 and April/May 2009 (AWC, 2009, pp. 84–5) could serve as the basis for an *ex post* analysis to indicate any variation in the levels of knowledge. However, such assessment would be crude and blind to other factors that might facilitate or impede understanding of devolution. Furthermore, given that the MPs' expenses scandal was at its peak when the second survey was conducted, public perception might have been skewed by the media frenzy around Westminster politics especially. Instead, we focus on the 'soft' impact, exploring the maturing debate promoted by the Convention, and its innovative ways of reaching out to the general public.

THEORETICAL BACKGROUND

This article builds on previous attempts to contextualize the work of independent commissions in Britain (Rowe and McAllister, 2006) and in Wales in particular (McAllister, 2005; McAllister and Stirbu, 2008). McAllister (2005) has suggested that the role of independent commissions has increased with the shift from government to governance, and with the wider network of agencies and social actors being involved in policy-making. Less institutionalized, ad hoc commissions and conventions play similar roles, though the literature offers a wider rationale, connected with government reluctance to take controversial or difficult decisions (Herbert, 1961). Commissions can also be a tactic for sidelining sensitive issues, especially within the trend towards evidence-based policy-making and the need to accumulate independent research and information that the government does not have the time, the expertise or (perhaps) the inclination to acquire on its own (McAllister, 2005). We approach commissions, alongside other similar participatory initiatives, as potentially integral components of deliberative democracy (Bohman and Rehg, 1997). Goodin and Dryzek (2008) argue that these institutionalized forms of democratic deliberation (also included here are citizen juries, consensus conferences and deliberative polls) inform policy-making, by using 'mini-publics' to test and legitimize policy debates, and to build consensus around policy options.

   The article also represents a first attempt to locate the work of the Convention against a theoretical backdrop of institutionalism, which assumes that political institutions are central to explaining political phenomena because they shape political actors' behaviour (March and Olsen, 1989). Moreover, relevant for our discussion on the Convention, institutions are often seen to be validated by outsiders and protected by insiders (March and Olsen, 2006). This continual validation and re-validation game plays an important role in ensuring the legitimacy of political institutions and in sustaining deliberative democracy.

CONTEXT FOR THE CONVENTION

Longitudinal opinion polling in Wales (NAfW Public Attitude Survey, 2008; BBC Wales/ICM, 2010) has shown a low level of knowledge about politics in general. Although a UK-wide problem (as continuously shown by the Hansard Society Annual Audit of Political Engagement, 2004–10), this has greater significance in Welsh politics for two reasons: first, the perceived limited legitimacy of the Assembly as a result of the marginal vote in favour in the 1997 referendum (Taylor and Thompson, 1999) and, second, the complexity of the ensuing constitutional arrangements for devolution in Wales, which, it might be argued, make intelligibility difficult (McAllister, 2000; Rawlings, 2003).

The other key contextual aspect is Wales's limited exposure to public deliberation on constitutional matters. Prior to devolution, Wales had experienced scarcely any debate over its constitutional future, especially when compared with Scotland. There had been a very small-scale Constitutional Conference in 1995, organized by the Parliament for Wales Campaign, that adopted a *Democracy Declaration* (Osmond, 1995, p. 171). However, it was not until after the establishment of the National Assembly that constitutional deliberation permeated from political and academic elites to having some (albeit limited) resonance with the general public.

In the first decade of devolution, Wales has seen a number of important commissions of inquiry (apart from the Convention itself) reviewing various aspects of its constitution: the Richard Commission (2002–4), established to examine the appropriateness of existing constitutional arrangements, and the Holtham Commission (2008–9), which investigated the financing of devolution in Wales (Holtham Commission, 2009).

In recent years, both regional and UK-wide constitutional arrangements have come under reconsideration. Apart from the reviews in Wales, the Scottish National Party (SNP) government in Scotland launched the National Conversation in August 2007, whilst the Scottish Parliament appointed the Calman Commission to investigate the role and position of Scotland within the Union (Calman Commission, 2009). Additionally, the House of Lords Select

Committee on the Barnett Formula reviewed the system of financing the nations of the UK (House of Lords, 2009), while the Lords Constitution Committee conducted a review of the Welsh Legislative Competence Orders process and its impact on Westminster (House of Lords, 2008).

This fluid constitutional and institutional context, marked by attempts to tackle issues of legitimacy, is emblematic of Wales. It is against this context that we try to understand the operation of the Convention and its role and impact on constitutional debates.

THE NARRATIVE: THE OPERATION OF THE ALL WALES CONVENTION

Set-up, membership and terms of reference

Despite there being no mention of a Convention in any of the party manifestos, our interviewees saw its establishment after the 2007 Assembly election as a natural progression for the debate on devolution. One interviewee highlighted this, commenting on some confusion and lack of clarity surrounding its establishment:

> It came out of a political need, to implement the One Wales Agreement. They [the government] might have had something like the Scottish Constitutional Convention in mind, but that was direct consequence of the civic society initiative. (Interview, November 2010)

Two other interviewees perceived it as an expected development in Wales's politics and a necessary excuse for the government in view of the crucial decision to require a referendum before moving to Part IV of the 2006 Act. Apart from the fact that it takes Legislative Competence Orders between six and twenty-four months to receive Royal Assent, which bolsters intellectual arguments for a move to Part IV, the alibi was needed to confirm there was enough consensus and public support for such a move.

The membership of the Convention had to carry sufficient weight to influence Westminster and Whitehall, as well as Wales. The appointment of Sir Emyr Jones Parry, who was born and educated in Wales and had chaired the Security Council of the United Nations for four terms, was felt to have the right profile and to carry sufficient weight.

In the context of the wider debate on legitimacy, the perceived representativeness of the Convention was crucial. The appointment procedure for the members of the Convention broadly followed that of the Richard Commission (McAllister, 2004), seeking to ensure substantial representativeness. The only change to the Richard Commission appointment approach was a mechanism for recruiting four members of the general public through open competition. In theory at least, the representativeness of the Convention could not be challenged. The Convention's members had to fulfil a broad spectrum of roles ranging from the traditional commission roles (gather expert evidence and gauge the views of the public, inform government's decision making) to roles more common to public educational campaigns (raise awareness and increase understanding). Despite the complexity and the amalgamation of roles, the members we interviewed did not think these were conflicting, seeing them instead as 'challenging' and naturally complementing each other. Having said that, some of the interviewees agreed that the budget and support allocated did not necessarily match the broad portfolio they had to cover, thus raising questions about capacity (especially on the external communications side).

The Convention as educator: the issue of complexity
The terms of reference envisaged raising awareness and promoting understanding of the current constitutional arrangements in Wales: the operation of the Assembly in general and the legislative process in particular.

Unsurprisingly, the Convention realized early on that fulfilling its educational role would be very difficult. It was, first of all, a matter of self-education. Only once the Convention's members understood the detailed devolution landscape themselves could they engage in a meaningful debate. Although the Convention engaged actively in understanding the legislative process – by commissioning research on the issues, by meeting lawyers and government and Assembly officials, and by liaising with academics – it soon came to appreciate the complexity of the current system and realized the lack of knowledge among lay people as well as among the professionals:

> we talked to lots of professionals in different sectors and realized that the complexity and the ignorance surrounding the devolution in Wales go hand in hand (especially in what the legislative process is concerned). (Interview, July 2010)

The complexity of the existing devolution arrangements in Wales is significant since one of the Convention's tasks was to distil the information on constitutional arrangements in Wales and transmit it to the general public in a simple and comprehensible form. As one of our interviewees noted, that was extremely difficult because 'language can distort' and, given the mass ignorance uncovered in its early days, one thing the Convention could not afford to do was to present a distorted image of the devolution arrangements in Wales to the general public.

The Convention undertook two pieces of social research (based on telephone surveys and discussion groups) in order to gauge the level of public understanding of devolution in Wales. As one member mentioned, one of the most staggering findings was that:

> virtually no one in Wales [from the general public] knew the difference between the National Assembly for Wales and the Welsh Assembly Government [that is between the executive or government and the legislature or parliament]. (Interview, July 2010)

Therefore, in the process of public constitutional deliberation in Wales, simply asking people whether they would support a move to Part IV of the 2006 Act without carefully explaining the current setup would have been pointless.

The educational role was significant for two reasons. The first was linked with the legitimacy question. Constitutional experts have already pointed out that devolution arrangements in Wales have been unintelligible and complex to the extent that they were at threat of undermining the very principles of democracy (see Rawlings 2003, 2005). Other studies link the lack of knowledge about politics with the low level of public engagement in politics and the low turnout in elections (Hansard Society, 2004–10). In this context, 'educating' the public, by engaging the ordinary people in a discussion about devolution, seeks to redress that knowledge deficit, in turn increasing the legitimacy of the political system as a whole.

Second, from the perspective of evidence-based policy-making, the Convention's task was to inform the government on whether a referendum would be winnable or not (AWC, 2009). This type of assessment needed accurate data on what people's views were, and people's lack of knowledge on the matter would have skewed the data presented to the Convention, thus shedding doubts on the robustness of the evidence presented to the government.

It is difficult to assess whether the Convention had fulfilled its educational role since there were no strict criteria for success set out in the first place. One of the members noted:

> one of the things that Convention did not do, was to put right all the public ignorance about the Welsh devolution. We didn't have the appropriate expertise and the resources to turn the Welsh public into devolution literates overnight. (Interview, July 2010)

We use this as a starting point in judging the Convention's success in fulfilling its educator role. The Convention Report highlighted low levels of public understanding of constitutional arrangements (AWC, 2009), and significantly, given a backdrop of limited data, backed their findings with solid evidence and measured arguments.

The Convention as public engagement facilitator

The complexity and the lack of understanding of the devolution arrangements in Wales and of the referendum issues in particular were just one solid obstruction that added up to a typically Welsh reluctance to engage in a discussion about constitutional matters, as one of our interviewees noted:

> The All Wales Convention was about involving the Welsh public. But to what extent you can get a working country like Wales to express a view on the constitution, was very hard. (Interview, July 2010).

Nevertheless, the Convention's work would suggest that people can be reached and that at least some of the public would engage in a serious debate given the opportunity. The Convention was relatively imaginative in creating such engagement opportunities. Its communication and consultation strategy envisaged reaching 'as wide a cross section of the Welsh public as possible' (AWC, 2009, p. 11). The Convention used stakeholders' own networks to tap into many Welsh communities (e.g. Wales Council for Voluntary Action, Welsh Rugby Union, local authorities, Urdd Gobaith Cymru). It conducted formal public meetings and evidence sessions, launched a wide communications campaign which included advertising in local newspapers and media, and held meetings in all local authorities in Wales. Less formally, the Convention engaged in talking to people in supermarkets, attending curry nights, visiting schools, going on road shows, attending community events (Urdd Eisteddfod in Cardiff) and the use of social networking (interactive website and Facebook page) (AWC, 2009).

Public meetings were generally well attended (on average between 60 and 150 attendees). Nevertheless, one member acknowledged the rather 'forced' format of the public meetings:

> it was as if people were trying to be official and the officials [the members of the Convention and the Convention secretariat] were trying to be the ordinary people. (Interview, July 2010)

Some of our interviewees agreed that another fundamental problem with the public meetings was the fact that they attracted only people who were strongly in favour or deeply hostile to the referendum, leaving a wide opinion gap in the middle. One interviewee noted that:

There were also people with a very fixed agenda and that is fair enough because the convention was an arena where they could express themselves. It was clear that some people were not there only to give evidence but also to persuade the other participants. (Interview, July 2010)

This is not unusual for this form of formal public engagement. Arter (2004) highlights the fact that public hearings in Scandinavian Committees are sometimes hijacked by political vendettas, while McAllister and Stirbu (2007) have discussed the volume of anecdotal evidence amassed by some of the Assembly committees in their consultation exercises. Irrespective of the way public consultations and inquiries are conducted and who conducts them, all public hearings and consultations are susceptible to vendettas or to polarization of opinion. It is the task of secretariats and members of such bodies to make sense of the evidence and to widen the pool of opinions and expertise into which they give access.

Given the systemic shortcomings of formal types of engagement (public meetings, evidence gathering), it is no surprise that they rarely reach beyond the 'usual' suspects. It is a credit to the Convention that it sought to create new avenues to hear different people's views. Despite some commentators' scepticism about the Convention's ability to reach ordinary people (Shipton, 2008), the Convention members considered the road-shows, the informal chats with people in supermarkets, and the curry night in Port Talbot to be important and meaningful consultation experiences. The curry night initiative left some in the Welsh media deeply unimpressed by the merits of such a public engagement tool (Shipton, 2009) but one member of the Convention noted that initiatives like this represented

the most important and honest consultation ... that went beyond the cynicism of journalism and people genuinely expressed what they felt. It's never been done before. (Interview, July 2010)

The Convention also established an important presence through articles it published on websites and newsletters belonging to various stakeholder organizations (such as Funky Dragon, Wales Council for Voluntary Action, Council of Ethnic Minorities Voluntary Organizations, TUC Wales) and in the local media (AWC, 2009, pp. 112–113). Our interviewees highlighted some difficulties in reaching out and communicating to and through the media, especially the printed media. These stemmed from a certain reluctance in the printed media to publish political content that they thought would not necessarily appeal to their general public.

Nonetheless, the Convention showed some imaginative and innovative approaches to engaging the public in what remains a technical, constitutional debate. While this has value in its own right, it does raise issues of 'appropriateness'. One of the interviewees stated that:

> in ordinary democracies, people do not need to know the nitty gritty details of how things works. But Wales is no ordinary democracy. Interview, July 2010)

So, why go to such lengths to reach the uninterested, who might be deemed 'unreachable'? It can be argued that the narrow referendum vote in 1997 left a question mark hanging over the legitimacy of the Assembly, and that the National Assembly has long been trying to answer that question by championing new forms of public engagement and participation in the political process. As one of our interviewees noted:

> it was this vulnerability (limited legitimacy and public appeal) that eventually made the Assembly so strong in engaging with the public and especially with communities that have traditionally felt excluded from the political process. It comes as no surprise that the Hindu or the Muslim communities in Wales chose to celebrate their holy days in the Senedd. (Interview, July 2010)

From a deliberative democracy perspective, the Convention's contribution to enhancing public participation in the political process – if only for the period of the Convention's existence – is extremely significant. Rather than adopting a 'one size fits all' approach to the consultation process, the Convention's targeted communication and its consultation strategy suggest a focus on meaningful engagement with the public. Our interviewees confirm that some of these engagement mechanisms were indeed important and honest.

Looked at from an institutionalist perspective, any change in complex institutional settings where the legitimacy of the institution has been questioned reinforces the need for wider consultation and for evidence-based decision-making. In the case of Wales, some authors argue that the particularities of devolution (limited powers, complexity, hybrid constitutional arrangements) acted as facilitators for enhanced public consultation and engagement (McAllister and Stirbu, 2007). In the present case, matters are overly complicated by the fact that the decision to hold a referendum had to be made on the basis of evidence gathered from people who were, and have long been, ill-informed, sceptical or uninterested in devolution.

The Convention as an excuse

To some extent, the Convention's role in informing the Welsh Assembly Government in its decision-making process is a natural progression from the other roles and 'identities' imposed by the terms of reference. Apart from the conclusion that 'a "Yes" vote is winnable' (AWC, 2009, p. 7) but with no guarantees, two other simple yet important messages stood out: first, how complex current devolution arrangements were and how little they were publicly understood; and second, how difficult it was to communicate the political process to the public.

In line with the Convention's widening participation ethos, the report was presented in a readable fashion; it was holistic and coherent throughout, and had an easy-read version for the general public. It received favourable media responses on the whole (BBC News, 2009), although it was criticized for being an expensive undertaking in 'stating the blatantly obvious' (Jonathan Morgan AM, quoted by BBC News, 2009). To this, the Convention could justifiably retort that it was the first time these 'obvious' conclusions were solidly grounded in evidence. Within the policy process, the report could be seen as valuable empirical research that would assist politicians in making decisions. Other sustained criticism came from 'True Wales' (a group campaigning for 'no more powers to the National Assembly'), who accused the Convention of being a 'Yes' campaign in disguise, funded from public money (WalesOnline, 2010). Nonetheless, our interviews found a clear determination among the Convention members to act neutrally and objectively.

Notwithstanding the Convention's evidence-based approach, a number of related questions arise. First, is this the best method of meaningfully engaging the public in constitutional debates, particularly as such exercises often end abruptly as soon as the commissions report and as the issues in question are of such technical nature?

Second, should a government base a crucial political decision on one relatively narrow snapshot measurement of the public's mood taken more than sixteen months prior to the actual staging of the referendum? One interviewee noted that the Convention merely

> scratched the surface ... and the other key thing about it is that it gives a picture of the status of the public opinion at the last moment of the writing of the report. It was a snap-shot. (Interview, July 2010)

Literature on commissions of inquiry shows that, despite the high profile of some commissions, the impact of their recommendations on policy varies from case to case (Rowe and McAllister, 2006). In Wales, the Richard Commission produced a comprehensive constitutional blue-print (Richard Commission, 2004) with a holistic set of recommendations for improvements in devolution supported by new evidence (Rawlings, 2004; Osmond, 2005). Yet its recommendations were understandably cherry-picked by the then Labour government in the production of the *Better Governance for Wales* White Paper in 2005. The current constitutional changes thus follow the Richard trajectory, rather than its actual recommendations. The trajectory was in many ways inevitable since the 2006 Act formalized what was occurring *de facto* in the Assembly (Stirbu, 2009).

Contribution to ongoing constitutional debates

Clearly, assessment of the Convention's contribution to constitution building is a matter of interpretation of what a successful contribution is. Some of our interviewees considered it as an important and worthwhile debate that reached out to the general public more than other exercises of this kind. To some of our interviewees, success meant a 'good reception' for the report, which most of them believed it had gained (Interviews, July 2010). Nevertheless, most of our interviewees also agreed that the report had had a very limited influence on more recent debates about the timing of the referendum. Commenting on the substantive impact of the report, one interviewee noted that:

> the Convention was never expected to influence the future debates on the timing of the referendum and on the framing of the referendum question. It encouraged the government to trigger a referendum, but with the timing of it, let's not forget that there were very few choices left. (Interview, November 2010)

The Secretary of State for Wales hardly made any reference to the Convention when she triggered the legal procedures for the referendum. The Electoral Commission took note of the Convention's Report and its in-depth analysis of the complexity of the referendum issue, and the lack of knowledge on constitutional arrangements in Wales (Electoral Commission, 2010, pp. 4, 6). A few academic submissions (for example, see those by McAllister and by Wyn Jones) to the Electoral Commission did mention the Convention's work but, overall, debates on the timing and the framing of the referendum question had limited references on the Convention (Electoral Commission, 2010).

There is some evidence to suggest that that the Convention's Report had some weight in the decision to trigger the referendum, as the First Minister, Carwyn Jones, 'acknowledged [its] depth of analysis' in Plenary (NAfW Record of Proceedings, 2010a). However, perhaps more significantly, the Convention's recommendation regarding 'efforts to ensure that the administration of justice in

Wales better reflects devolution' (AWC, 2009, p. 6) caught the First Minister's attention (NAfW Record of Proceedings, 2010a). This is an indication of the more profound implications of the Convention's work, aside from its influence upon debates around the referendum question and timing.

The Convention's perceived limited impact might be put down to a limited institutional legacy. The Richard Commission report had stimulated the establishment of Cymru Yfory/Tomorrow's Wales, a cross-party, cross-sectoral group that emerged from the publication of the Richard Report in March 2004. Equally, some former members of the Richard Commission remained active in making the case for the Richard recommendations (Lord Ivor Richard and Sir Michael Wheeler-Booth at Westminster, Professor Laura McAllister in the media and through academic publications).

Nevertheless, given the different remits of the two bodies, this may be an unfair comparison since the Richard Commission was in effect charged with assessing the appropriateness of the constitutional arrangements in Wales, and with proposing recommendations for a possible constitutional change, whereas the Convention's role was more that of an public educator, to help capture the appetite for further steps in the devolution journey. One interviewee noted that, for most of the members, the Convention was a public service duty and that to continue to advocate either in the name of the Convention or in the spirit of its recommendations might have muddied subsequent political waters (Interview, July 2010).

If the perceived impact seems modest, the contribution of the Convention to the maturing constitutional debate in Wales is more meaningful; not only in the light of the widespread public debate instigated and conducted by the Convention, but also in the light of the comprehensive investigation into how the current legislative system works in Wales, and how little devolution is understood by the general public. In addition to this, the Convention touched upon things that were not strictly within its remit but which were nevertheless significant findings of the public deliberations: the legal system, policing and criminal justice etc. As illustrated above, the issue of the legal system's need to reflect the realities of devolution has already been taken up by the First Minister.

Theoretical discussion

Our discussion of the operation of the Convention brought forward issues such as legitimacy, constitutional change, participation and the complexity of constitutional arrangements in Wales. From an institutionalist perspective, major changes are prompted by either major failures within the system, or a radical ideational shift outside the institution (March and Olsen, 2006). In the case of political institutions – such as constitutions, legislatures or executives

– 'legitimate' and well-informed changes are crucial in ensuring the future sustainability of the political process (Stirbu, 2009). Literature on institutional change asserts that institutions are often validated by outsiders and protected by insiders (March and Olsen, 2006).

In this vein, the Convention can be seen as playing a dual role: first as facilitating a thorough and mature public debate over the current devolution and institutional arrangements in Wales by which devolution would be 'validated' or not. Given that the report's findings suggest limited knowledge of the devolution arrangements in Wales, but quite substantial support for devolution and, indeed, for primary powers, we are able to connect with a certain 'institutional change' validation.

Second, the 'defence' of the institution (Wales's constitutional settlement) is down to the Convention's contribution to increasing people's understanding of devolution. The extent to which the Convention managed to 'defend' devolution in Wales by increasing the level of understanding within the general public remains a point of dispute. As Sir Emyr Jones Parry noted in his submission to the Electoral Commission, exercises such as the Convention end abruptly, thus impeding the process of 'popular learning' (Electoral Commission, 2010). Drawing on Freire's (1985) theories of popular education, we argue that, for the political and constitutional emancipation of Wales, the educator role that the Convention carried out for a while should become more permanent and institutionalized. Invoking the Welsh devolution mantra, 'a process not an event', we argue that the Convention made an important shift towards making raising awareness and understanding of politics and constitutional arrangements, a continuous process, not an event.

Looked at from a more rational choice perspective, legitimizing institutional change by engaging the public in the process, or by evidence-based decision-making, is indeed the perfect excuse for politicians who want to maximize their chances for re-election, yet minimize the electoral cost of this (North, 1990) – and taking controversial decisions on constitutional matters would be such a cost. The concern over the 'weight' the Convention would carry both in Wales and in Westminster and Whitehall seems to support the excuse hypothesis.

Complexity and systems theory have been invoked in making sense of the development of constitutionalism and constitutional orders (Ratnapala, 2002). The argument put forth is that complex social and political order can be sustained only by a handful of simple laws (Hayek, 1973). On this account, a handful of simple and straightforward constitutional principles sit at the heart of modern liberal democracy: separation of powers and checks and balances, rule of law, independence of judicial review, limitations on government powers and protection of individual rights (Ratnapala, 2002). The absence of such simple laws leads to chaos or political anarchy, whilst an abundance of complex laws makes political systems unadaptive to changing environments (Hayek, 1973). This point is relevant in the context of designing or fundamentally changing political orders.

The establishment of the National Assembly can be regarded as major landmark in the evolution of the Welsh social and political sphere. Hence, the ongoing fluidity of the constitutional settlement in Wales is part of an adaptive process, governed by a handful of constitutional rules. However, in the case of Welsh devolution, it is difficult to argue that 'simple constitutional rules' establish order in the chaos. On the contrary, if one looks at the powers and functions of the National Assembly (see how the transfer of functions was made[2]), or at the LCO process,[3] we can argue that the constitutional rules governing Welsh devolution bring more chaos than order.

It was this context that the Convention had to break through, to distil the complexities of the Welsh constitutional arrangements into simpler and manageable concepts and terms and then transmit the message to the people of Wales. One of the Convention members drew attention to the dangers of adopting a rather superficial method of understanding the Welsh devolution by making clumsy comparisons with Scotland:

> I think there is a clumsy aspiration that after the referendum Wales would be more like Scotland. But this referendum would still not resolve the constitutional conundrum that is the difference between Wales and Scotland: Scotland has everything except what is reserved, whereas Wales is the mirror of that. (Interview, July 2010)

The Convention sought to avoid that by a careful analysis of the current devolution system in Wales, in what Kirsty Williams, the Welsh Liberal Democrats' leader, called 'a devastating critique of the existing, half-baked settlement' (quoted by BBC News, 2009).

Throughout this evaluation of the need for a Convention in the first place, we have posed fundamental questions. From a pure deliberative democracy stance, any such exercise involving public education and consultation is worthwhile. Social activist theorists would argue that participation is valuable in its own right (including Arnstein, 1969; Pateman, 1970). The Convention's participatory style and some limited but innovative mechanisms for engagement, as well as the whole ethos of its operation, commend it as an example of a gradually maturing constitutional debate in Wales.

From an institutional change perspective, the coalition partners of 2007 (Labour and Plaid Cymru) were presented with a significant window of opportunity to advance the debate on Wales's constitutional future even further. Nonetheless, the conditions around the establishment of the Convention and its subsequent terms of reference suggest caution; the early days of an untested coalition government left little room for risking a controversial debate over the size of the Assembly and on the electoral system. This suggests an appetite for incremental, gradual change, around which consensus might be fairly easily built.

CONCLUSIONS

In offering an early narrative on the Convention's operation, as well as an evaluation of its contribution to the ongoing constitutional development of Wales, we have contextualized this within the devolution 'journey'. The article also represented a first attempt to locate the Convention against a theoretical backdrop based on principles of deliberative democracy and institutionalism. Our evaluation was framed around three core tenets of deliberative democracy: evidence-based policy-making, public participation and civic self-governance (see Bohman and Rehg, 1997). We then used these as a framework to test the likely legacy of the Convention. This was a useful match with the principal roles that the Convention was meant to fulfil (as educator, as facilitator of greater public engagement with devolution, and as an informant to the government on future policy). It is against this framework that we offer a judgement on the Convention's impact.

The Convention as an educator
Arguably, the most challenging role that the Convention had to fulfil was its educational function. Devolution contributed to addressing the institutional democratic deficit through establishing new, democratically elected and accountable political institutions (Kay, 2003). Nonetheless, the unfolding of the process also revealed other important gaps, such as people's low levels of knowledge of and disengagement with politics, as well as the limited knowledge and confusion surrounding the powers and operation of the Assembly (AWC, 2009). This is particularly significant in Wales given the low levels of initial public support for devolution in the 1997 Referendum (Taylor and Thompson, 1999). Of course, whilst the Convention was never likely to be able to close that gap, it did further expose it through the production of a thorough and evidence-based report (AWC, 2009).

The Convention can be seen as a post-devolution model of a 'national conversation' taking a snapshot of people's views, knowledge and preferences as to the profile of the Assembly and devolution more widely. It also acted as a tool to further legitimize such debates, thus signalling a certain maturing of the constitutional debate in Wales.

The Convention satisfies at least two of the three ideals of deliberative democracy: a focus on evidence-based policy-making, and greater engagement with the public. Nevertheless, it is significant that the Convention was effect-ively a top-down initiative and not a civil-initiated constitutional debate (as had existed in Scotland between 1988 and 1995). Therefore, it could not be said that the civic self-governance ideal of deliberative democracy was met.

Another defining issue was the relatively short timescale for its operation, with unsurprisingly only limited impact on boosting levels of political know-ledge. The Convention's findings with regard to low levels of public knowledge about constitutional arrangements (AWC, 2009) suggest that Wales's new democracy needs regular and longitudinal public engagement in order to further legitimize itself and its political institutions.

The Convention as a public engagement facilitator
From the perspective of deliberative democracy, any form of public engagement and deliberation is to be welcomed, especially in the context of new or fragile democracies where political institutions have yet to establish their legitimacy. Wales is such a case. Some of the Convention's innovative approaches to involv-ing the public in constitutional debates convey and underline the Assembly's participatory focus especially in reaching out to groups historically excluded (McAllister and Stirbu, 2007). Some of the participatory initiatives promoted by the Convention might be used for remodelling by Assembly Committees in the context of their enquiries, and by the government in its separate consultation processes.

The impact of the Convention
We conclude that, whilst the Convention might be judged as a 'perfect' excuse for government in its decision-making process (a unanimous, evidence-based report, involving relatively wide public participation), it had, by any measure, a very modest, substantive impact on the timing of the referendum and the ques-tion used.

The Convention's overall contribution to Wales's maturing constitutional debate must thus be judged as modest. Its successes and strengths lie specific-ally in its contribution to encouraging wider public awareness and participation. This, at least, added another layer of intelligence and potential legitimacy to ongoing debate on Wales's constitutional future.

NOTES

[1] The Convention organized thirty-seven stakeholder events and twenty-four public events across Wales (discussion groups, question time, road shows, family days). It also received 544 written and online submissions (from members of the Welsh Assembly Government, the National Assembly and the Wales Affairs Committee, and from organizations, politicians and members of the public) to its consultation.

[2] The powers of the Assembly, previously held and accumulated by the Secretary of State for Wales in a piecemeal fashion over a long period of time, fell into eighteen broad 'fields', or areas of competence, as initially listed in Schedule 2 of the Government of Wales Act 1998. The transfer of these functions was done in an incremental manner: field by field, statute by statute, section by section, contributing to a complex jigsaw-like system that eventually needed a Technical Guide to the Transfer of Functions Order of 500 pages (Rawlings, 2003).

[3] Using the LCO (Legislative Competence Order) process a new 'matter' is added into the relevant field in Schedule 5 of the Government of Wales Act 2006, thus enhancing the jigsaw legislative competences of the National Assembly.

REFERENCES

Arnstein, S. R. (1969). 'A ladder of citizen participation', *Journal of the American Institute of Planners*, 35, 4, 216–24.

Arter, D. (2004). *The Scottish Parliament: A Scandinavian-Style Assembly*, London: Frank Cass.

AWC (2009). *All Wales Convention Report*, Cardiff: AWC.

BBC News (2009). 'More powers for Wales says report', 18 November, http://news.bbc. co.uk/1/hi/wales/wales_politics/8350333.stm (accessed November 2010).

BBC Wales/ICM (2010). 'ICM Poll for BBC Cymru Wales', http://www.icmresearch. co.uk/pdfs/2010_mar_bbc_wales_poll.pdf#search=%22welsh%20assembly%22 (accessed November 2010).

Bohman, J. and Rehg, W. (1997). *Deliberative Democracy*, Cambridge, MA: MIT Press.

Calman Commission (2009). *Serving Scotland Better: Scotland and the United Kingdom in the 21st Century*, the Report of the Calman Commission, Edinburgh: Commission on Scottish Devolution.

Dahl, R. A. (2002). *How Democratic is the American Constitution?*, New Haven, CT: Yale University Press.

Electoral Commission (2010). *Report on Referendum on the law-making powers of the National Assembly for Wales*, London: Electoral Commission.

Freire, P. (1985) *The Politics of Education: Culture, Power and Liberation*. South Hadley, MA: Bergin & Garvey.

Goodin, R. E. and Dryzek, J. S. (2008). 'Deliberative impacts: the macro-political uptake of mini-publics', *Politics and Society*, 34, 2, 219–44.

GWA (2006). *Government of Wales Act*, London: HMSO.

Hansard Society (2004–10). *Audit of Political Engagement* (1–7), London: Hansard Society.

Hayek, F. A. (1973). *Law, Legislation and Liberty: Rules and Order*, vol. 1, Chicago: Chicago University Press.

Herbert, A. (1961). 'Anything but action? A study of the uses and abuses of committees of inquiry', in R. Harris (ed.), *Radical Reaction: Essays in Competition and Affluence*, London: Hutchinson.

Holtham Commission (2009). *First Report: Funding Devolved Government in Wales: Barnett and Beyond*, Cardiff: Independent Commission on Funding and Finance for Wales.

House of Lords (2008). *Select Committee on the Constitution Report (HL Paper 17): Scrutiny of Welsh Legislative Competence*, London: HMSO.

House of Lords (2009). *Select Committee on the Barnett Formula (HL Paper 139): The Barnett Formula*, London: HMSO.

House of Lords (2010). *Select Committee on the Constitution Report (HL Paper 99): Referendum in the United Kingdom*, London: HMSO.

Kay, A. (2003). 'Evaluating devolution in Wales', *Political Studies*, 51, 51–66.

McAllister, L. (2000). 'The new politics in Wales: rhetoric or reality?', *Parliamentary Affairs*, 53, 591–604.

McAllister, L. (2004). 'The Richard Commission: Wales's alternative constitutional convention?', *Contemporary Wales*, 17, 128–39.

McAllister, L. (2005). 'Proving the potential of independent commissions: a review of the Richard Commission on the powers and electoral arrangements of the National Assembly for Wales', *Public Administration*, 83, 2, 493–512.

McAllister, L. and Stirbu, D. (2007). 'Developing devolution's scrutiny potential: a comparative evaluation for the National Assembly for Wales's subject committees', *Policy and Politics*, 35, 2, 289–310.

McAllister, L. and Stirbu, D. (2008). 'Influence, impact and legacy: assessing the Richard Commission's contribution to Wales's evolving constitution', *Representation*, 44, 3, 209–24.

March, J. G. and Olsen, J. P. (1989). *Rediscovering Institutions: The Organisational Basis of Politics*, New York: Free Press.

March, J. G. and Olsen, J. P. (2006). 'Elaborating the "new institutionalism"', in R. A. W. Rhodes, S. A. Binder and B. A. Rockman (eds), *The Oxford Handbook of Political Institutions*, Oxford: Oxford University Press.

NAfW Public Attitude Survey (2008). 'The National Assembly for Wales: public attitudes 2008', http://www.assemblywales.org/abthome/abt-commission/about_us-public_attitudes_2008.htm (accessed November 2010).

NAfW Record of Proceedings (2010a). *National Assembly Record of Proceedings*, 9 February, http://www.assemblywales.org/bus-home/bus-chamber/bus-chamber-third-assembly-rop.htm?act=dis&id=166366&ds=2/2010 (accessed November 2010).

NAfW Record of Proceedings (2010b). *National Assembly Record of Proceedings*, 9 November, http://www.assemblywales.org/bus-home/bus-chamber/bus-chamber-third-assembly-rop.htm?act=dis&id=202350&ds=11/2010 (accessed November 2010).

North, D. C. (1990). *Institutions, Institutional Change and Economic Performance*, Cambridge: Cambridge University Press.

One Wales (2007). *A Progressive Agenda for the Government of Wales*, an agreement between Labour and Plaid Cymru Groups in the National Assembly, Cardiff: Welsh Labour Party and Plaid Cymru.

Osmond, J. (1995). *Welsh Europeans*, Bridgend: Seren.
Osmond, J. (2005). 'Virtual parliament', *Agenda: The Journal of the Institute of Welsh Affairs*, Summer, 25–29.
Pateman, C. (1970). *Participation and Democratic Theory*, Cambridge: Cambridge University Press.
Ratnapala, S. (2002). 'The idea of constitution', *Policy*, Summer, 199–202.
Rawlings, R. (2003). *Delineating Wales: Constitutional, Legal and Administrative Aspects of National Devolution*, Cardiff: Cardiff University Press.
Rawlings, R. (2004). 'Richard's radical recipe', *Agenda: The Journal of the Institute of Welsh Affairs*, Summer, 27–31.
Rawlings, R. (2005). 'Hastening slowly: the next phase of Welsh devolution', *Public Law*, 824–52.
Richard Commission (2004). *The Report of the Richard Commission on the Powers and Electoral Arrangements of the National Assembly for Wales*, London: The Stationery Office.
Rowe, M. and McAllister, L. (2006). 'The roles of commissions of inquiry in the policy process', *Public Policy and Administration*, 21, 4, 99–115.
Shipton, M. (2008). Speech at the Devolution Conference at All Nations Centre, Cardiff, 6 November, http://crossofstgeorge.net/forums/viewtopic.php?t=22500&start=0&postdays=0&postorder=asc&highlight= (accessed July 2011).
Shipton, M. (2009). 'All Wales Convention hold first public meeting', *WalesOnline*, 15 January, http://www.walesonline.co.uk/news/wales-news/2009/01/15/all-wales-convention-holds-first-public-meeting-91466-22696749/ (accessed November 2010).
Stirbu, D. (2009). 'Instituting constitutions: the internal reconfiguration of the national assembly for Wales from 2005 to 2007', *Contemporary Wales*, 22, 95–112.
Taylor, B. and Thomson, K. (eds) (1999). *Scotland and Wales: Nations Again?*, Cardiff: University of Wales Press.
WAG (2009). 'Welsh Assembly Government welcomes the publication of the All Wales Convention Report', Cabinet statement, 18 November, http://wales.gov.uk/newsroom/firstminister/2009/091118allwalesconventionreport/;jsessionid=xntTMjdRhThZt2vQ0CdWy6rmlJnhXQPhr5nM8Fr26Z6WmHPhLy2b!320120316?lang=en (accessed November 2010).
Wales Office (2010). 'Welsh Secretary sends draft referendum question to Electoral Commission for consideration', press release, 23 June, http://www.walesoffice.gov.uk/2010/06/23/welsh-secretary-sends-draft-referendum-question-to-electoral-commission-for-consideration/ (accessed November 2010).
WalesOnline (2008). 'All-Wales Convention members named', 4 July, http://www.walesonline.co.uk/news/welsh-politics/welsh-politics-news/2008/07/04/all-wales-convention-members-named-91466-21226462/ (accessed November 2010).
WalesOnline (2010). ' "No" campaign leader warns about Assembly powers', http://www.walesonline.co.uk/news/wales-news/2010/02/01/no-campaign-leader-warns-about-assembly-powers-91466-25730317/ (accessed November 2010).

5. WALES IN A GLOBAL NEIGHBOURHOOD: THE IMPACT OF GLOBALIZATION ON TWO WELSH MARKET TOWNS

Corinna Patterson

ABSTRACT

The paper examines how two Welsh market towns, Llangefni and Machynlleth, have been affected by processes of globalization and in particular how local residents and business owners perceive and experience these changes, showing the uneven effects of globalization on locations, economies and cultures. This multi-dimensional, place-based analysis contributes to understanding how people living in small rural historic market towns engage with the local and the global in their day-to-day lives, and consequently how empowered they are and feel as local and/or global citizens.

INTRODUCTION

Globalization is an all-encompassing subject, which by its very definition affects the *entire* world, so it is no wonder that most books, articles and research on the subject tackle the phenomenon from a macro perspective: the 'McDonaldization of society' (Ritzer, 1993), cultural standardization (Bauman, 2000), global economic and corporate dominance (Klein, 2001) and changes to the meanings of time, space and travel (Castells, 2000). However, it is at the local level that these globalizing forces are implemented, their effect is felt and policy reactions and adaptations to globalization are administered. Still, as Albrow observes (1997, p. 118), 'scant attention has been paid to everyday life' in the field of globalization studies. Comparatively little research has been carried out at the micro level, though there is now a growing interest and recognition within a number of disciplines that, in order to gain a greater understanding of how globalization is affecting people and places, we need to refocus our attention towards the local (Albrow, 1997; Cvetkovich and Kellner, 1997; Woods, 2007). Furthermore, there is a distinct lack of research into how globalization is affecting rural locations in particular, with the majority of micro research concentrating on urban areas (Castells et al., 1997; Savage et al., 2006). This has led Woods to coin the term 'global countryside' to highlight how interlinked the concepts are and to emphasize that, although the effects may be less overt in rural areas, nevertheless they are felt and responded to (Woods, 2007, p. 486).

The concept of citizenship, too, is being remoulded in light of the advancements of globalization, which, for theorists such as Scholte (2000) and Ohmae (2000), is undermining the nation-state structure in relation to management of national economies and powers of self-determination and civic engagement, and in turn threatens the democratic process itself, making the rights and responsibilities associated with citizenship less clear. Simultaneously, globalization, through the advancement of communication technologies such as the Internet, has also potentially aided the advance of global citizenship and democratized information. Today, citizenship is then not a static concept, but is becoming ever more difficult to define.

In Britain, the erstwhile Labour government devoted effort to reinforcing notions of 'active' and 'responsible' local citizens and introduced 'global citizenship' as a theme into the national curriculum in 2002. In 2006, the then Chancellor of the Exchequer, Gordon Brown, warned that 'globalization could mean a free-for-all, a turning inwards, a new protectionism, even a break up of family life' (Brown, 2006) and spoke of the need to build 'stronger communities' in recognition that people today feel insecure because their local communities are changing so rapidly. He championed the 'active involvement and engagement of local people themselves' (Brown, 2006). The relationship between the local and the global and our understanding of citizenship and the associated rights and responsibilities is therefore under scrutiny and is being actively reshaped and remoulded in response to the pressures of globalization.

The emerging emphasis, to study how the global is affecting the local, is not before time and there is a great deal to be learned from local studies about how communities, cultures, identities and the meanings of place are influenced by the forces of globalization. Woods puts forward what he calls a new multi-dimensional place-based micro research agenda that would adopt the hypothetical concept of the 'global countryside' and examine rural places in relation to their historical identities. He also calls for rural locations to be analysed in relation to power and political engagement in order to understand how places and identities are shaped in response to global forces (Woods, 2007, p. 503). The research discussed here addresses these agendas by examining the situation in two Welsh rural market towns, Machynlleth and Llangefni, with the aim of understanding better how rural locations and the people who live in them are affected by, and respond to, local and global forces. Like Woods, it assumes that people and locations need to be understood within their multi-dimensional existences; and that only through analysing people's local life-worlds can we adequately assess and develop effective policies in relation to both the local and the global.

LOCATING THE RESEARCH

Though most of its population is concentrated in urban areas, in some senses Wales continues to be a significantly rural country, with a distinctive culture, language and history steeped in its own mythology. Its spectacular mountainous scenery has, according to some, such as Bowen (1959) and Day (2002), played a key part in maintaining the distinctiveness of Welsh history and culture over a long period of time, helping Wales preserve much of its identity through keeping many of its villages and towns relatively inaccessible (until fairly recently); the remoteness of some of these rural areas (referred to often as the Welsh heartlands) has protected rural Wales from the full impact of many external forces and pressures.

Over the last few decades, the economic, demographic, communication and transportation changes that have taken place have significantly altered the face of rural Wales, linguistically and culturally. The decline of traditional industries and the restructuring of essential services that have been taking place since the 1980s and 1990s (privatization of public transport, the rationalization of the public sector services such as the selling off of council housing in the 1980s, the closing of small post offices, the decline in local shops and amenities in response to the growth of 'high street' retail outlets in larger towns and out-of-town shopping complexes) has resulted in an outward migration of young people in search of better employment and higher education prospects. At the same time, there has been a population growth from people moving into Welsh villages as places to commute to work from or to retire to, placing a great deal of pressure on community structures, the Welsh language and local and Welsh identities (Cloke et al., 1997, pp. 3–4). These changes have not, however, been homogeneous, but have affected regions and communities in a variety of ways. For example, different locations in Wales attract different socio-demographic flows of in-migrants and these socio-economic trends also change and evolve over time (Day, 2010).

As Day (2002, p. 258) remarks, 'it is apparent that over recent years Wales has been changed, profoundly and irreversibly' by the processes of globalization, altering it economically, demographically, technologically and culturally. Wales today is globalized, with the mass of the population wearing brand-named clothing made in places such as China, with global high street shops, such as

Boots pharmacy, New Look, Debenhams and Costa Coffee, locating themselves in most of the main town centres. Most people have cars made in Germany or Japan, watch American films, fly abroad for their summer holiday and shop in supermarkets where they buy food from New Zealand, South Africa and India. In more rural areas, the changes may be apparent in the absence, or centralization, of local services, and changes in the economic, technological and transportation infrastructure, which have meant that the diverse people now living in Wales bring with them a whole host of meanings to living in the countryside, in Wales, in a market town, in a community, thus leaving rural Wales less uniform than it previously was, and raising, as Day points out, issues for policy-makers around the meaning of 'rural' and, for that matter, the meanings of 'community' and 'identity' (Day, 2006).

EXPLORING RURAL WELSH MARKET TOWNS

Market towns are the traditional service centres for their rural hinterlands, attached to which are often strong historical and local identities. Small towns and market towns have found themselves recently in the policy and media spotlight, as politicians, retail giants, campaign groups and grassroots movements all clamour over issues relating to cuts in services and amenities and the economic 'rationalization' of services such as schools, hospitals and post offices, which has seen the dispersal of services away from central community locations such as town centres to nearby larger towns or cities. Recognized as sites of distinct policy intervention, market towns are facing many challenges as a result of changing economic and demographic trends: social deprivation and exclusion, the closure of major employers and the competition facing local retailers from larger towns, supermarkets and other big-name retailers. These all have a direct knock-on effect on communities in their surrounding rural hinterland (Wales Rural Observatory, 2007, p. 5). According to some reports, as many as 2,000 independent retailers a year are closing down in the UK (APPSSG, 2006, p. 8) as a result of being unable to compete with big-name high street shopping outlets and supermarket giants such as the market dominance of the 'big four' (Tesco, Asda-Walmart, Sainsburys and Morrisons). Reports show Britain's towns either becoming cloned or turning into 'ghost towns' (Local Works, 2003) or 'shopping deserts' (Sillito, 2007), as independent retailers close their shops as their businesses become unviable, resulting in many town centre outlets becoming boarded up or the premises being reopened as charity shops, painting a bleak picture.

A *Guardian* headline, 'Condemned to History' (Brown, 2007), laments the death of many traditional market towns as government policies to build new houses on green-field locations on their outskirts turns them increasingly into primarily locations for accommodation, whilst other nearby larger towns or cities become the replacement main service, employment and social centres. An increasing commuter culture is seen as resulting in the purpose of many market towns, as traditional providers of services and amenities to their residents and hinterlands, becoming defunct. Calls for a Local Communities and Sustainability Bill by Local Works (2003) or grassroots organizations such as the Slow Food Movement, 'think global, act local' movements, not to mention the numerous local campaigns to save schools, hospitals and other services and provisions, all demonstrate how changes affecting small and market towns have become a focus of fierce topical debate.

The condition of rural Welsh market towns is now recognized as a distinct policy issue (Wales Rural Observatory, 2004, p. 1) and as a result they are being reconstructed in light of new influences and pressures. The relationship between the local and the global is reflected within policy documents, such as *Planning Policy Statement 4: Planning for Sustainable Economic Growth* (Department for Communities and Local Development, 2009), that seek to address issues of community cohesion, identity, participation and sustainability as well as meeting environmental objectives, though the principal emphasis remains the development of local economies.

In order to investigate some of these processes, two market towns, Machynlleth and Llangefni, were chosen as potentially interesting case studies, primarily because, on the basis of a limited prior knowledge, they appeared visually to be very different from each other and to have very different social atmospheres, prompting numerous questions about how far they really differed and why. Both are situated in rural locations where Welsh remains the first language for many or most of the residents, and have strong historical identities and similarly sized populations. In the past, the towns had played a central role in local people's lives, as they had been host to weekly or twice-weekly traditional town markets as well as a livestock market, where people could buy their groceries, socialize and sell and buy livestock. Today, the whole of Machynlleth and one ward in Llangefni (Tudur) are designated Communities First areas. Llangefni was situated within a European Objective 1 designated area and at the time of research Machynlleth was in an Objective 2 area (evolving into 'Convergence Regions' in 2007). Both are within similar commuting distance from larger urban centres, the university towns of Bangor and Aberystwyth.

Llangefni is situated in the centre of the island of Anglesey (Ynys Môn), in the north, where the surrounding countryside consists of fields and fairly gently rolling hills and Machynlleth is in mid-Wales, on the edge of Powys, bordering both Gwynedd and Ceredigion, the countryside here consisting of steeper fields and hills or small mountains and very wooded (see Map 5.1).

Map 5.1
Welsh counties and the market towns (redrawn from http://www.walesdirectory.
co.uk/counties.htm).

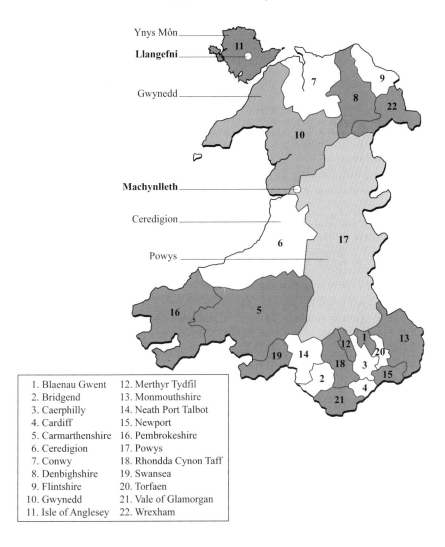

1. Blaenau Gwent	12. Merthyr Tydfil
2. Bridgend	13. Monmouthshire
3. Caerphilly	14. Neath Port Talbot
4. Cardiff	15. Newport
5. Carmarthenshire	16. Pembrokeshire
6. Ceredigion	17. Powys
7. Conwy	18. Rhondda Cynon Taff
8. Denbighshire	19. Swansea
9. Flintshire	20. Torfaen
10. Gwynedd	21. Vale of Glamorgan
11. Isle of Anglesey	22. Wrexham

Through in-depth semi-structured interviews with local residents, local business people and community workers, a picture of people's lifestyles and opinions was gained which reveals people's relationship with their local and the global. The aim was to discover if and how they perceived globalization to be affecting their towns and their lives, what affiliation they had towards local and global issues and whether they felt empowered as local or global citizens. The target population were men and women aged eighteen plus and who were resident in each town. They were contacted primarily through snowball sampling, including an element of stratified sampling to ensure that a good cross-section of the populations was represented. This enables a comparative analysis to be undertaken not only of the two market towns as such, but also between the social groups within and between each town.

PROFILING THE MARKET TOWNS

Profiling Llangefni

According to the 2001 Census, Llangefni has a population of 4,662 and 82 per cent of its population can speak, write and read Welsh fluently, the majority of whom speak it as their first language. In 2006, the town was named 'the Welshest place in Wales' by a survey looking at the origins of residents' names (Western Mail, 2006a).

Llangefni is steeped in history, with links back to the age of the Vikings, and has close connections with Llewelyn the Great (Llewelyn Fawr) (Evans, 2008, p. 1). Llangefni was initially a small village that developed as an agricultural market town in the late eighteenth century, its first market being held in 1785. It grew to become the main agricultural trading centre for Ynys Môn and its second largest commercial centre (the largest being Holyhead). In 1899, Llangefni became Ynys Môn's administrative centre. It has also become the second largest centre of employment on Ynys Môn (after Holyhead) and has the largest industrial estate on the island, initially developed in the 1950s and 1960s and continuing to expand since (IACC, 1999, p. 7). Today, the industrial estate comprises a mixture of large international factory units such as Grampian Prepared Meats, Glambia Cheese and Eastman Peboc and a range of small and medium-sized businesses.

Llangefni still retains its position as the second biggest commercial centre on the island, but, since the closure of the livestock market (where the supermarket store Asda is now situated) in December 1997, the town is now referred to primarily as the island's administrative centre, home to Ynys Môn/Isle of Anglesey County Council, the major employer in the town. Although Llangefni still has its twice-weekly street market, held on a Thursday and Saturday in a car park at the side of the large Town Hall and clock, the town does not look as though it is prospering. In a report by the Planning and Economic Development Department of the local authority in 1999, Llangefni was described as 'potentially a very attractive town set in a scenic rural landscape' (IACC, 1999, p. 6). Amid its

Grade II listed buildings is a mixture of high street brands and independent shops, as well as boarded-up shops and charity shops, and its generally neglected appearance gives the visitor the strong impression that the town has seen better days. The 1999 report identified some of the threats facing Llangefni as:

- Diminishing role as an important market town
- Trade being lost to other prominent regional centres
- Enhanced by-passing of town once A55 had been completed
- Continuing loss of young people if new employment opportunities are not created
- Social problems may grow unless effective community-based initiatives take place (IACC, 1999, p. 13).

Today, in Llangefni over 55 per cent of families are on income-related benefits (WAG, 2004, p. 12), with 7.4 per cent unemployment (IACC, 2006, p. 3) and 34 per cent of the population have no qualifications. The town is split into three wards: Cefni, Cyngar and Tudur (see Map 5.2). The Tudur ward has been designated as having multiple deprivation and is a Communities First area.

The town became notorious locally during the 1990s as having a severe drugs problem and more recently as experiencing a problem with 'anti-social behaviour' and was designated an 'alcohol free zone' on 15 December 2005 (IACC, 2005, p. 1), which was described by an Anglesey Council spokesman as meaning a 'crackdown on everything from vandalism and graffiti to boy-racers playing music in the town centre and nearby car park' (BBC, 2007). More recently, though the town has enjoyed the success generated by regeneration of its Dingle nature reserve, which runs along the river Cefni; the development of Oriel Môn, a museum, arts and events gallery situated just outside the town itself; the redevelopment of the Grade II listed Bull Hotel, situated next to the Town Hall in the centre of the town; and the controversial planning permission for an Asda supermarket to be built on where the old livestock market used to be held, and the subsequent redevelopment of the area. The town has also started to host its own festival: 'Gwyl Cefni' (Cefni Festival). Llangefni currently is in the process of being rebranded, which may include losing its market town status and image to reflect 'the major decrease in the number of market stalls and consumers coming to the town on a weekly basis' (Williams, 2010, p. 4).

Profiling Machynlleth

According to the 2001 Census, Machynlleth's population is 2,147 and 58 per cent of its residents speak Welsh. Machynlleth's market dates back to 1291, documented in a charter by King Edward I to Owen de la Pole, granting him permission for a market to be held every Wednesday. Machynlleth is, however,

Map 5.2
Isle of Anglesey County Wards, showing Llangefni's wards in the centre of the island (redrawn from http://www.anglesey.gov.uk/doc.asp?cat=4524).

more famous for being the location of Wales's first parliament, held by Owain Glyndwr after he was crowned Prince of Wales in the early 1400s (Davies, 2000, p. 7), and still retains many of its historic buildings.

The railway, which is still running today and remains one of the town's main access routes, first came to Machynlleth in 1863 (Davies, 2000, p. 7). An important building in the town is Plas Machynlleth, gifted to the people of Machynlleth by the seventh Marquis of Londonderry on 2 December 1948 (Davies, 2000, p. 13), which for a while was the location for Celtica, a Celtic heritage visitors' attraction that opened in 1995, closing in the spring of 2006 shortly after the research commenced, and reopening in April 2008 as a multi-purpose community centre. Laura Ashley, the fabric designer, opened her first shop in the town in the early 1960s and later opened a factory in nearby Carno, becoming an important local employer and internationally renowned designer (Davies, 2000, p. 39). The closure of the factory in 2004 resulted in the loss of 220 jobs (BBC, 2004).

The traditional industries of the area have been farming, slate quarrying in nearby Corris and Aberllefenni, forestry and the railway, though these industries have been in decline over the latter half of the twentieth century or, in the case of the railways, have more recently started to sub-contract to companies from elsewhere who bring workers in (Communities First Bro Dyfi, 2004, p. 13), and the more recent closure of the Laura Ashley factory has placed increasing economic pressures on the local economy. These industries have steadily been replaced, largely by tourism over the last thirty years, which is now worth about £333.2 million to the local economy and generates around 11,193 jobs (TPMW, 2008, p. 6). Machynlleth has also become renowned for developing a niche economic market and identity for itself, based on environmental sustainability. Described as 'eco-pioneers' (Lerner, 2006), the Centre for Alternative Technology (CAT), located just outside the town in nearby Corris, was established in 1973 as an educational and demonstration centre and has had a profound influence upon the town. There have been several CAT spin-offs in the town: Dulas Engineering established in 1982, whose focus is on developing renewable technologies, and Ecodyfi, a regeneration organization, established in 1998 to promote sustainable community regeneration in Machynlleth, both economically and environmentally, aiming to meet the needs of the local community with that of the environment and working in partnership with Communities First. The overall focus of these three organizations in Machynlleth is both local and global. Dubbed as being amongst the 'greenest people in Wales' in a local newspaper article in 2006 (Western Mail, 2006b), Machynlleth has become renowned for its environmental profile and many businesses have been developed locally on the back of this reputation.

In 2005, at the beginning of the research, Machynlleth had 4.8 per cent unemployment (BBC, 2005), while 35.7 per cent of the population have no qualifications compared with 29.1 per cent of England and Wales as a whole (Communities First Bro Dyfi, 2004, p. 20). It has a relatively high proportion of people aged over seventy-five (11.9 per cent compared with the average of 7.6 per cent for England and Wales; Communities First Bro Dyfi, 2004, p. 20), which is the result of the out-migration of many of its young and the in-migration of people moving to the area to retire (Communities First Bro Dyfi, 2004, p. 10). The major issues currently are: affordable housing, which has been exacerbated by house price inflation created by the demographic changes; the out-migration of younger people as a result of both the housing shortage and lack of 'conventional' employment and education opportunities (factory and office work); the cost and lack of availability of public transport, which have been identified as often making the rural poor worse off than their urban counterparts; education initiatives and improved childcare facilities (Communities First Bro Dyfi, 2004).

Machynlleth is generally considered to be 'a pretty town' by its citizens

(Communities First Bro Dyfi, 2004, p. 15). As you come into the town from the north over the river Dyfi, there is a Methodist chapel, 'The Tabernacle', which has been converted into an arts and cultural centre, attached to another building which houses the Museum of Modern Art (MOMA) (Wales). There are numerous independent shops painted a variety of colours. Machynlleth also holds a number of annual events, such as a carnival, the Light Festival, a week of activities that include a lantern parade, the Pink Snowball Film Festival and the Machynlleth Music Festival.

Interestingly, therefore, while Llangefni and Machynlleth both have long established historical identities which evolved to fulfil a similar service to their rural hinterlands, more recently the towns appear to be developing along diver-gent paths in response to a combination of local and global influences.

NARRATIVES OF THE LOCAL AND THE GLOBAL: RESPONDENTS' VIEWS OF THE MEANING OF PLACE

From the onset of the research, it became apparent how important 'place' con-tinues to be within people's imaginations and sense of belonging. In both towns, identities were structured territorially. Interview narratives provided a revealing insight into people's feelings about the places they inhabited, worked in and ran businesses from, and their perceptions of the positive and negative factors cur-rently influencing market towns and the lives of their inhabitants. Respondents were asked to describe the town, what they liked and did not like about it, what changes had taken place and how they felt about them. The aim was to allow people's own agendas and priorities about their local life-worlds to come to the fore.

The changes that people identified in Llangefni were directly associated with the features they did not like about the town today. Narratives were structured primarily around the problems faced by the town. The loss of Llangefni's live-stock market was perceived as marking a downturn in local identity, prosperity and community, changing it from being perceived as a lively market town and service centre, with its own unique identity, in which community engagement would take place and relationships could be formed amongst the independent shops, market stalls and livestock sales on market days. By contrast, the town now is seen as an 'administrative hub' and a commuter town (a location to reside or work in) from which respondents appear relatively detached.

The economic and social costs of the closure of the livestock market was at the fore of narratives describing how the town has lost its purpose and become a generic 'non-place' with 'non-people' (Ritzer, 2004). The replacement of

independent shops with high street branches meant not only visual homogenization, but also a social homogenization, as service has become increasingly
standardized and personality-less, no longer generating community involvement and engagement to the extent that it once did. These changes were seen as
threatening, evoking protectionist and defensive sentiments in many:

> The cattle market being removed from the town killed the town. The farmers and
> their family used to come in together. It used to be busy. (Ceinwen)

> Supermarkets have destroyed the independent shops ... [there are] no personal-
> ized staff in the big shops. (Jeanie)

> When we first opened the shop it was a nice little town – homely and friendly, but
> over the last eleven years it has just died. The first thing that happened is that they
> made it look like anywhere else. (Aled)

Meanwhile, in Machynlleth, interviewees identified very few major changes
to have taken place in the town, and some of the changes that were identified
were closely associated with aspects of the town which people reported liking.
The emphasis on the narratives was positive in Machynlleth, but negative in
Llangefni. For Machynlleth respondents, the town's purpose and identity was
still as a 'market town' fulfilling its traditional role as service centre to its
citizens and its surrounding rural hinterland. The major change people noted
to have affected the town was the establishment of the Centre for Alternative
Technology (CAT), which was recognized as having a significant and predominantly positive influence on the town's economic and cultural development.
Specifically, it was suggested that CAT was attracting into the town educated,
environmentally conscious people who have established additional eco-busi-
nesses and other ethical developments, hybridizing the town culturally and
economically in the process but also ensuring that it retains a unique identity
and purpose. Adjectives such as 'colourful' and 'vibrant' were often used in
people's description of the town, which contrast sharply with those sometimes
used to describe Llangefni such as 'grey', 'visually depressing' and 'decaying'.
In other words, people's narratives of the place are, what Ritzer (2004) would
term 'something-full', indicating a unique place capable of generating community engagement:

> What I like about it is that it still has a small town atmosphere, it still has small
> independent shops. I think it is important to preserve those – it is a market town,
> it has a vibrancy connected with that. (Frank)

You still haven't got your chain stores in the town, which is very unique in that sense – you can walk up and you won't see a Woolworths, a Smiths or a Boots. (Daniel)

For a small Welsh town it's very vibrant ... It's the best experience I have really had of living in a small town, I have lived in a village, I have lived in the countryside and I have lived in cities, but it's the first kind of small town and have met so many friendly people, but also there is quite a lot happening really, you can do something every night, either go out and do something or hang out with your friends, there is no reason to be bored, there is always something going on. (Nat)

As well as differences between each town, local life was experienced very differently by different social groups within each town, which correlated with the social class, cultural and educational backgrounds of the respondents. Compared with those with higher incomes or educational achievements, those on low incomes and with few educational qualifications appeared to be denied equal participation in, if not excluded from, the advantages of globalization (Internet, travel, breadth of information or networks), leaving many to feel disempowered. This means that, for those who are excluded from these processes, their locality, as Bauman (2000) would argue, is being stripped of social meaning, as is the case in Llangefni, or, as in Machynlleth, is being changed despite and without them. In the case of Machynlleth, many residents had moved or chosen to remain there as a lifestyle choice, choosing to sacrifice (at least temporarily) their careers or well-paid jobs (many of these interviewees were well educated) in order to be part of a like-minded community that was concerned about similar local and global issues to themselves: fairtrade, environment, vegetarianism, 'buy local think global'. The reality of borders and boundaries, therefore, is largely a 'class stratified phenomenon' (Bauman, 2000, p. 12).

PERCEPTIONS OF GLOBALIZATION: VIEWS OF GROUPS WITHIN THE TOWNS

Knowledge of globalization and people's responses to it differ greatly between Llangefni and Machynlleth. This unevenness is revealed both geographically and between social groups. For most people in Llangefni, their awareness of globalization was limited and their life-worlds were very locally focused. Despite being locally focused, however, they did not have a conscious local agenda through community organization, which for the local population was symbolized by the lack of a carnival. The majority listened to Welsh radio stations and watched local Welsh television programmes (their wider tastes on the whole only extended to British soap operas) and read mainly local newspapers. In Machynlleth, despite the majority of people being on low incomes as they were in Llangefni, they were generally more educated and accessed a far broader range of media. They were far more globally focused, but also with a conscious local agenda (manifest in support for local businesses, carnival and Light Festival). Overall, the impression gained was that, the more informed people were, the more empowered they appeared to be, not only in using and accessing global communication, such as the Internet, but also in resisting the negative aspects of globalization, seeming therefore to have more control over the town's economic and community development. The educational initiatives of CAT and Ecodyfi in particular seemed central to Machynlleth respondents' awareness of the interconnectivity of the local and the global. As a result, people seem inspired to resist big business, by supporting their local economy and balancing their budgets with their ethical concerns.

What emerged from both sets of interviews was the success of and potential for education awareness campaigns and clear policy directives. People in Machynlleth appear to be empowered by their knowledge, believing that their actions make a difference both locally and globally.

I try and buy my veg off the market store. I try and buy locally, organic, non-American rice. (Shirley)

We've got some quite good sources of local food, like that deli and we've got a community co-operative thingy-stall on the market which is great and they sell all seasonal veg and jam and cakes and eggs and all that kind of thing ... so I try and buy off that. The market provides quite a lot of our food – fruit and veg. and fish comes off the market. And the rest of the time I have to go in the Co-op – we eat quite healthily really. (Lauren)

Well it's a combination of being on a low income, so I am restricted by my low income, I try and eat as healthily and ethically as I can within my boundaries – sometimes I have to stray and buy things that perhaps I don't want to because of financial restrictions. I try and buy fair-trade, because here it's been such high profile – it's in the school and off the kids and everything and it's really good because you've got the influence of them – 'is this coffee fair-trade?' sort of thing – so you have to comply – it is the way to get through isn't it. (Lauren)

Whilst this degree of global consciousness is lacking in Llangefni, the initiatives and suggestions raised by a number of the interviewees there (such as car sharing, education programmes and the dropping of recycling costs for small businesses), indicates that there is support for a range of measures to highlight the interconnectivity of the local with the global, when initiatives are seen to benefit local people and local places as well as people and the environment elsewhere:

> But, you know, with education in schools and the university wanting to do some work in school and with communities at the moment, setting up workshops, bringing that awareness in and I think that people locally would really appreciate that kind of work because younger people are open to new ideas and working with other people. I think a global consciousness would be welcome, but at the moment I think it's very difficult to keep a total broad perspective of your place in this big world all the time but there are elements of awareness that get triggered every now and again. People forget that we are on a globe, you know, in a big universe. (Dafydd)

A local business owner explained:

> We recycle cardboard – well, we try to anyway. But there again you see it's not encouraging, you have to pay to get rid of our empty boxes ... we used to offer them to the companies that deliver them ... but nobody seems interested in having them back. They should do more to encourage us, they should help, especially small businesses, it's such a struggle these days, between your rent, your rates, your water, gas, it's gone and things like that. (Ffion)

> I remember when there was foot and mouth, they did it in the council where you shared cars, a car pool, with other people from your town, for people working all through Gwynedd and all through Anglesey ... and it was fantastic for that period because it made such a huge difference to the levels of traffic. So I've been asking them if they could do something like a bonus that was linked into sharing your car with somebody else because it could make a difference you know, but they're not interested. You could start something like cycling to school or walking to school, but then we're part of this as well – I don't live very far from the school and we pick them up in a car too. (Cllr. Rhian)

Social class, income, education, lifestyle and perhaps greater social diversity all appear to have a direct influence on how aware and engaged people are with the processes of globalization, not only in how people utilize and interact with global processes but also in how they resist the more negative elements of globalization, giving them greater control over their towns' development and empowering them with more life-style choices.

THE IMPORTANCE OF COMMUNITY AND IDENTITY

As Day (2002) notes, Wales does not have a homogenous identity, and neither does Llangefni or Machynlleth. Their social structures are diverse and complex, and are formed along lines of class, ethnicity, culture, interest, occupation and age. In such situations, 'social identities are not given, but constructed out of the intersection of a variety of memberships and commitments' (Day, 2002, p. 212). In both market towns, community networks are altering in response to the demographic and economic changes that have taken place, undermining traditional social structures and creating spaces for new networks to develop. These social networks were defined by the interviewees and were often observable as distinct social groups, with different social networks wearing specific clothing, hair styles and demonstrating body language particular to them. Whilst it would be wrong to argue that everyone fitted neatly into *one* social group, what the interviews confirmed was that people were keen to affiliate themselves with a specific social group in the town, a desire that fits neatly with Maffesoli's (1996) depiction of 'neo-tribes' to describe how community networks are formed along lines of common interests, beliefs and desires.

Interviewees in Llangefni did not perceive there to be any overarching town community. Instead, a range of independent social networks were identified and only amongst one of these social networks (the 'Welsh and from Llangefni' group) was a community structure recognized as existing (Figure 5.1).

In Machynlleth, meanwhile, though community was also identified as existing on different levels, amongst separate social groups, these were also seen to exist within an overarching community spirit in the town, which came together to feed into what could be referred to as 'the town's community' (Figure 5.2).

The 'traditional' members of both towns, identified as being specifically Llangefni/Machynlleth 'born and bred', and perceived to be part of the town's former community structure, are now an ageing and diminishing social group (the 'Welsh and from Llangefni' group and in Machynlleth the 'original townspeople' and the 'Welsh and speak Welsh' groups). For these groups, the local is historically constructed, and changes are often experienced in negative terms

Figure 5.1
Structure of social groups in Llangefni.

Figure 5.2
Structure of social groups in Machynlleth.

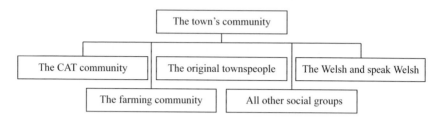

as being forced upon them, instilling feelings of defensiveness and nostalgia. Principally in Llangefni, but also to a lesser extent in Machynlleth, this was seen as revolving around being Welsh and speaking Welsh, though identity and belonging can be narrowed – for example, to being 'Llangefni born and bred' – and broadened to include Wales as a nation, depending on the context and the person. Identities are not fixed concepts, but are negotiated and are formed in opposition to other social groups, such as, in this case, largely the 'English'. The threat to community and belonging is not perceived as a consequence of globalization, but is often seen as an extension of English colonization and social policies. Thus, interviewees in Llangefni explained:

Well it's a very Welsh community here isn't it, you know? I think there are about 75 per cent Welsh people in Llangefni. Quite close knit I find, I am not from Anglesey originally, I am from Blaenau Ffestiniog, which is a quiet place, another tight community place. But people on the island here, I find to be very insular. It takes some time for you to be accepted here if you are not from the island, you know, but ... I have been involved with Rotary, the Choir, Town Company ... I have been here since '84. (Dilwyn)

I came to Llangefni in 1984 when I got married – I'm from Bangor – Whilst ... I've lived here for twenty years ... I don't see myself as a local still in the sense that I was from Bangor, and ... I have always worked over the bridge ... so I have not spent a lot of time here ... in the day ... , and I don't speak Welsh, though I can understand it. The farming community is very Welsh – still very Welsh – very Welsh community and when I met David, there was this kind of idea, I remember him saying, his uncle who was a farmer saying 'Oh, you don't want to marry her, she's a towny', there was very much you know this kind of community, working and Welshness. (Kate)

Because there are a lot of new people coming here to Llangefni to live, whether that's because they needed to be re-housed, or the fact that a lot of people have settled here it has changed a lot ... I mean the drug culture it has affected every community, just like everywhere else, it has affected Llangefni, there was a time when you were younger, where you could rely on communities to work together. Gone are the days when you could leave your back door open. (Sandra)

In Machynlleth, respondents often spoke of the social divisions that ran along linguistic and national lines:

Bea: I hardly know any of the Welsh speakers, which sometimes I find a bit, well I don't know, it's not really disappointing, but it's not a good thing ... in the town if you go to the pub, you don't really, I mean I'm thinking, most of my friends, or nearly all the people I go to the pub with or involved with the stall with, or anything, they're all English.

I: Why do you think that is?

Bea: I don't want to say it's because they are not as open to new ideas and things because that sounds wrong, but maybe that is part of it ... All the Welsh people I do know, they're all farmers' sons, they're all lovely, but they don't interact with the English in such a strong way. They do on a very personal level, but there's a dividing line. For example if you go out on a Friday night it's all us lot and on a Saturday night it's all Welsh ... which is really weird.

When discussing this with a local community worker who had tried to build 'partnerships' between the town's different social groups, he commented that 'it's difficult to get them to mix' (Owen). When asked why this was the case, the interview went as follows:

Owen: I think it's pure prejudice personally.

I: On both sides?

Owen: I am not convinced that it is on both sides, I think people are afraid of language.

I: So do you think this is coming from the non-Welsh speakers?

Owen: The non-Welsh speakers yes. I think people are afraid of the language ... possibly because there are too many people to live their lives without touching the language ... We're getting a lot more strangers into the town and probably the Welsher side of it, you know, can't accept it, but others do ... whereas you knew everybody before you don't know them now ... There are a lot here who are very weary of these people, who come in for the Centre for Alternative Technology, which has been good for the town in lots of ways, but the older generation feel that they are taking over, though they have been good for the town, you know, like putting on pantomimes and various other things in the community, they are always willing to participate and do something.

For these 'traditional' social networks, identity and community were historically and geographically bounded to place, evidence which is at odds with the conclusions of Savage et al.'s (2006) urban research of regions of Manchester, in which it was found that there was 'very little evidence that the local is historically constructed in this way as a kind of defensive identity' (Savage et al., 2006, p. 204).

On the other hand, Savage et al.'s (2006) concept of 'elective belonging' is very relevant to the CAT community in Machynlleth, who have been and are still active in constructing a form of 'community' upon which are superimposed certain ideological principles and identities, but which also draw on romantic images of the town's Celtic heritage and its people, 'y gwerin'. Members of this social group are often transient, yet the importance of place, and the feeling of belonging that they attach to it, is no less important or significant for them. This group's members, proportionately well educated and/or often from middle-class backgrounds are, as Bauman (2000) calls them, 'the global' – they have the education and income that enables access to travel, information technology and knowledge or 'cultural capital' (Bourdieu, 1997) to have choices, to be mobile. For them, the 'local' can be an elected place, whereas for others, especially those from the more disadvantaged social groups, localization can be a symbolism of poverty and exclusion, creating ghettoized areas such as the Bro Tudur council estate in Llangefni.

As Cresswell (2004) notes, place still appears to be an important concept to people even if many locations are losing their sense of 'place', and the threat that locations face in becoming 'placeless', identity-less zones often results in them taking on an added importance in people's imagination. As life still exists for most people at the local level, the space where, as Ray (2007) puts it, 'life gets done' remains an important arena within which people impose meanings, values and construct their identities, and is mourned by those who feel that their 'local', in this instance their market town, is losing its sense of place. For the respondents who participated in this research, 'community' is closely associated with place, to a romantic image of belonging, identity and communal social structures. Identity and community and people's sense of belonging were all constructs that people directly located within a territorial boundary. Even if some groups within the towns, such as some members of the CAT community in Machynlleth, may be transient and globally mobile, while they live in the town and become integrated into one of its social networks, 'place' becomes imbued with meaning, upon and around which identities and relationships are constructed.

CITIZENSHIP AND EMPOWERMENT

Market towns have become designated as sites of 'distinct policy areas' (Caffyn, 2004) for locations in need of regeneration, and policy strategies have been set out which incorporate a host of objectives that emphasize partnership working, active civic engagement and participation, local and global responsibility, sustainable employment and community. The recognition of the relationship between the local and the global is woven into most policy documents; however, the contradictions that exist within and between such documents not only work against each other, making their objectives difficult to achieve or even unachievable, but can also undermine civic empowerment and democratic participation. The principle policy document that affects these two market towns is the Wales Spatial Plan (Welsh Assembly Government, 2004), which sets out the tailored policy strategies for areas of Wales, and which all other policy documents feed into; it is focused primarily on developing local economies. Since Machynlleth's local economy has recently been built up around 'green industries' (Dulas Engineering, CAT, green tourism), helped significantly by the existence of Ecodyfi, then the Spatial Plan's environmental and community building policies can be applied more fully here. Llangefni meanwhile, as part of the 'Menai Hub' strategy area, is seen as an employment location and a commuter town. The emphasis here is on encouraging direct inward investment, from retail outlets to manufacturing facilities. The flexibility that exists within the Spatial Plan means therefore that there is no consistent or coherent universal strategy for areas. Policy priorities are then given different weight in different locations depending on the Spatial Plan's economic strategy for an area. This can result in some policy priorities (e.g. developing sustainable local businesses versus attracting direct inward investment) competing with or counteracting others. The emphasis on community development, democratic enhancement or environmental sustainability not only is unequal between places, but can also undermine the ability to achieve these objectives at a national level, let alone a local one.

Hence in Llangefni, community development, meaningful civic participation and developing an ethos of local and global responsibility do not appear to be key priorities, whereas in Machynlleth they are, because the identity and uniqueness of the town is recognized as its prime economic asset. Therefore despite both towns being at the time in European priority (Objective 1 and Objective 2) areas and recognized as being or containing Communities First wards, the support given to these schemes is not equal. Gardner (2003) notes similar contradictions existing in the Rural White Paper (and accompanying documents) that sets out a programme for community development and governance on rural planning policy. The policy documents contain statements emphasizing their commitment to include, for example, committees in decision-making processes, but as the documents fail to give local authorities additional planning powers, and because the main focus is economic and there is an agenda to reduce costs through the rationalization of services, such as schools and post offices, they inhibit local authorities from enacting fully on the policy objectives to include communities in the decision-making process (Gardner, 2003). Such policy strategies serve to further undermine communities and are having their biggest impact on society's most vulnerable, and so run contradictory to community development policies and programmes, such as Communities First, or to meeting environmental objectives, raising major concerns about Westminster's and the Welsh Assembly's commitment to civic empowerment and participation.

Thus the independence of Ecodyfi as a development agency, its commitment to working in partnership with Machynlleth's Community's First programme and through it actively encouraging and facilitating civic participation in the development of the town and on issues that are both local and global in scope, such as an interactive online 'ideas book', for members of the local community to be able to add their suggestions to how the local community, economy and environment could be improved (Ecodyfi, 2008), appears to be pivotal to the success, development and community cohesion of Machynlleth, as Ecodyfi's statement on local and global sustainability demonstrates:

> Local needs must be met within a long-term vision. This implies attention to global as well as local environmental quality and sustainability (e.g. climate change), to the robustness of the local economy (e.g. encouraging local purchasing) and to the capacity of local people to take responsibility for the future. (Ecodyfi, 2008)

The development of local areas and the success in policy implementation also appeared to be uneven between locations because of the discrepancies in efficiency, skills and commitments in and between both local authority departments and local authorities themselves. The success of community involvement also therefore appears to be dependent on the commitment and abilities of elite agents, such as community workers, corroborating Edwards et al.'s (2003, p. 128) findings that 'the key role of particular elite agents in the regeneration process highlights the difficulty of generating a more collective engagement that is capable of involving the wider community and delivering the rhetoric of New Labour collective empowerment'. Community development and engagement is therefore a very uneven process.

Though interviewees often perceived themselves as not being 'political', associating 'politics' with the formal political process, and seeing it as unrepresentative, undemocratic and archaic, in reality respondents from both towns were found to be very politically aware, but not party political, though levels of empowerment differed enormously between towns and ran along education, class and poverty lines. For example, many people in Llangefni appeared apathetic and defeated by issues that concerned them, whilst respondents in Machynlleth were active in responding to local and global issues.

Although there were enormous differences between respondents' understandings of and engagements with the concept of citizenship, a common thread was that it was understood as referring in some way to 'belonging'. People's definition of what they understood citizenship as meaning they belonged *to*, however, encompassed a wide range including the town or village a person came from; the local community from which they were part of; a nation – which for some was being Welsh and for others was being British; being European; and belonging to the world. However, more broadly the emphasis in Machynlleth was on *participation* whilst in Llangefni it was on *rights*.

The different levels of empowerment experienced between people in Llangefni and Machynlleth are illustrated in the analogy given by Christine, who has lived in both locations:

Machynlleth is more touristy, people are more relaxed because people are on holiday. *You don't feel as skint in Machynlleth as you do in Llangefni even if you are*. In Llangefni the Welsh is slightly different, the people there are harder – they are not laid-back, there is a shortage of jobs and money is tight. Llangefni is less friendly. (Christine: emphasis added)

This statement is reflective of how empowered people feel in the two towns in terms of their own lives and local life-worlds, but also of how empowered they are to bring about or resist change in their towns or even further afield. People in Llangefni mostly felt powerless and consequently were reactive to things that affected them, whilst people in Machynlleth were empowered as both local and global citizens and were instead pro-active locally and globally (there was, for example, a campaign during 2005–8 to ensure that, after the closure of Celtica in 2006, the building, Plas Machynlleth, remained the property of the townspeople and was used for the benefit of the residents of Machynlleth; the FairTrade group; 'think global, act local' campaigns; the 'slow food' campaign; the organization of annual community events such as pantomimes, carnivals and the Light Festival). What appears to be occurring is that citizenship power is increasingly being seen and used in terms of 'consumer power' to support the local economy or to boycott unethical companies. To be globally responsible is also regarded as being a privilege for those who can afford to be, though in Machynlleth efforts were made by many of its residents, even those on low incomes, to buy local, organic, fairtrade or environmentally friendly products where possible, juggling their principles with their income. It may be, as Desforges (2004, p. 567) suggests, that 'social capital, time resources and communicative abilities available to those in Britain who are interested in global development may be limited, such that a more fiscal form of citizenship fits neatly with any desire for involvement in global politics', and the same could be applied to local developments and politics.

CONCLUSION

People's relationship with and experience of the local and the global depend very much on how empowered or unempowered they feel as citizens. The participatory level of local agents within the towns appears crucial in raising global awareness, in community development and in generating local or global civic activity. For those who took part in this study and who had a good comprehension of globalization, citizenship participation is generally seen as needing to operate at the international global level, since rights, responsibilities and notions of belonging are perceived as being shared between people locally and internationally. For others who do not have a good understanding of globalization, the idea of citizenship is still confined to the national, if not to the local, level. Representative civic participation is then reduced disproportionately to the middle classes, the educated and members of single-issue groups and not society as a whole, which raises concerns not only for democratic participation in general, but also for civic engagement and empowerment in people's own individual lives, in their local area as well as globally.

This inequality in participation will limit the scope for achievement of the new coalition government's 'Big Society' objective of developing a civic ethos that encompasses rights and responsibilities if significant proportions of the population are excluded, disempowered and unrepresented within the local, national and global political arenas. Globalization appears to enhance democracy for some but undermine democracy for others. There are then scales of citizenship and civic engagement. Globalization and post-modernism have 'brought citizenship to the political *and* intellectual agendas' (Isin, 2000, p. 5). Notions of citizenship are currently being simultaneously eroded and remade and thus have to be seen as part of an evolutionary process which is currently being reshaped by civic and political agents, nationally as well as internationally.

How people and places respond to global influences and the 'grobalization' (Ritzer, 2004) machine, how the local interactions take place, is uneven and is dependent upon a range of local dynamics, which can result in some places losing their identities (becoming homogenized) like Llangefni, whilst others evolve, mixing new and old identities and cultures (become hybridized) like Machynlleth. However, Machynlleth's independence is not a sealed fate, as the aggressive expansive nature of the capitalist and consumerist element of globalization, termed 'grobalization' by Ritzer (2004) means that the threat of homogenization remains ever present, as represented for example by Tesco's recent plan to locate itself in the town.

Globalization is not reducible to being a 'good' or 'bad' set of processes, and neither can it be reduced to creating either homogenization or hybridization. Whilst the aggressive 'grobalization' machine of capitalism and consumerism is undoubtedly powerful, globalization also facilitates communication, understanding, global accessibility and interpretation. However, the effects of globalization are uneven and unequal. This study revealed that those who are educated and middle-class are far more empowered as a social group at the local and global levels than those from lower economic backgrounds and who have limited educational attainment. The educated have greater ability to access information and are more empowered as citizens; for them, globalization provides access to ideas, people, places, cultures: it can enable and empower them, allowing them to create for themselves the community and lifestyle that they want, as we have seen the CAT community is doing in Machynlleth. They are what Bauman (2000) refers to as the global. Others meanwhile, who do not have the skills, knowledge or finance to access and engage with the many processes of globalization, can become the globalized (Bauman, 2000), restricted to their local out of necessity, rather than out of choice. For these social groups, their lack of civic empowerment means that things happen *to* them, for good or for bad. For its citizens, the homogenization of Llangefni weakened the town's purpose, meaning and identity, turning it into a 'non-place', with 'non-people' selling 'non-things'. Their social, economic and educational disempowerment makes them vulnerable. It makes them victims. Given this, these finding show us that the 'sociological problems of power and social division such as social class, gender, nationality, ethnicity, institutional organization and capitalism remain as central as they have ever been' (Ray, 2007, p. 200).

REFERENCES

Albrow, M. (1997). 'Travelling beyond local cultures', in J. Eade (ed.), *Living the Global City: Globalization as a Local Process*, London: Routledge.

APPSSG (All-Party Parliamentary Small Shops Group) (2006). *High Street Britain: 2015*, London: House of Commons, http://www.nfsp.org.uk/uploads/pdfs/High%20Street%20Britain%202015%20report.pdf (accessed 11 November 2008).

Bauman, Z. (2000) *Globalization: The Human Consequences*, Cambridge: Polity Press.

BBC (2004). 'Laura Ashley shuts home factory', 25 October, http://news.bbc.co.uk/1/hi/wales/3951377.stm (accessed 6 October 2008).

BBC (2005). 'Wales: facts and figures', 24 November, http://www.bbc.co.uk/wales/mid/sites/machynlleth/pages/census_2001.shtml (accessed 11 November 2008).

BBC (2007). 'Island town looks at booze ban', 4 March 2007, http://cdnedge.bbc.co.uk/1/hi/wales/north_west/3536667.stm (accessed 10 November 2008).

Bourdieu, P. (1997). 'The forms of capital', in A. H. Halsey, H. Lauder, P. Brown and A. S. Wells (eds), *Education, Culture, Economy, Society*, Oxford: Oxford University Press.

Bowen, E. G. (1959). 'Le pays de Galles', *Transactions of the Institute of British Geographers*, 26, 1–23.

Brown, G. (2006). 'Speech to Labour Party Conference', 25 September, http://news.bbc.co.uk/1/hi/uk_politics/5378312.stm (accessed 19 October 2006).

Brown, P. (2007). 'Condemned to history', *The Guardian*, 7 February.

Caffyn, A. (2004). 'Market town regeneration: challenges for social policy and implementation', *Local Economy*, 19, 1, 8–24.

Castells, M. (2000). *End of Millennium, The Information Age: Economy, Society and Culture*, Cambridge, MA: Blackwell.

Castells, M., Boraja, J., Belil, M. and Benner, C. (1997). *Local and Global: Management of the Cities in the Information Age*, London: Earthscan Publications.

Census (2001). *Parish Headcounts*, http://neighbourhood.statistics.gov.uk (accessed 11 November 2008).

Cloke, P., Goodwin, M. and Milbourne, P. (1997). *Rural Wales: Community and Marginalization*, Cardiff: University of Wales Press.

Communities First Bro Dyfi (2004). *Towards an Action Plan*, http://commfirstpowys.org.uk/f2/file/Reports/towardsactionplane.doc (accessed 6 October 2008).

Cresswell, T. (2004). *Place: A Short Introduction*, Oxford: Blackwell.

Cvetkovich, A. and Kellner, D. (eds) (1997). *Articulating the Global and the Local*, Oxford: Westview.

Day, G. (2002). *Making Sense of Wales*, Cardiff: University of Wales Press.

Day, G. (2006). 'A community of communities?' Civil society and rural Wales', in G. Day, D. Dunkerley and A. Thompson (eds), *Civil Society in Wales*, Cardiff: University of Wales Press.

Day, G. (2010). 'The Englishing of rural Wales? Migration, conflict and integration in community life', in P. Milbourne (ed.), *Geographies of Rural Wales: Society, Economy and Environment*, Cardiff: University of Wales Press.

Davies, W. D. (2000). *Machynlleth Town Trail: A Historical Guide to the Town*, 2nd edition, Aberystwyth: Cambrian Printers.

Department for Communities and Local Development (2009). *Planning Policy Statement 4: Planning for Sustainable Economic Growth*, Whitehall: DCLG.

Desforges, L. (2004). 'The formation of global citizenship: international non-governmental organisations in Britain', *Political Geography*, 23, 549–69.

Ecodyfi (2008). *Communities First: What Is a Regeneration Programme?*, http://www.ecodyfi.org.uk/regeneration.htm (accessed 18 October 2008).

Edwards, B., Goodwin, M. and Woods, M. (2003). 'Citizenship, community and participation in small towns: a case study of regeneration partnerships', in R. Imrie and M. Raco (eds), *Urban Renaissance? New Labour, Community and Urban Policy*, Bristol: Policy Press.

Evans, G. (2008). 'A stroll around historic Llangefni', *BBC Home: North West Wales*, http://www.bbc.co.uk/wales/northwest/sites/llangefni/pages/buildings.shtml (accessed 7 January 2008).

Gardner, G. (2003) '(Re)thinking power in rural studies: from organic community to political society', in M. Kneafsey and L. Holloway (eds), *Geographies of Rural Cultures and Societies*, Farnham: Ashgate

IACC (Isle of Anglesey County Council) (1999). *Revitalizing Llangefni Conference: Background Report*, Llangefni: Planning and Economic Development Department.

IACC (Isle of Anglesey County Council) (2005). *Llangefni Alcohol Free Zone Comes into Force*, http://www.anglesey.gov.uk/doc.asp?cat=99&doc=2243 (accessed 4 October 2008).

IACC (Isle of Anglesey County Council) (2006). *Local Development Plan Evidence*, http://www.anglesey.gov.uk/upload/public/attachments/48/Ecomony_and_Employment.pdf (accessed 3 October 2008).

Isin, E. (ed.) (2000) *Democracy Citizenship and the Global City*, London: Routledge.

Klein, N. (2001). *No Logo*, London: Flamingo.

Lerner, S. (2006) *Eco-Pioneers: Practical Visionaries Solving Today's Environmental Problems*, Cambridge, MA: MIT Press.

Local Works (2003). *Bringing the Global Economy Home*, London: New Economics Foundation.

Maffesoli, M. (1996). *The Time of the Tribes*, London: Sage.

Ohmae, K. (2000). 'The end of the nation state', in F. Lechner and J. Boli (eds), *The Globalization Reader*, Oxford: Blackwell.

Ray, L. (2007). *Globalization and Everyday Life*, London: Routledge.

Ritzer, G. (1993). *The McDonaldization of Society*. Newbury Park, CA: Pine Forge Press

Ritzer, G. (2004). *Globalization of Nothing*, London: Pine Forge Press.

Savage, M., Bagnall, G. and Longhurst, B. (2006). *Globalisation and Belonging*, London: Sage.

Scholte, J. A. (2000). *Globalization*, London: Palgrave.

Sillito, D. (2007). 'The fall of Fenny Stanford's high street', *BBC News*, http://news.bbc.co.uk/1/hi/uk/6261227.smt (accessed 25 September 2008).

TPMW Business Plan 2008/2009 (2008). *Tourism Partnership Mid Wales 2008/2009: Final Draft*, http://tpmw.love-media.co.uk/files/178.doc (accessed 22 November 2008).

Wales Rural Observatory (2004). *Key Findings: Paper 4 – A Survey of Rural Services in Wales*, http://www.walesruralobservatory.org.uk/reports/english/Key%20findings%204-%20A%20survey%20of%20Rural%20Services%20in%20Wales%20version%202.pdf (accessed 10 August 2011).

Wales Rural Observatory (2007). *Small and Market Towns in Rural Wales and Their Hinterlands: Research Report*, *http://www.walesruralobservatory.org.uk/reports/english/Market%20Towns%20report%20final2.pdf* (accessed 21 November 2008).

Welsh Assembly Government (2004). *People, Places, Futures: The Wales Spatial Plan*, http://new.wales.gov.uk/about/strategy/spatial/sppublications/walesspatial?lang=en (accessed 12 September 2008).

Western Mail (2006a). 'The Welshest place in Wales – and proud of it', 11 September, http://www.walesonline.co.uk/news/wales-news/tm_objectid=17720981&method=full&siteid=50082&headline=welshest-place-in-wales---and-proud-of-it-name_page.html (accessed 17 September 2006).

Western Mail (2006b). 'The greenest people in Wales', 14 June 2006, http://www.redorbit.com/news/business/538000/the_greenest_people_n_wales/index.html (accessed 6 October 2008).

Williams, F. (2010). 'Llangefni to lose its market town image', *Bangor and Anglesey Mail*, http://www.icnorthwales.co.uk (accessed 10 August 2011).

Woods, M. (2007). 'Engaging the global countryside: globalization, hybridity and the reconstruction of the global', *Progress in Human Geography*, 31, 485–507.

6. ECONOMIC RENEWAL AND THE GENDERED KNOWLEDGE ECONOMY IN WALES

Alison Parken and Teresa Rees

ABSTRACT

The Welsh Assembly Government's Economic Renewal Strategy aims to develop Wales into a 'knowledge economy'. 'Knowledge economies' depend upon close networks and effective collaboration between the members of the 'triple helix' of universities, government and industry. The Assembly Government is obliged, under the Government of Wales Act (2006), to pay due regard to equality of opportunities in all its policies, a commitment underlined by the requirements for equality impact assessments under new British equalities legislation. In this paper, we conduct a political arithmetic of the gender of key players in the 'triple helix' in Wales. Will the Economic Renewal Strategy promote equality or unintentionally reproduce already rigid patterns of gender segregation in the labour market?

INTRODUCTION

The European Union in its economic strategy, *Europe 2020*, is promoting the idea that Member States develop into a 'knowledge economy' (European Commission, 2010). It argues that the three priorities for Europe should be 'smart growth' (developing an economy based on knowledge and innovation); 'sustainable growth' and 'inclusive growth' (European Commission, 2010, p. 8). Hence, critical to this economic strategy is the aim to ensure that moving to a knowledge economy promotes social inclusion by combining welfare and child-care policies and gender employment policies alongside knowledge and innovation. An inclusive knowledge economy necessitates an ongoing analysis of the gender beneficiaries of investment and addressing the causes and consequence of gender segregation in the labour market to avoid reproducing inequalities.

The Welsh Assembly Government is also committed to developing a knowledge economy. It could equally be expected to address attention to the inclusivity of its economic renewal strategy given the requirements of the Government of Wales Act (2006, s. 77) that Ministers pay 'due regard' to equality for all, in all that they do. Indeed, under new British statutory equality duties for gender, race and disability (cf. Equality Act, 2010), public policies, including spending cuts and investment, are now subject to equality impact assessments.[1] This should imply regular analysis of relevant gender-disaggregated statistics, particularly as there is a commitment in the Assembly Government both to promoting equality and to an evidence-based approach to developing policy. However, in practice, 'promoting equality' is an inexact science – and as policy-making processes are rarely linear, arguably, they are therefore never entirely evidence-based.

This paper seeks to offer some background gendered analysis of the labour market in Wales as a backcloth for the Economic Renewal Strategy (Welsh Assembly Government, 2010). It draws upon research conducted for EURODITE, a five-year, European Commission 6th Framework Programme research project on regional trajectories to knowledge economies, in which Wales was a case study region (Parken and Rees, 2009).[2] Strategies designed to foster knowledge economies focus on certain 'innovative' sectors. It is the knowledge created at the interface of actors in universities, business and the government sector, known as the 'Triple Helix' (Etzkowitz and Leydesdorff, 1997) that is viewed as the platform for creating knowledge intensity in a region, leading to economic growth. Good networks between these actors are crucial to facilitating investment by venture capital in new or expanding businesses and developing new markets – but policies developed to promote a knowledge economy overlay existing patterns of gender segregation, both in those sectors regarded as relevant for support and investment and among those actors playing key roles in decision-making. Here we explore the gendering of the 'triple helix' in Wales, and the challenge faced by the Welsh Assembly Government (WAG) in its aim of promoting a knowledge economy which also promotes gender equality.

Overall, the EURODITE research team investigated knowledge generation, use and transfers within twenty-two case studies in nineteen countries in the 'knowledge economy sectors' of automotive, food, information and communication technologies (ICT), new media, tourism, bioscience, and 'knowledge intensive businesses' (KIBs). The sectors that have been selected by the Welsh Assembly Government in its Economic Renewal Strategy (WAG, 2010) are those which already have some presence in Wales: ICT, energy and environment, advanced materials and manufacturing, creative industries, life sciences and financial and professional services (WAG, 2010, p. 37).[3] Employment data for Wales illustrate that men have acquired most of the new high-quality jobs in these 'knowledge economy sectors' over the last decade, whilst women have attained two thirds of the jobs in the expansion of poorly paid care and personal services occupations. This is a difficult baseline for the Economic Renewal Strategy to build upon, especially if the Welsh government is to fulfil its obligation to pay due regard to equalities for all.

Within EURODITE, Cooke (2006) and Manniche (2010) have defined knowledge creation phases as exploration (broadly, analytic inquiry in universities), examination (synthesizing analytic knowledge with technical knowledge to engineer applications) and exploitation (use of symbolic knowledge in learning activities, commercialization, marketing and branding). Government funding to universities and businesses is heavily concentrated in the first two phases. However, it is in the last knowledge phase where the greater involvement of women has been identified through the EURODITE case studies.

This paper draws upon a range of data sources, largely secondary analysis of the Office for National Statistics' *Regional Labour Market Statistics* and datasets from WAG's Statistics Wales (see 'Data sources' below) to explore the extent to which women are positioned to benefit from the Economic Renewal Strategy's focus on 'knowledge economy' sectors. To consider who Wales's 'knowledge workers' are, an innovative and indicative dataset was created in collaboration with Statistics Wales based upon gender participation by occupation in the 'knowledge phases' described above.

We further explored the gender make-up of the 'triple helix' players in Wales. This 'political arithmetic' of potential participation is measured first through an account of the presence of men and women among the various industrial sectors in recent years. Second, we examine gender participation in the 'triple helix' in universities, and beneficiaries of one of the main tools of the knowledge economy so far in Wales, the 'Knowledge Transfer Partnership Programmes'. The paper is offered as a worked example of how gender-disaggregated data can be collected and analysed for the purposes of promoting gender equality and informing public policy.

THE GENDERING OF THE LABOUR MARKET

The term 'gender' does not, of course, refer to given, fixed or biological attributes but rather is used to describe how society is stratified by a particular social and economic division, in a similar way to class, age, disability or ethnicity. It is important to understand how gender regimes operate in organizations, in networking and in institutional systems and practices, in order to consider how such practices produce advantage or disadvantage for men and/or women.

Research within sociology and organization studies has demonstrated that jobs are not gender-neutral spaces (Acker, 1990; Adkins, 1995; Cockburn, 1985, 1988, 1991). A 'gendered presentation of self', or rather a 'hetero-gendered presentation of self' (Parken 2003, 2010a), can be assumed within the employment contract (Gheradi, 1995). Studies across occupations have considered the performance of gender as integral to the goods or services being consumed (Leidner, 1991). Indeed, both the masculinized performances of management (Collinson and Hearn, 1996) and the feminized 'sale' of services (Adkins, 1995; MacEwan Scott, 1994; Taylor and Tyler, 2000) have been mapped.

Thus, gender is an active process, 'an ongoing activity embedded in every day interactions in which we do gender' (West and Zimmerman, 1987, p. 45). We produce a performance appropriate to the dominant discourses of gender in each occupation. Through our jobs and tasks, we build our gendered identities. In these processes and social practices, we reproduce the gendering of occupations. Therefore, we are constantly, if subconsciously, studying the 'gendering of everyday life' (Horelli, 2000) at both workplace and institutional levels.

Gender segregation in the labour market remains extraordinarily robust, vertically, horizontally and contractually. The European Union Treaty of Amsterdam (1999, Article 3) committed member states to a policy of gender mainstreaming in order to reduce the impact of gender on occupational and other life chances, through promoting equality in all policies. Gender mainstreaming is defined by the European Commission as:

> mobilising all general policies and measures specifically for the purpose of achieving equality by actively and openly taking account at the planning stage of their possible effects on the respective situations of men and women. (Commission of the European Communities, 1996)

The extent to which Member States have adopted and implemented this strategy remains highly variable, however. Chaney's review of equal opportunities and human rights in the first decade of devolution in Wales (Chaney, 2009) demonstrates a much more pro-active approach to equalities by WAG than by the previous Welsh Office. While he characterizes the early years of the Assembly as 'declaratory' in relation to equalities, in later years, he argues, the range of equality dimensions included in policy-making has increased and the policy process has become more sophisticated than before in addressing equality dimensions. This suggests a context in which the gendered dimension of a knowledge economy would be on the agenda.

The knowledge economy: a gendered concept?

The concept of a knowledge economy is widely contested and how it is defined has implications for how to explore its gendered dimensions. Knowledge economy research projects funded by the Economic and Social Research Council (Hudson, 2006, table 2) are described as supporting the shift from an industrial to an information age through the application of knowledge and skills to innovation in order to gain competitive advantage. Indeed, many definitions include 'innovation' as a concept, which itself is hard to define. Blake and Hanson (2005) observe that 'innovation' has been truncated to refer to technology, while Ball argues (2010) that it should refer more widely to change or renewal of ideas within any sector or discipline. It could even refer to the application of existing innovative ideas regarding service delivery to new spatial domains (Blake and Hanson, 2005).

Sociological and cultural interpretations describe the effects of information and communication technologies (ICTs) on producing a 'knowledge based society' (Brinkley, 2006; Burfitt et al., 2007), but the United Nation Development Programme (UNDP) and the United Nations Development Fund for Women (UNIFEM) (2004) have reported upon the 'gender digital divide' in Europe. A narrower definition of knowledge economies, predominant in regional economic development and in economic geography, focuses upon technology and high-status occupations:

> technology and knowledge based industries reflecting R and D intensity, high ICT usage, and the development of large numbers of graduates and professionals and associate professional workers – the knowledge workers. (Rudiger and McVerry, 2007, p. 11)

In addition, the Work Foundation concentrates on the value of knowledge-based outputs from workers in just three occupational strata, namely Managers and Senior Officials; Professional and Associate Professional; and Technical (Brinkley, 2006). There are fewer women than men in these top three strata and those who are in the 'top three' are clustered in a narrow range of industries and occupations. Hence, relatively few women are in a position to benefit from research monies targeted in these sectors, occupations or lead researcher roles. However, the Work Foundation (Brinkley, 2006; Mahdon et al., 2007; Rudiger and McVerry, 2007) also includes older industries in its definition, where workers use ICTs both extensively and routinely in their studies (Brinkley, 2006). They also incorporate intangibles such as brand values, human capital and processes for knowledge transfer (Mahdon et al., 2007, p. 4), which some argue have become as important as controlling land and labour in the emerging economy (Cooke, 2006). Hence:

general purpose technologies have combined with intellectual and knowledge assets 'the intangibles' of research, design, development, creativity, education, science, brand equity and human capital to transform economies across Europe. (Rudiger and McVerry, 2007, p. 11)

It is in these branding and marketing roles, where value in innovation is realized, that we find more women involved (Parken, 2010b). However, by focusing on the senior and technical occupational strata, an examination of 'knowledge work' at lower levels of the occupational hierarchies is precluded. Thus the polarization of work in Britain, into what Goos and Manning (2003) describe as 'lousy and lovely jobs', is obscured. Against this background Perrons (2004, 2005) describes the 'new economy' as an alternative frame of analysis as opposed to the knowledge economy. She demonstrates divergent gender participation between knowledge jobs and care jobs – further stratified by other social divisions such as class and income. Whilst higher-order jobs have mostly provided growth in male employment, a similar rise in poorly paid social care jobs, characterized by part-time contracts and low earnings, has been largely taken up by women. This divergence has been replicated in Wales. While social care work requires considerable *application* of knowledge, it does not conform to the idea of knowledge work as narrowly defined, and is not valued or rewarded as such.

What are the gender dimensions of these definitions of knowledge economies? A wider definition might have a broader industry base and include knowledge work in management and service delivery in the public sector. This would have the effect of including more women workers, who are primarily concentrated in public administration, educational and health jobs throughout Wales, and indeed the rest of Europe. It can be argued that the restrictive sectoral approach misses much that is both innovative and applies new technologies in traditionally female work. A wider definition goes further than the very narrow association of the knowledge economy with innovation only in technology by including, for example, knowledge transfer in food, tourism, new media and knowledge-intensive businesses, as well as automotive, bioscience and ICT. Evidence from the EURODITE case studies shows women's contribution in vital support roles in these sectors. However, rather than driving innovation from leadership roles in the triple helix, they are more likely to contribute in customer-facing administrative and marketing functions to the value chain (Parken, 2010b).

Gender and the knowledge economy sectors in Wales
The first ten years of devolution (1999–2009) have been characterized by a commitment by the Welsh Assembly Government to creating a 'small clever

country'.[4] Since the 1970s, the economy of Wales, like those of similar regional areas within Europe, has transformed from a heavy dependence on energy and heavy industry, mining and manufacturing to a service economy. The National Assembly for Wales was set up with devolved administrative and policy powers including those covering health, the economy, transport, education, local government and the environment. In 2006 it was granted some primary legislative powers but it cannot as yet raise taxes or set welfare provision limits. Wales was part of the UK National Reform Programme for the European Employment Strategy, which had as its goal to 'make Europe the most competitive knowledge based economy in the world by 2010'.[5] The new European Union 2020 strategy is also heavily reliant on world-class research universities and research and development in leading businesses for growth (European Commission, 2010). It specifies the importance of social inclusion in the transition to knowledge economies. However, this is not emphasised in the Economic Renewal Strategy (WAG, 2010).

During the long period of deindustrialization in Wales between 1975 and 1994, there was a 61 per cent decrease in men's employment in the Standard Industrial Classification (SIC 1980) 'extraction/metal manufacture; minerals/metals', down from 103,000 to 40,000 workers (Rees, 1999, p. 9). Women's employment fell in this grouping by almost 50 per cent but from a low base of 13,000 to 7,000. Mining and manufacturing jobs have continued to fall. Manufacturing jobs decreased by 7 per cent between March 2008 and March 2009 to represent just 13 per cent of all employee jobs in Wales (Statistics Wales, 2009a, p. 7). Although the unemployment rate in Wales has been lower than that of the UK as a whole, unemployment has been high in the Valleys and West Wales, where rates of economic activity have been low. These areas have attracted Objective 3 European Structural Funds (and subsequently Convergence Funds).[6]

The significance of spatial economic geographies to gender relations has been illustrated in relation to mining. For example, Styck et al. (2008) detail how the mining companies in Limberg in Belgium historically promoted large families as a source of labour. In so doing they instituted dependency and male dominance through the mine as the source and centre of cultural and economic life, spilling over from the landscape to encompass work, family and leisure. Engineers' wives were obliged, through their husband's employment contracts, not to undertake paid work but to provide the service of a housewife, ensuring their husband's readiness for work. This type of measure was unnecessary for miners as their wages were too low to purchase household services in the (informal) market. In short, employment contracts and wage levels instituted a gender and class regime which confined women to caring and reproductive activities (De Rijck and Van Meulder, 2000, in Styck et al., 2008, p. 77). This example illustrates the contextual constitution of gender relations, and how their legacies can operate as gender cultures (Pfau-Effinger, 1998) embedded in social practices repeated over time within communities. Gender relations, then, are influenced by employment contexts and provision of public services, and in turn shape employment choices, which are not fixed 'naturally' but change temporally and spatially. Greed (2005) shows how women's current employment 'choices' are constrained by spatial planning decisions, when cognizance of how gender roles affect daily life is not 'mainstreamed' into transport planning and city design by local planning authorities. Women more often undertake lateral journeys incorporating a series of activities rather than the journeys taken by men, which tend to influence planning – straight to and from work in peak hours (Greed, 2005, pp. 720–1).

In 2005, 'knowledge based services' represented 68 per cent of UK services exports (ONS, 2006, from Hudson, 2006), the most significant of these being in business, financial and computer services. In Wales, financial and business services constituted 16 per cent of employment in 2007 compared with 21 per cent UK-wide (Statistics Wales, 2009b). In 2007, Wales's higher education institutions (HEIs) ranked technology transfer as a significantly lower priority than HEIs in the other nations and regions of the UK, and recorded lower income from intellectual property than all other UK nations and regions apart from Northern Ireland (HEFCE, 2008, pp. 12–24). In 2007, gross value added (GVA) per head of population in Wales was £14,877, representing 75 per cent of the average for the UK regions (Statistics Wales, 2009b: 10).[7] This is the lowest GVA per head of the UK regions. This all creates a challenging context for developing a knowledge economy.

MEN AND WOMEN IN THE TRIPLE HELIX IN WALES

Who are the players in the triple helix of universities, government and industry in Wales as well as in the labour market more generally? First, Table 6.1 shows the gendered distribution of employment in Wales. Women have low levels of self employment compared with men but are over-represented in temporary employment.

In 2008, men held almost two thirds of all full time jobs in Wales (64 per cent) but just 23 per cent of part-time jobs (Office for National Statistics, 2009, table 11). Women are much more likely to work part-time and to have a second job than men. The current figures reflect a long history of women's low self-employment and lower entrepreneurial activity (Harding et al., 2007). Women's employment rates are:

Table 6.1
Employment in Wales (thousands), October 2007–September 2008

	Total	Employees	Self-employed	Full time	Part time	Second job	Temporary
All in employment	1,338	1,151	175	978	357	56	74
Men	709	577	127	625	84	24	33
Women	628	575	48	354	273	32	41

Source: Office for National Statistics (2009, table 3).

significantly affected by the presence of dependent children, their number and ages. Overall gaps in economic activity and employment rate between women and men in Wales are 6 per cent and 5 per cent respectively (ONS, 2009b) but the employment rate gap between men and women who have dependent children under the age of 5 years in Wales is 32 per cent (LFS, 2008). Ninety per cent of these fathers of children under 5 are working, compared to only 58 per cent of mothers. (Parken et al., 2009, p. 23).

The UK has a mixed economy of childcare. As elsewhere, childcare in Wales is of variable quality, but on average more expensive than in England (particularly in rural areas) and insufficient places are available (Bevan Foundation, 2005). Provision does not meet the European Union's Barcelona agreement on childcare targets, set within the European Employment Strategy (90 per cent coverage for pre-school children over three years old, and 33 per cent coverage of those under three, by 2010). Recently, the National Assembly passed the Carers Strategies (Wales) Measure (2010), which includes a child poverty duty, requiring local authorities to extend their provision of free childcare to two-year-olds in deprived areas.[8] Besides providing these children with improved education chances, the aim is to facilitate women's economic activity. However, as provision of only fifteen hours per week of care is on offer, only part-time working will be possible.

Current patterns of gender segregation by industry in Wales (horizontal segregation) are set out in Table 6.2.

Men constitute 86 per cent of workers in the 'agricultural, fishing and farming industries' category and 76 per cent of manufacturing workers (Office for National Statistics, 2009b). Gender balance is almost achieved in the very broad classification of 'distribution, transport, finance, business etc.'. Women dominate the education, health and public administration sectors, totalling 69 per cent of this category, which mostly comprises public sector jobs (Office for National

Table 6.2
Wales: employee jobs by industry (thousands), December 2008

	Totals, seasonally adjusted	Men	Women
Agriculture, forestry, fishing and farming	7,000	6,000	1,000
Mining, energy, waste supplies	7,000	5,000	2,000
Manufacturing industries	152,000	116,000	35,000
Construction	48,000	41,000	7,000
Distribution etc., transport etc., finance and business services	483,000	241,000	243,000
Education, health, public administration and other services	448,000	139,000	309,000

Source: Office for National Statistics (2009, table 5).

Statistics, 2009b). While the public sector, particularly education and health, remains excluded from knowledge economy support and investment, very few women will be in a position to participate. When considering the hierarchy of occupations, the effect of vertical gender segregation means that there are few women amongst the top three strata – the knowledge workers (Table 6.3) – and fewer still in those occupations in the growth sectors prioritized in the Welsh Assembly Government's Economic Renewal Strategy (WAG, 2010).

Men numerically dominate management and professional positions in the 'agricultural, manufacturing and construction' industries. No women senior managers were recorded in the sub-category 'energy and water', signalling that the new industries of 'renewables' may become particularly characterized by vertical gender segregation (see Cooke and De Laurentis, 2010 on the growing importance of bio-mass industries in Wales). Men also dominate in senior management positions in the 'services' category ('distribution etc.') but there is a near gender balance within the 'services' professions. However, of the 67,700 professional women employed in this category, 57,500 were working within occupations in public administration, education, health and other services. This accounts for fully 82 per cent of women professionals in the larger occupational category ('distribution etc.').

No women professionals were recorded in the 'agriculture, fishing etc.' category or in 'transport and communication'. In 'associate professional and technical' jobs, 62,500 of the 87,000 women in 'distribution and other industries' were working within 'public administration, education and health'. Overall, this is a picture of extreme gender segregation; one which has changed little over time, even with the growth of services and the substantial increase in women's percentage of employee jobs in these occupations. Indeed, recent statistical analysis from the European Commission demonstrates that, far from improving,

Table 6.3
Top three occupational strata: industry sector analysis

	Total	Men	Women
Managers and senior officials – all industries	*174,600*	*111,400*	*62,800*
Managers and senior officials – agriculture, fishing; energy and water; manufacturing; construction	47,400	39,200	8,000
Managers and senior officials – distribution, hotels, restaurants; transport and communication; banking, finance and insurance etc.; public administration, education, health and other services	127,200	72,300	54,800
Professionals – all industries	*158,300*	*87,800*	*70,500*
Professionals – agriculture, fishing; energy and water; manufacturing; construction	23,100	20,500	2,300
Professionals – distribution, hotels, restaurants; transport and communication; banking finance and insurance etc.; public administration, education, health and other services	135,100	67,400	67,700
Associate professional and technical – all industries	*172,800*	*79,300*	*93,500*
Associate professional and technical – Agriculture etc.	22,600	16,200	6,500
Associate professional and technical – Distribution etc.	150,200	63,100	87,000

Source: Annual Population Survey January 2008–December 2008. Wales. NOMIS. Data Run: 195009, extrapolated 22 July 2009.

industrial gender segregation has become even more entrenched in the last decade (European Commission, 2009).

The number of 'top jobs' in Wales grew significantly between 2001 and 2006 (Statistics Wales, 2007), with women gaining an almost equal share of the 23,000 new 'Manager and Senior Official' positions and the majority of the 13,000 'Professional' and 25,000 'Associate Professional and Technical' jobs (Statistics Wales, 2007, p. 4). So, whilst vertical segregation by gender has decreased, segregation by industry has not (Statistics Wales, 2007, p. 4).

There was little change in middle-ranking occupations ('administrative and skilled trades'), except for a large increase in 'Personal Service Occupations'. Moreover, 'plant and process, and elementary jobs' declined. However, women took over two thirds of the newly created 15,000 jobs in 'personal services' (Statistics Wales, 2007). These are mostly part time and caring related, substantiating Perrons's (2004) analysis of a gender divided 'new economy'. Without commenting on the growing gender disparity, the Statistics Wales review of job quality notes that there has been 'a shift away from machine based jobs, [and a] shift towards working with people' (Statistics Wales, 2007, p. 3).

Within the EURODITE research project, partners articulated knowledge transfer within symbolic, analytic and synthetic knowledge production (Cooke, 2006; Manniche, 2010). However, it is clear from the following analysis of synthetic and symbolic jobs in Wales that few women are engaged in synthesizing knowledge for commercial application. More are contributing by adding value in the downstream, consumer facing, marketing and brand-building tasks of exploiting new knowledge in technologies and services.

Part of the difficulty of analysing knowledge workers is the lack of a discrete occupational index for them across sectors (Brinkley, 2006, 2008). However, an innovative dataset was constructed by Statistics Wales, using the knowledge phases described in EURODITE and drawing upon occupations such as 'production, works and maintenance managers, ICT managers, electronics engineers, engineering technicians, and design and development engineers' for synthetic knowledge occupations, and 'solicitors and lawyers, judges and coroners, chartered and certified accountants, management consultants, actuaries, economists and statisticians, public relations officers and marketing associate professionals' in cross-sector symbolic knowledge occupations. Table 6.4 shows an overwhelming masculinization of synthetic knowledge generation and transfer processes in the UK and in Wales. Women are more evidently contributing to symbolic knowledge processes.

Given women's paucity of participation in knowledge transfer occupations in business, and in senior roles in government, we now turn to consider whether and where women are engaged in analytic knowledge phases within the university axis of the 'triple helix' of knowledge generation and use. In other words, how are women involved in the exploration for innovation and commercialization in Wales? Although preparedness for knowledge work is not confined to the study of science, technology, engineering and mathematics subjects (STEM), there has been and continues to be a view that these knowledge areas signify the locus of economic growth (Brinkley, 2006). Higher education qualifications show a gender divide between men and women, with more men in engineering and physics, while women predominate in social science, education and health-related subjects. Women continue to be the majority of graduates in Wales, constituting 57 per cent of first degree graduates in 2007/8 (Table 6.5).

Table 6.4
Synthetic and symbolic knowledge jobs by occupation group and gender (thousands)

	Wales			UK		
	Males	Females	Total	Males	Females	Total
Synthetic	71.2	10.0	81.2	1,921.6	322.8	2,244.5
Symbolic	64.4	42.9	107.3	2,011.7	1,299.7	3,311.4
All occupations	724.7	653.6	1,378.3	16,273.0	14,308.0	30,581.0

Source: Annual Population Survey Year to March 2009.

Table 6.5
Study by subject at all levels (first degree and postgraduate) by subject and gender,
Wales 2009

Subject	Women	Men	Total
Subjects allied to medicine	2,865	560	3,470
Business and administrative studies	2,880	3,495	6,445
Engineering and technology	260	1,910	2,200
Social studies	1,475	900	2,395
Computer science	235	940	1,195

Source HESA: Table 7a – Qualifications obtained by students on HE courses at HEIs in the UK by location of institution, level of qualification obtained, gender and subject area, 2007/08(1).

Gendered subject choice is apparent, with men dominating 'engineering and technology and computer science', as well as within subjects. Although women dominate 'social studies' as a subject area, men dominate in 'economics and politics'. Table 6.5 shows that the biggest single subject category of study for women and men is 'business and administrative studies'. The next most popular subject for men is 'engineering and technology' – and, for women, 'subjects allied to medicine'. This category includes subjects such as anatomy, pharmacology and ophthalmology, but their domination of this subject area is due to the majority studying nursing.

The Higher Education Funding Council for England (2008) survey of university and business interaction for 2006/7 (which also provides data for Wales, Scotland and Northern Ireland) details the participation of university staff in commercialization activities. However, the data on the 170 staff engaged with commercial partners in dedicated business or community units were not gender disaggregated. Individual Welsh HEIs report their highest rates of engagement being with the automotive, manufacturing, energy and construction, transport and public administration sectors (HEFCE 2008, Annex 1, Q2). They are less engaged with the financial, property, wholesale and retail sectors.

This examination was achieved by commissioning new data from the Higher Education Statistics Agency demonstrating academic grade (professoriate) with academic subject and gender.

Table 6.6 summarizes the gender of participants in academic disciplines allied to the knowledge economy sectors studied within the knowledge economy sectors identified by EURODITE.

Gender segregation among the professoriate in Wales is clear; of the total professors in Wales, women and men account for 110 (11.7 per cent) and 840 full person equivalent positions respectively (HESA, 2009). In the disciplines selected for analysis, women are absent from several of the subjects traditionally linked to the development of a knowledge economy. In science, engineering,

Table 6.6
Gender disaggregation of Welsh HEIs professoriate in selected academic 'industrial, business and professional disciplines' (2007/8)

Discipline	Women	Men
(B2) Pharmacology, toxicology and pharmacy	0	12
(C1) Biology	1.0	23.4
(C4) Genetics	2.0	9.0
(C7) Molecular biology, biophysics and biochemistry	2.0	22.8
(C5) Microbiology	0	16.4
(F1) Chemistry	1.0	28.6
(F3) Physics	1.8	34.1
(G1) Mathematics	0	39.4
(G4) Computer science	1.0	11.3
(H2) Civil engineering	1.0	13.4
(H6) Electronic and electrical engineering	0	19.0
(K4) Planning (urban, rural and regional)	0	6.0
(M2) Law by topic	2.4	13.9
(N1) Business studies	1.0	8.0
(N2) Management studies	1.0	11.4
(N3) Finance	1.0	3.0
(N4) Accounting	0	11.0
(N5) Marketing	1.0	5.0
(N6) Human resource management	0	5.0
(P3) Media studies	0	2.0

Note: Full-person equivalent: Individuals can hold more than one contract with an institution and each contract may involve more than one activity. In analyses staff counts have been divided amongst the activities in proportion to the declared full-time equivalent (FTE) for each activity. This results in counts of full person equivalents (FPE). Staff FPE counts are calculated on the basis of contract activities that were active on 1 December of the reporting period (using the HESA staff contract population).

Source: Higher Education Statistics Agency, *Gender disaggregation of Welsh HEIs professoriate*, commissioned data run, 21 August 2009, from the HESA staff record.

technology and mathematics (STEM), there are fewer than three women professors of physics in Wales, and none in mathematics or electrical engineering (HESA, 2009).[9]

Historical vertical gender segregation in the physical sciences persists, especially in disciplines related to biosciences where we might expect to find more women given their dominance of related subjects at undergraduate level. However, shifting gender composition has been shown to affect the valuing of several occupations over time, for example in printing, radiography and clerical work (Cockburn 1983, 1985, 1988; Savage and Witz, 1992). Evidence from EURODITE case studies suggests women predominate as 'lab rats' in biosciences. In Catalonia, government competition policy aimed at reducing wage costs in biosciences had a direct effect on gender composition (Colobrans Delgado, 2008).

Decision making

The necessity to involve women in decision-making structures and networks has long been a goal of equality mainstreaming strategy within WAG and the National Assembly for Wales (NAW, 2004). The impetus is both social justice and the 'business case' for promoting equality. A recent account of the latter demonstrates the continuing need for focus in this area:

> In 2007, both McKinsey's and Catalyst's analyses made a significant contribution to the business case for women leaders. Both reports demonstrated a correlation between women's representation at board level and the financial performance of companies worldwide, pin-pointing a 30 per cent turning point at which women's representation has a significant impact across a set of corporate performance indicators. (Lewis and Rake, 2009, p. 4)

Wales has had near gender balance amongst members of the National Assembly and currently (May 2011) has six male and three female Ministers in the WAG Cabinet. Such a gender balance in elected assemblies is rare. However, not all areas of Welsh life are as gender balanced as the National Assembly or previous Cabinets have been. For example, Table 6.7 lists Boards and Committees that have influence over economic policy and investment in economic growth in Wales shows how women's representation at economic decision-making level does not meet the 40/40 gender balance 'ideal' (Lewis and Rake, 2009).

A survey of regional development agencies through Europe shows that this pattern of under-representation of women in economic policy making is replicated (Parken, 2010c).The Equality and Human Rights Commission's annual review of *Who Runs Wales?* reports that men in Wales constitute 100 per cent of University Vice Chancellors, 84 per cent of Heads of Further Education Colleges, 84 per cent of secondary school head teachers (although in the last category they are only 26 per cent of overall teaching staff) and 100 per cent of chief executives of the top 100 private companies (Equality and Human Rights Commission, 2009, pp. 9–11).

This review has shown that the majority of participants in the 'valued' areas of knowledge transfer activities, and the key decision-makers in the economy, business, government and the universities are men. This suggests the incorporation

Table 6.7
Gender balance in public bodies in Wales

Body	Men	Women	Total
Ministerial Advisory Group for Children, Education, Lifelong Learning and Skills	3	4	7
Economic Research Advisory Panel	6	1	7
Welsh Industrial Development Board	4	2	6
Wales Employment and Skills Board	9	3	12
Economy and Transport Ministerial Advisory Group	4	0	4
Design Commission for Wales	4	1	5
South Wales Sea Fisheries Committee	9	0	9
North West and North Wales Sea Fisheries	7	0	7
Social Enterprise Ministerial Advisory	5	2	7
Child Poverty Expert Group	2	2	4
Welsh Financial Inclusion Strategy Group	0	4	4

Source: Public Appointments Division, Welsh Assembly Government, August 2009.

of subjectivity into systems and structures where judgements are made relating to where 'value' lies in the economy, and potentially a lack of reflection on the different lives and social divisions which shape participation. Such reflection, and a wider view of the value of women's predominately customer-facing businesses, might be more likely with a more diverse range of decision makers.

Knowledge transfer partnership projects
The Welsh Assembly Government has invested heavily in a new group of economic programmes designed to stimulate exploratory knowledge in universities that might have commercial application. Under the banner Academy for Business (A4B), this includes fostering collaboration between universities and establishing the infrastructure they need to communicate with businesses (Department for Economy and Transport, 2009).

The Welsh Assembly Government contributes funding to the National Knowledge Transfer Partnership. This body decides policy and allocates its own – and, in partnership, Technology Strategy Board – funding to knowledge transfer partnership between academies and commercialization partners. An indicative analysis of named lead researchers for project in Wales (Table 6.8) demonstrates the effect of having so few women in universities in positions where they can compete for research funds.

Not all monies went to Welsh HEIs: some supported projects in English HEIs. However, in Wales, women academics received just 11 per cent of the

Table 6.8
Welsh funding to knowledge transfer partnerships in higher education allocated between 2003 and 2007

Knowledge/technology	Total projects	Project lead men	Project lead women
Environmental sustainability/sustainable technologies	2	2	0
Services	4	3	1
Creative industries	2	1	1
ICT	11	11	0
Design	8	8	0
Agriculture	1	1	0
Food processing	3	1	2
High-value services	4	2	2
Built environment	1	0	1
Chemical science	2	2	0
Medicine and healthcare	2	2	0
Electronics, photonics, electrical technology	1	1	0
Bioscience	4	3	1
Advanced materials	1	1	0
High-value manufacturing	3	3	0
Totals	49	41	8

Source: Compiled from the Knowledge Transfer Partnership Projects Database, online, viewed 30 June 2009. Some lead researchers had more than one project. Further education projects not included as innovation project administrator was recorded, not lead researchers.

funding allocated between 2003 and 2007, totalling £413,000. Men received £3.5 million.

There were no knowledge transfer partnerships (KTPs) led by women in ICT, design or high-value manufacturing, and just one woman led a bioscience KTP – despite the preponderance of women in technician roles in biosciences throughout the EU (European Commission, 2009). There appeared to be a number of women running KTPs in management science within one further education college in Wales. However, following enquires, it became apparent that the administrator for innovation had been listed as the contact rather than the lead researcher.

In short, the current distribution of funding for KTPs further contributes to reproducing patterns of gender segregation. An interview with a knowledge transfer partnership manager working for the Welsh Assembly Government revealed that projects in retail, charity and the third sector are coming on stream. More women may be in position to bid for these.

CONCLUSION

This paper has described the recent and current patterns of gender segregation in higher education, employment and government related to the developing strategy for a knowledge economy in Wales. Women are much more likely to be working and learning in sectors not typically considered to be part of the 'knowledge economy'. They are not found in senior roles in universities or among the professoriate in those disciplines identified as crucial to knowledge economy sectors in Wales. There is little evidence of women's participation in or deriving direct benefit from participation in knowledge networks in the 'triple helix' of partners in government, education and business, where decisions are made concerning the focus of knowledge economy development, and the allocation and expenditure of resources. Women are largely absent from the sectors and knowledge types that are supported for 'growth' and 'competitiveness'.

Regional policy designed to promote a knowledge economy needs to capitalize on the potential of the available workforce. Women, as the majority of graduates from Welsh HEIs and as participants in the labour force in jobs that explore, examine and exploit knowledge, need to be included in policies designed to promote knowledge economies. Gender-blind policies are likely to reproduce the status quo, undermining the impact of investment. Indeed, non-compliance with statutory duties to promote equality, which require the government to address such inequalities in their economic strategies, policies, programmes and distribution of funds and investment, may simply reproduce gender segregation in the labour market, with all the waste that that implies. Gender-disaggregated statistics on the labour force, in particular those sectors designated as key players in the knowledge economy, as well as among the participants in the triple helix and beneficiaries of knowledge economy initiatives should play a major role in the Economic Renewal Strategy.

ACKNOWLEDGEMENT

The research reported on in this paper was funded by the European Commission Sixth Framework Programme project EURODITE, 2005–10.

NOTES

[1] This will remain the case under the forthcoming Public Sector Equality Duty (Equality Act 2010) when it is implemented.
[2] http://www.eurodite.bham.ac.uk/

[3] As an aside, the EURODITE analysis found that this strategy of clustering of knowledge-intensive businesses, patents, education levels, science and research and development intensity in a region did not necessarily lead to regional economic growth (Carrincazeaux and Gaschet, 2010, slide 10).

[4] http://wales.gov.uk/topics/international/news/smallclever/?lang=en

[5] http://www.eurofound.europa.eu/areas/industrialrelations/dictionary/definitions/europeanemploymentstrategy.htm

[6] http://ec.europa.eu/regional_policy/policy/object/index_en.htm

[7] Figures have been rounded up to the nearest full percentage point.

[8] http://www.legislation.gov.uk/mwa/2010/5/enacted

[9] HESA Full Person Equivalent figure for women professors of physics in Wales is 1.8. Owing to the rounding methodology HESA prefers the phrase 'fewer than three'.

REFERENCES

Acker, J. (1990) 'Hierarchies, jobs, bodies: a theory of gendered organisations', *Gender and Society*, 4, 2, 139–58.

Adkins, L. (1995). *Gendered Work: Sexuality, Family and the Labour Market*, Milton Keynes: Open University Press.

Ball, J. (2010). 'Improving what we already do', *Agenda*, 40, Spring, 49–50.

Bevan Foundation (2005). 'A childcare revolution in Wales', Policy Paper 6, February, by Anthea Symonds and Anne Kelly.

Blake, M. and Hanson, S. (2005). 'Rethinking innovation: context and gender', *Environment and Planning A*, 37, 681–701.

Brinkley, I. (2006). *Defining the Knowledge Economy*, report, The Work Foundation, http://www.theworkfoundation.com/research/publications/publicationdetail.aspx?oItemId=65&parentPageID=102&PubType= (accessed 16 June 2009).

Brinkley, I. (2008). *Knowledge Economy and Enterprise: A Knowledge Economy Working Paper*, London: Work Foundation.

Burfitt, A., Collinge, C. and Staines, A. (2007). 'Knowledge and the economy: cross-disciplinary perspectives and the knowledge economy thesis', research paper for Eurodite.

Carrincazeaux, C. and Gaschet, F. (2010). 'Knowledge and regional diversity: a comparative analysis of European regions', speech to Conference of European Association of Regional Development Agencies, 6 May, Brussels, http://www.eurodite.bham.ac.uk/ (accessed 15 December 2009).

Chaney P. (2009). *Equal Opportunities and Human Rights: The First Decade of Devolution in Wales, Executive Summary*, Cardiff: Equality and Human Rights Commission.

Cockburn, C. (1983). *Brothers: Male Dominance and Technological Change*, London: Pluto Press.

Cockburn, C (1985). *Machinery of Dominance: Women, Men and Technical Know-How*, London: Pluto.

Cockburn, C. (1988). 'The gendering of jobs', in S. Walby (ed.), *Gender Segregation at Work*, Milton Keynes: Open University Press.

Cockburn, C. (1991) *In the Way of Women: Men's Resistance to Sex Equality in Organizations*, Basingstoke: Macmillan.

Collinson, M. and Hearn, J. (1996) *Men as Managers, Managers as Men*, London: Sage.

Colobrans Delgado, J. (2008). *Territorial Knowledge Dynamics for Catalonia Region and Bio Sector*, Final WP5 final and including WP6 synthesized findings, University of Barcelona, EURODITE: Regional Trajectories to the Knowledge Economy: A Dynamic model, Project no. 006187.

Commission of the European Communities (1996) *Incorporating Equal Opportunities for Women and Men into All Community Policies and Activities*, Communication from the Commission, COM(96) 67 (final), Luxembourg: Office for Official Publications of the European Communities.

Cooke, P. (2006). 'Markets and networks in the knowledge value chain', research paper, EURODITE: Regional Trajectories to the Knowledge Economy: A Dynamic model, Project no. 006187.

Cooke, P and De Laurentis, C. (2010). *Work Package 6: Final Firm Knowledge Dynamic Report*, EURODITE: Regional Trajectories to the Knowledge Economy: A Dynamic model, Project no. 006187.

Department for Economy and Business (2009). 'Academic expertise for business, Cardiff: Welsh Assembly Government', http://new.wales.gov.uk/topics/businessand-economy/a4b/?lang=en (accessed 21 August 2009).

Equality Act (2010).

Equality and Human Rights Commission (2008). *Who Runs Wales? The Road to Equality for Women*, Cardiff: EHRC.

Etzkowitz, H and Leydesdorff, L. A. (1997). 'Universities and the global knowledge economy: a triple helix of university–industry–government', *Research Policy*, 29, 2, 109–23.

European Commission (2009). *SHE Figures: Statistics and Indicators on Gender Equality in Science,* Luxembourg: Publications Office of the European Union.

European Commission (2010). *Europe 2010: A Strategy for Smart, Sustainable and Inclusive Growth*, Communication from the Commission, Brussels, 3 March, COM(2010) 2020, http://ec.europa.eu/europe2020/index_en.htm (accessed 20 May 2010).

Gheradi, S. (1995) *Gender, Symbolism and Organizational Culture*, London: Sage.

Goos, M. and Manning, A. (2007). 'Lousy and lovely jobs: the rising polarization of work in Britain', *Review of Economics and Statistics*, 89, 1, 118–33.

Government of Wales Act (2006).

Greed, C. (2005). 'Overcoming factors preventing gender mainstreaming in spatial planning', *Urban Studies*, 42, 719–48.

Harding, R., Hart, M., Jones-Evans, J. and Levie, J. (2007). *Global Entrepreneurship Monitor: UK 2007 Monitoring Report*, n.p.: GEM.

Higher Education Funding Council for England (2008). *2007 Higher Education: Business and Community Interaction Survey for UK Higher Education Institutions*, Bristol: HEFCE.

Horelli, L. (2000). 'Creating the infrastructure of everyday life in the context of European, local and regional development', paper presented to the ESRC Seminar Series: The Interface between Public Policy and Gender Equality. Seminar 5: Women in local and regional development: gender equality issues in participation and consultation, Sheffield Hallam University, 7 April.

Hudson, J. (2006). 'Inequality and the knowledge economy: running to stand still?', *Social Policy and Society*, 5, 2, 207–22.

Leidner, R. (1991) 'Serving hamburgers and selling insurance', *Gender and Society*, 5, 2, 154–77.

Lewis, R. and Rake, K. (2009). *Breaking the Mould for Women Leaders: Could Boardroom Quotas Be the Key?* London: Fawcett Society.

MacEwen Scott, A. (1994) 'Gender segregation in the retail industry', in A. MacEwen Scott (ed.) *Gender Segregation and Social Change*, Oxford: Oxford University Press.

Mahdon, M., Rudiger, K., Brinkley, I. and Coats, D. (2007). *Intangible Assets and the Knowledge Economy*, London: Work Foundation.

Manniche, J. (2010). 'Types of knowledge and learning', in H. Halkier, M. Dahlström, L. James, J. Manniche and L. Smed Olsen (eds), *Knowledge Dynamics, Regional Development and Public Policy*, Aalborg: Department of History, International and Social Studies, Aalborg University.

National Assembly of Wales (2009). *The Economic Contribution of Higher Education in Wales*, report from the Enterprise and Learning Committee, http://www.assembly-wales.org/cr-ld7730 (accessed 18 July 2011).

Office for National Statistics (2009). *First Release, Regional Labour Market Statistics, Annual Population Survey*, Newport: UK Statistics Agency.

Parken, A. (2003). 'Gender mainstreaming: "outing" hetero-sexism in the workplace', unpublished PhD thesis, University of Wales, Cardiff.

Parken, A. (2010a). 'A multi-strand approach to promoting equalities and human rights in policymaking', *Journal of Policy and Politics*, 38, 1, 79–99.

Parken, A. (2010b). *Syntheses of Gender Data from Eurodite Partner's Research Reports*, EURODITE: Regional Trajectories to the Knowledge Economy: A Dynamic model, Contract no. 006187.

Parken, A. (2010c). 'Gender, knowledge dynamics and regional policy', in H. Halkier, M. Dahlström, L. James, J. Manniche and L. Smed Olsen (eds), *Knowledge Dynamics, Regional Development and Public Policy*, Aalborg: Department of History, International and Social Studies, Aalborg University, http://vbn.aau.dk/files/20055382/knowledge_dynamics_regional_development_public_policy.pdf (accessed 14 July 2011).

Parken, A. and Rees, T. (2009). *Gender and the Knowledge Economy in Wales*, a case study for EURODITE: Regional Trajectories to the Knowledge Economy: A Dynamic model, Project no. 006187.

Parken, A., Rees, T. and Baumgardt, A. (2009). *Options for an Equal Pay Duty in Wales*, research report for the Welsh Assembly Government, Cardiff: Welsh Assembly Government.

Perrons, D. (2004). 'Understanding social and spatial divisions in the new economy: New Media clusters and the digital divide', *Economic Geography*, 80, 10, 45–64.

Perrons, D. (2005). 'Gender mainstreaming and gender equality in the new (market) economy: an analysis of contradictions', *Social Politics: International Studies in Gender State and Society*, 12, 3, 389–411.

Pfau-Effinger, B. (1998) 'Gender cultures and the gender arrangement: a theoretical framework for cross-national gender research', *Innovation: The European Journal of Social Sciences*, 11, 2, 147–66.

Rees, T. (1999). *Women and Work: Twenty Five Years of Gender Equality in Wales*, Cardiff: University of Wales Press.

Rudiger, K. and McVerry, A. (2007). *Exploiting Europe's Knowledge Potential: 'Good Work' or 'Could Do Better'*, a report prepared for the Knowledge Economy Programme, London: Work Foundation.

Savage, M. and Witz, A. (1992) 'Theoretical introduction: the gender of organisations', in M. Savage and A. Witz (eds.), *Gender and Bureaucracy*, Oxford: Blackwell.

Styck, K., Luyten, S., Kesteloot, C., Meert, H., and Peleman, K. (2008). 'A geography of gender relations: role patterns in the context of different regional industrial development', *Regional Studies*, 42, 1, 69–82.

Taylor, S. and Tyler, M. (2000) 'Emotional labour and sexual difference in the airline industry', *Work, Employment and Society*, 14, 1, 77–95.

United Nations Development Programme Regional Centre Europe and UNIFEM Europe (2004). *Bridging the Gender Digital Divide: A Report on Gender and ICT in Central and Eastern Europe and the Commonwealth of Independent States*, Bratislava: UNDP and UNIFEM.

Welsh Assembly Government (2010). *Economic Renewal: A New Direction*, Cardiff: Department for Economy and Transport, Welsh Assembly Government.

West, C. and Zimmerman, D. (1987). 'The social construction of gender', *Gender and Society*, 1, 2, 125–51.

Data sources

National Assembly for Wales (2004). *Mainstreaming Equality Policy Review*, final committee report of the Equality of Opportunity Committee, July, Cardiff: National Assembly for Wales, http://www.assemblywales.org/bus-home/bus-committees/bus-committees-second/bus-committees-second-eoc-home/bus-committees-second-eoc-policy/bus-committees-second-eoc-policy-sub2.htm (accessed 14 July 2011).

Office for National Statistics (2009). *First Release, Regional Labour Market Statistics*, NOMIS: Newport, Wales.

Statistics Wales (2007). *Statistics on Job Quality in Wales: Statistical Article*, 27 October, Cardiff: Welsh Assembly Government.

Statistics Wales (2009a). *Key Economic Statistics for Wales*, Statistical Bulletin, SB 48/2009, 14 August, Cardiff: Welsh Assembly Government.

Statistics Wales (2009b). *Workplace Employment by Industry in Wales 2001–2007*, Statistical Bulletin SB45/30 July, Cardiff: Welsh Assembly Government.

7. THE ROLE OF GOVERNMENT IN CORPORATE SOCIAL RESPONSIBILITY AMONG SMES IN WALES

Simon Brooks and Owen Evans

ABSTRACT

The Department for the Economy and Transport (DE&T) at the Welsh Assembly Government (WAG) has taken on leadership of the corporate social responsibiity (CSR) policy agenda in Wales. The key aim of DE&T is to establish a clear, focused and accessible policy on CSR that is relevant and appropriate to the economy and people of Wales. This paper reports on four key research objectives of a study undertaken to inform CSR-related policy in Wales, with particular reference to small and medium-sized enterprises (SMEs). The paper sets out to make a contribution not only to policy and practice in this field but to the building of theory. Research into CSR among SMEs is growing, but still under represented in relation to work on larger firms. In addition, research on the role of governments in this agenda is scarce.

This qualitative study of 114 SMEs in Wales shows that there is a large variety of CSR undertaken, and that, although awareness is high, there is an appetite for 'light touch' government intervention. The contribution of this paper to theoretical development is evaluated and tentative recommendations for policy development are set out.

INTRODUCTION

Research into corporate social responsibility (CSR) has been predominantly focused on the role of business, as the discourse has developed and practice has evolved. However, the role of government and policy has begun to attract attention in the last decade (see, for example, Moon, 2004; Albareda et al., 2007, 2008). It is argued by Albareda et al. (2008) that this developing field can be broadly divided into research that takes a global view of the relationship between business and government and that which focuses more closely on the development and implementation of policy in particular regions and countries. It is to this latter debate that this paper makes a contribution.

This paper reports on key elements of a scoping study undertaken to inform CSR-related policy in Wales, with particular reference to small and medium-sized enterprises (SMEs). As will be explored below, CSR in SMEs is also an evolving area of research, since not only has the emphasis been on business, but research to date has predominantly concerned itself with larger firms. The balance is being partially redressed (see, for example, Brooks, 2004; Jenkins, 2006; Moore and Spence, 2006; Spence, 2007) but, as Morsing and Perrini (2009, p. 2) recently argued, 'more research is needed to understand in detail the conditions and strategies for SMEs to adopt CSR practices'. This is not to say, however, that SMEs do not engage in CSR without policy incentives, for, as this paper will show, the situation in Wales is encouraging in this regard. This research, then, has the opportunity to make a contribution to practice as well as theory in the area of CSR and SMEs. The main objectives around which the study was designed can be seen immediately below.

The objectives of the study
The research aims reported in the paper were agreed with the Welsh Assembly Government (WAG) at the inception of the research and are as follows:

1   to establish the level of awareness and understanding of CSR among business in Wales;
2   to determine what CSR activities companies are currently involved in within Wales;
3   to ascertain what businesses see as the business benefits and business constraints associated with CSR activities;
4   to establish what businesses in Wales think the Welsh Assembly Government could do to promote and enable CSR.

The rest of this paper is structured into the following sections. First, the context for the research will be briefly explored, setting out the policy background and drivers that have led to the study. Second, we will explore the theoretical development of CSR and SMEs, taking a broadly chronological approach, and this is followed by the methods in the third section. Fourth, the findings are examined, taking each objective in turn. Finally, the paper concludes with a discussion of its contribution to the debate on CSR and SMEs as well as a contribution to practice through a series of tentative recommendations for policy.

THE CONTEXT FOR THE RESEARCH

The Department for the Economy and Transport (DE&T) at WAG has taken on leadership of the CSR policy agenda in Wales. The aim of DE&T is to establish a clear, focused and accessible policy on CSR that is relevant and appropriate to the economy and people of Wales. This may include a rebranding of 'CSR' to terminology and language that has resonance in the Welsh context.

The study has been carried out in the light of recognition that the economy of Wales is proportionately more reliant on SMEs than the United Kingdom (UK) in general. Figures from the Department of Business Innovations and Skills (BIS) (2009) show that, in the UK, SMEs are responsible for 99.8 per cent of all enterprises, 48.4 per cent of employment and 47.2 per cent of turnover. The corresponding figures for Wales are 99.9 per cent, 77.4 per cent and 59.7 per cent respectively (BIS, 2009).

DE&T is therefore particularly interested to establish the extent of SME engagement in CSR, as well as the views of those SMEs on CSR and its practice in Wales. For the purposes of this research, the definition of firm size is taken from the Department of Business Innovation and Skills (formerly DTI and BERR) and is congruent with that used in Europe in terms of number of employees. These categories are set out in Table 7.1.

CORPORATE SOCIAL RESPONSIBILITY AND SMALL TO MEDIUM-SIZED ENTERPRISES

There are a large number of definitions of CSR to be found in academic and practitioner literature, making both theoretical development and the practicalities of measurement problematic (McWilliams et al., 2006). However, for the purposes of this study, we will use the European Commission definition, which is concise but retains an appropriately broad scope:

> CSR is a concept whereby companies integrate social and environmental concerns in their business operations and in their interaction with their stakeholders on a voluntary basis. (European Commission, 2006)

In addition, since this paper is not solely concerned with contributing to theory on CSR and SMES, but is designed to make a contribution to policy and practice in the field, it is arguable that a definition adopted from a governmental body such as the European Union is appropriate for this work.

To confer stability of language on the research, we took an a priori view of

Table 7.1
Definitions of firm size

Descriptor	Number of employees
Micro business	Fewer than 10
Small business	10 to 49
Medium-sized business	50 to 249
Large business	More than 250

the terminology and used 'corporate social responsibility' or 'CSR' throughout the study. This means that the term 'CSR' will be used in this paper unless other terms are deliberately to be discussed. Such consistency is important because the language used to describe what we are calling CSR is challenged by some respondents. Indeed, it is an aspect of the first objective of the study to ascertain whether the Welsh SME context calls for an alternative term to 'CSR'.

While we use this European Commission definition of CSR, however, it is important to note there is a large range of alternative definitions to be found among both academics and practitioners and that the very meaning of CSR is contested territory (Shamir, 2004; McWilliams et al., 2006). As well as this, the majority of the research into CSR is still conducted in the context of large firms, meaning that the most widely cited models of CSR are almost exclusively based on research that excludes SMEs (see, for example, Frederick, 1983; Carroll, 1991; Carlisle and Faulkner, 2004; Mirvis and Googins, 2006). Indeed, possibly the most widely cited proclamation on CSR was that of Milton Friedman in 1970, when he stated that the 'social responsibility of business is to increase its profits'. However, in this seminal article he overtly excludes owner-managed businesses as being exempt from arguments over the legitimacy of CSR as a business activity. Therefore, in the words of Spence, SMEs require a 'tailored perspective on CSR and similarly a bespoke research agenda' (2007, p. 533).

Initial research in this field was conducted in the United States of America. However, some caution is needed since there can be inconsistent measures for what constitutes a small business in this early work. For example, Wilson (1980) carried out a study of 180 small businesses using an upper size limit of twenty-five employees, whereas others define 'small' as being up to 500 employees (Holliday, 1995) or even 1,000 (see, for example, Dunfee et al., 1991; Robertson, 1991). Additionally, in these early studies, quantitative methods tended to pre-dominate (see, for example, Kedia and Kuntz, 1981; Brown and King, 1982; Chrisman and Fry, 1982; Chrisman and Archer, 1984; Besser and Miller, 2001) and some also based their research on duplications of prior studies on large firms.

Returning to the notion of a bespoke approach, as Tilley puts it, 'small firms are not little big firms' (2000, p. 33) and so we need to understand what the differences are. Spence (1999) has usefully summarized a number of characteristics of small businesses from a variety of earlier papers, including Curran and Blackburn (1994), Holliday (1995) and Rutherfoord et al. (1997), arguing that issues of ethics and responsibility in smaller firms may be different from larger organizations. For example, smaller firms are said by Curran and Blackburn (1994) to be more independent in terms of ownership structure and to enjoy autonomy from the local community. This claim of independence from community is contestable, however. The Bolton Report (1971) characterizes small business owners as being *more* embedded in communities than their counterparts in larger organizations, a position broadly reinforced by subsequent research (Spence, 2007).

It is also suggested by Spence (1999) that smaller firms may lack strategic focus, as managers are more likely to take responsibility for operational functions as well as organizational leadership. Furthermore, smaller firms are likely to experience reduced power distance and a greater degree of informality in terms of the personal relationships and control structures that develop. North *et al.* (1998) imply that externally imposed procedures may be antithetical to practices in small firms, although Tilley claims that small businesses in her study 'demonstrated a preference for external forms of regulation, as opposed to self-regulation, as a means of controlling the environmental behaviour of businesses' (2000, p. 36).

More recent research on CSR among SMEs in the UK can be found in the field of business ethics, although the label 'corporate social responsibility' has become more prevalent over time. Spence and Rutherfoord (2001) conducted a qualitative study of social responsibility and ethics among small-firm owner-managers based in the south east of England. Their work showed how owner-managers were rarely concerned only with profit maximization and tended to be flexible in their priorities, focusing on social issues and community from time to time as contexts changed. Of interest for us here is that Spence and Rutherfoord pointed to the need for policy-makers to acknowledge this dynamism and not assume that profit maximization was the only driver for SMEs.

More recently, Spence and Rutherfoord (2003) call for more empirical research into ethics among smaller companies, arguing that a sociological approach has much to offer. This call is being partially answered by an emerging literature relating ethics and social responsibility to notions of social capital (see, for example, Spence et al., 2003; Fuller and Tian, 2006).

The need to acknowledge the specific social context of small businesses has begun to be addressed by Jenkins (2004a,b). She has been careful to point out that, while we might agree on a definition of what is small or medium-sized, the SME 'sector' is far from homogenous. Certainly the variety of CSR practices found by Joseph (2000) would seem to support the notion that each SME is a creature of its own context, at least when it comes to practising CSR. The Bolton Report in 1971 had already attempted to explain this variety by hypothesizing a close link between the values of a dominant owner or owner-manager, and the predominant values and management style found in the SME. This would imply that the owner or owner-manager would have a large influence on the type of CSR carried out by smaller businesses. There are other complexities to factor in, however. Bolton (1971) proposed that SMEs are more embedded in their communities, as noted above, but others such as Curran et al. (2000) suggest that the idea of what is 'local', or what is meant by 'community', is not a simple question.

Comparatively little is written on what actually drives SMEs to engage in CSR, although Jenkins has made some progress, finding that a large number of her respondents 'used moral and ethical arguments to justify why CSR was important to them' (2006, p. 249). In terms of instigating and implementing CSR, the predominant feature in her study is that senior management or the owner-manager was usually responsible, echoing the claims of Trevino (1986) and Hemmingway and Maclagan (2004) that senior managers make decisions based on their own values. Jenkins (2006) goes on to say that in many of the firms in her study, respondents found it difficult to quantify and measure the benefits that accrued from CSR, reinforcing the work of Spence and Rutherford (2001) noted above.

More recent work has included Spence (2007), as well as a variety of contributions to a special issue of *Business Ethics* published in January 2009. The contribution from Spence in 2007 is especially apposite for our study here. Her review of European Commission policy on CSR concludes that the Commission's ambition for CSR to contribute to (for example) improvements in public health, employability, positive perceptions of business, and progress towards the millennium goals might be lost on SMEs. Spence uses her analysis to propose a research agenda for SMEs and CSR. She labels these as the 'five Cs', namely the *Credibility* of CSR/SME research, *Comparative* work with larger firms, research within the *Confines* of the SME, *Change* in CSR in SMEs and finally the *Character* of owner-managers (Spence, 2007). Having provided some analysis of the dominant themes from the extant research into CSR and SMEs we now briefly explain the methods used in this study.

METHODS

The research strategy used to gather and analyse data in this study is broadly qualitative, seeking as it does the opinions of respondents on such issues as drivers and barriers to CSR, as well as the meaning they attach to the language of CSR. There is, therefore, an element of constructionism in this study (see Berger and Luckman, 1967, and more recently Burr, 2003) as we explore the language used around CSR by SMEs. Overall, we argue that a qualitative approach provides the richer, contextualized findings needed by most of the objectives of this study (see, for example, Easterby-Smith et al., 2002; Denzin and Lincoln, 2003; Rubin and Rubin, 2004). While the data-gathering techniques were qualitative, the number of respondents interviewed allowed the presentation of some basic frequency data.

The sample of organizations used in this study was taken from a number of sources, as listed below:

- The University of Glamorgan Consultancy Services database of company directors in Wales. This comprises over 1,000 companies spread across Wales.
- The Federation of Small Businesses Welsh membership, comprising some 10,000 companies. These first two databases provided the respondents for the telephone interviews.
- Business in the Community (BITC) membership database, providing access to approximately 180 organizations with which BITC is in regular contact. This was used to establish the respondent sample for the semi-structured interviews.

The sampling was designed to ensure representation from all regions of Wales, as well as to ensure an appropriate spread of firm size. Table 7.2 shows the percentage breakdown of respondents by standard industry classifications.

There were two main data-gathering techniques used in this study, namely telephone interviews and in-depth face-to-face interviews. The option of conducting both methods in Welsh was made available, although no one availed themselves of this facility.

Initial contact with all potential respondents was made by email, and recipients were asked to reply by email to the research team indicating their willingness to take part. The response rate exceeded the numbers necessary to fill the quota agreed with DE&T at the inception of the research. The team therefore proceeded through the positive responses, arranging telephone interviews or face-to-face interviews as appropriate until the quota was fulfilled. One hundred telephone interviews and fourteen face-to-face interviews were conducted by the research team over a period of three weeks. The interviews were semi-structured in nature, based on a schedule designed around the four main objectives of the research.

The face-to-face interviews were less structured than the telephone interviews, allowing emergent findings to come to the fore. The conversations were

Table 7.2
Research respondent sector (SME)

2007 SIC: main classification headings

Section	Description	Percentage of respondents
A	Agriculture, forestry and fishing	0
B	Mining and quarrying	0
C	Manufacturing	10
D	Electricity, gas, steam and air conditioning supply	0
E	Water supply, sewerage, waste management and remediation activities	5
F	Construction	13
G	Wholesale and retail trade; repair of motor vehicles and motorcycles	12
I	Accommodation and food service activities	17
H	Transportation and storage	9
J	Information and communication	11
K	Financial and insurance activities	4
L	Real estate activities	4
M	Professional, scientific and technical activities	2
N	Administrative and support service activities	6
O	Public administration and defence; compulsory social security	0
P	Education	0
Q	Human health and social work activities	2
R	Arts, entertainment and recreation	3
S	Other service activities	4
Total		100

centred on objectives 1 to 5 of the study as set out above but did not necessarily closely follow a scripted survey. This is because data gathered through such interviews is valued for its depth and the insights on offer, rather than for the ability to draw statistically based findings (Denzin and Lincoln, 2003). The interviews were organized such that a wide geographical spread was covered, encompassing south east, west and north Wales.

The interviews were recorded for the purposes of analysis. The resulting texts were content analysed using the main themes around which the research has been structured. As well as being structured around these key themes, the analysis remained sensitive to what 'interpretive repertoires' were used by the respondents to discuss CSR. An interpretive repertoire has been defined by, for example, Potter as 'systematically related sets of terms, often used with stylistic and grammatical coherence, and often organized around one or more central metaphors' (1996, pp. 115–16).

FINDINGS

The findings of the research are set out below, taking each objective in turn.

Objective 1: To establish the level of awareness and understanding of CSR among SMEs in Wales

This objective was split into two subordinate aims. First, the study sought to establish how many firms were aware of the notion of some kind of 'responsibility' in relationships between business and society, whatever language they used to describe this. The second sub-objective was to explore the issue of language use in relation to CSR. The respondents were therefore deliberately asked to reflect on whether terms other than CSR or corporate social responsibility had more currency and resonance in a Welsh SME context. Part of the rationale for this was that previous research has shown that the term 'corporate' can be perceived by some SMEs as excluding them (see, for example, Brooks, 2004).

The awareness of CSR
Among the 100 telephone interviewees, only one firm claimed no awareness of the concept of CSR (or related terms). This was a micro-business employing fewer than nine employees. This shows a very high degree of awareness generally in Wales. The findings from the face-to-face interviews were disregarded for the purposes of this sub-objective since these respondents had been selected from the Business in the Community database and could therefore be assumed to have knowledge of CSR.

Studies conducted some five or six years ago showed lower levels of general awareness (see Brooks, 2004, for an example located in the Welsh context). We do not have the data to speculate on causality here but clearly there has been increased media attention to the activities of businesses in recent years. This is likely to have been a strong contributory factor.

The language of CSR
Of the 114 respondents, 90 per cent expressed some opinion on the language used to describe and discuss CSR.

Approximately 34 per cent of all interviewees expressly rejected or at least questioned the word 'corporate'. Reasons given included the feeling that this was 'designed for larger firms' and that the word 'corporate' would not be 'readily understood by customers when they deal with us'. One respondent felt that the word rendered the term 'one sided' and 'it's a term to suit business, not the public'. This sentiment was echoed by a small number of respondents, who thought that the whole term 'CSR' was (for example) 'contrived' and 'just business jargon.' Two interviewees also thought the term was overly academic. In contrast, 14 per cent of those expressing an opinion were happy enough to keep the term CSR, although, interestingly, a small minority felt that terminology really did not matter and three respondents said words to the effect of 'we just get on with it'.

Some alternatives to CSR were discussed in most interviews, although there was no dominant substitute to emerge. Some other terms were offered, including language around 'community' and 'community investment' or 'involvement', and the phrase 'responsible business practice' was suggested by some interviewees. There was some discussion in a small number of interviews that 'green' environmental language was not always helpful in that sustainability is such a potentially diverse term meaning many things in different contexts. Some felt that, in any case, environmental responsibility could be seen as a sub-set of wider business responsibilities.

To summarize, the fact that some 90 per cent of interviewees expressed opinions on the language implies that the language used in documents and other media designed to promote CSR is important. The key challenge for policymakers will be to find appropriate language for CSR that admits the scope of the concept while promoting common understanding.

Objective 2: To determine what CSR SMEs are currently involved in within Wales

This objective is divided into two main subordinate aims, these being first the extent of CSR activity and second the nature of that activity.

The extent of CSR activity

Of the 114 sampled, eighty-eight firms (78 per cent) are engaged in some form of CSR. This can be broken down further to show that all medium-sized firms engaged in CSR, 97 per cent of small firms engaged, and 73 per cent of micro businesses engaged, as summarized in Table 7.3.

The nature of CSR activity

A number of existing studies have attempted to categorize CSR activities, but CSR has been shown to be varied to the extent that categorization is often not simple. However, there are some useful divisions proposed, such as that offered by BITC. They divide CSR into activities concerned with community, employees, the marketplace and the environment (Business in the Community, 2011).

Table 7.3
Company engagement in CSR

Descriptor	Number of employees	Percentage that engage in CSR
Micro business	Fewer than 10	73
Small business	10 to 49	97
Medium-sized business	50 to 249	100

For this study, we were led by the responses received from the participants in order to build up as detailed a picture as possible of the variety of activities taking place in Wales. These are summarized in Table 7.4 in order of the number of times the activity was identified.

Table 7.4 is necessarily a simplification of the true picture to some extent since there are many varieties of CSR to be found. However, these categories emerged as offering some aggregation without losing too much detail. During both sets of interviews, we discussed with respondents the influences on the kind of CSR activity undertaken. One thing that emerges clearly is that CSR is very 'context dependent' and the main influencing factors to emerge are discussed here.

First, the size of the firm seemed to influence CSR in that the medium-sized firms often displayed more variety than small or micro firms. Medium-sized firm activities are also more likely to be 'generic' in that they may engage in ongoing projects led by demand from charities and other groups, for example. Smaller firms tend to engage in one or two specific activities, although there are some instances of smaller firms spreading their CSR across a number of initiatives. The second factor is related in that SMEs are likely to take what might be called a 'resource-based view' of CSR. In simple terms, they tend to do what they are equipped to do, using what resources and skills are to hand. In one example, a firm specializing in training communication skills offered free workshops to paramedics and other health professionals in their area as part of an arrangement with a local heath trust. There are also a number of occasions when the initiative for CSR came from staff, although it seems the owner-manager (or similar) remains the final decision-maker when it comes to allocating resources to proposed activities.

Third, SMEs are also more likely to have a local focus. This might be anticipated since SMEs will generally have a narrower geographic scope than larger firms. This might be illustrated by the fact that the third most popular activity in Table 7.4 is sponsorship of local sports clubs. One interesting feature of the Welsh context, though, is that in three cases firms stated that their focus was on the valley in which they were located. In some parts of south Wales it is easier

Table 7.4
The nature of CSR activities

CSR activity	Number of instances
Donations of money to charities	67
Involvement in schools or colleges in any kind of educational initiative	58
Sponsorship of local sports clubs	38
Recycling or similar waste management such as pollution reduction	37
Having an environmental policy	36
Sponsorship of local community groups	34
Donations of prizes for schools or fetes (or similar)	34
Reduced prices for local groups or charities.	22
Donations of equipment.	18
Supporting employee volunteering for charities or other groups through time off or similar.	17
Having an accredited environmental management system like ISO 14001	17
Ensuring suppliers have sustainability policies.	16
Pro-bono work (usually but not always professionals like lawyers or architects)	14
Creating opportunities for the economically inactive.	14
Helping other businesses through mentoring or similar.	14
Encouraging staff to car share or use alternative modes of transport.	13
Ensuring representation from diverse communities.	13
Staff involvement in community based activities like environmental improvement or renovating community buildings or similar.	12
Allowing community groups or charities to use your resources.	11
Payroll based giving.	8
Helping local community develop new businesses	2

to travel (broadly) on a north–south axis than to go from one valley to the next, which may partly explain this. However, in at least one case there was a sense of loyalty to community in the valley in which the firm was located, where the manager stated that the owner 'liked to look after where he came from'.

A fourth factor that needs further exploration is the influence of the owner-manager in SMEs. Interview conversations indicated that the preferences and interests of owner-managers are likely to influence the focus of the CSR activities. For example, serving as a school governor seemed in some cases to lead to deeper involvement in educational aspects of CSR. In other cases membership of Rotary or the Round Table had led to community involvement by the firm.

In summary, there are a wide variety of CSR behaviours being undertaken in Wales by SMEs. In particular, the fact that they often take a 'resource-led' approach to CSR means that in effect there are potentially as wide a variety of CSR activities from SMES as there are different SMEs. One implication from these findings is that government policies and the language in which they are couched needs to clearly acknowledge this variety. Attempts to place boundaries around what a 'responsible' business may look like risk excluding some activities and firms. That is not to say that CSR cannot be defined in a Welsh context, but, if, for example, some kind of measurement or accreditation tool was considered, such an initiative would need careful planning with appropriate expertise involved.

Objective 3: To ascertain what businesses see as the business benefits and business constraints associated with CSR

The next stage of the study is concerned with an analysis of the positive and negative drivers of CSR for firms in Wales. This will allow us to evaluate what businesses see as the benefits of engagement in CSR and what they see as the barriers to engaging in (or increasing) CSR activities.

The benefits of CSR

The main business benefits identified through the telephone interviews are summarized in Table 7.5. As with Table 7.4, these categories emerged from the interviews rather than being a priori.

One frequent finding was that businesses often engage in CSR for at least partially altruistic motives. Some 22 per cent of respondents spoke of this, and examples of language used include CSR being 'just what we do' or 'the right thing to do'. This answer to the question of what benefits might accrue from CSR was the fourth most commonly cited factor, as can be seen in Table 7.5. This was rarely the only reason cited for engaging in CSR, because there were often more tangible business benefits listed as well. This is interesting in that it implies that there is no perceived conflict between CSR being the 'right thing' to do and the realization of some eventual business benefit for the firm.

The benefits for the small number of companies who have moved beyond CSR as a 'bolt on' option to a whole new business model have been improved networking with large firms that are interested in their methods. For example, one renewable energy company assessed the carbon footprint associated with each job and have turned down business if the overall impact is negative, as the following illustrates:

we will walk away from potential work if the figures do not add up. If we are going to create more carbon travelling to the job than we will save through the installation then we will not do it.

Table 7.5
Benefits of CSR engagement

Example of benefit	Number of instances cited (ranked)
Improved community relations	63
Reduced waste costs	51
Improved customer perception	47
No benefit expected – it is the right thing to do	42
Access to new markets or customers	32
Better staff morale	27
Improved efficiency	23
Improved recruitment	21
Improved relationships with suppliers	17
Easier to 'sell ourselves' when we bid for work	17
Increasing staff skills	14
Good advertising	12
Better knowledge of local markets	8
Business networking opportunities	7
Improved innovation internally	5
Improved investor relations	5
Staff loyalty	4
No benefit gained	11

In addition, improved innovative processes have been identified in which social responsibility is adopted as a fundamental driver for company decisions and behaviours. These are variously thought to accrue from more flexible company cultures that allow space for mistakes as well as an acknowledgement that work should be a fulfilling exercise. The latter observation came from two firms that expressly set out to employ those who are considered long-term unemployed. One of these firms claimed to have reduced recruitment costs through seeking out local potential employees.

One firm operating a specialist project management consultancy pointed to pressures from a key client to be able to show social responsibility. As a result they had become involved in engineering-based projects in a local school. Although this had started out as what they described as a 'box ticking exercise of the worst kind' they had remained involved with the school because the staff enjoyed the activity and they derived satisfaction from it, despite the pressure from the client disappearing. A specialist media services and audio visual firm offered very heavily discounted equipment and services for charities but did not expect anything in return. The respondent did, however, mention that most of their publicity was 'word of mouth' and that this kind of work 'would not do them any harm' in terms of local reputation.

Overall, the business benefits articulated by the respondents showed that a significant number do not begin their CSR engagement with the intention of reaping benefits. This does not imply that business benefits might not accrue to the firm in time, but at inception there was more of an altruistic intent. This implies that CSR is not always something that is planned for. Indeed there were a number of examples of CSR ideas coming from staff, adding to the strong impression that few SMES take what might be termed a 'strategic' attitude to CSR. A strategy might *emerge* from CSR in practice, but the notion of a pre-planned approach was rare among SMEs.

For others, the business case is important, and is in some cases used to 'sell' CSR to internal stakeholders. External stakeholder pressure is also in evidence. For example, there are firms for which the business case for CSR is tied to acceptance for tenders, although even here the commitment to helping the community seems genuine, as far as can be ascertained from interviews.

Barriers to CSR
The current economic climate was perhaps unsurprisingly offered as a reason for non-engagement in CSR in a small but significant number of cases. Such observations were normally linked to a more general scarcity of resources, whether in terms of time or money. Indeed, there were thirty-two respondents to the telephone interviews who simply said that they did not have the money or resources to engage in CSR as much as they would like. For example, six firms said that they had too many requests for help from charities or community groups and found it difficult to prioritize. Two of these said they knew they should take a strategic approach and think how best to use CSR but 'we really don't have time for proper business planning, you know ... for core business ... let alone planning for CSR'.

A lack of knowledge either of CSR generally or of what constituted best practice was cited by thirty-five firms. One respondent said: 'I would love to know what others are doing, what does good CSR look like?' There was an appetite among many of these for some education, through seminar- or web-based knowledge sharing. In particular, some firms wanted to be convinced of the business case for CSR. This last point is related to the findings from three firms where there were enthusiastic individuals who wanted support to put together a convincing business case to persuade senior colleagues of the potential of CSR.

The spread of accreditation schemes for environmental management (for example, the ISO 14000 series) also acts as a barrier for some SMEs due to the perceived cost of attaining and maintaining them. It was noted by ten respondents that there are no accreditations aimed specifically at SMEs. One proposed that what was needed was a 'light touch scheme that does not take months to fill in and get the information for'. He has previous experience of working for a larger firm that had taken part in a CSR index managed by BITC.

A small but vocal number of the SMEs interviewed pointed to a lack of recognition for what was termed in one case the 'unspoken contribution' made by SMEs to their communities as being a potential barrier to increased engagement.

Objective 4: To establish what businesses in Wales think the Welsh Assembly Government could do to promote and enable CSR

Many of the potential answers to this objective are of course implied by and embedded in responses given to earlier questions, particularly on what drives engagement in CSR by SMEs. However, the question was overtly addressed with the respondents as part of the research and the findings are discussed here.

To begin with, a number of respondents, amounting to some 15 per cent, thought that it was not the business of the Welsh Assembly to interfere in this agenda. There is, however, a considerable overlap between those who claim not to engage in CSR and those who responded in this way. The relatively small numbers involved make it impossible to establish a clear statistical correlation through this study, but based on the data we have collected there certainly seems to be a relationship. These findings are divided into those derived from telephone interviews and those from the face-to-face interviews. This is because, of all four objectives, this is the one for which most depth of discussion emerged from the face-to-face interviews in comparison with the telephone interviews.

Telephone interviews
Telephone interviewees whose firms are active in CSR made a number of suggestions that can be grouped under the following headings (please note that, while these are broadly ranked, no statistical significance should be attached to the order here):

- Provide a means of linking SMEs together to discuss this agenda and share best practice.
- Provide a means of recognizing the good work that SMEs already do in the community through awards or metrics.
- Make it clearer what the business case for CSR actually is.
- Provide clear signposts to other resources that could help SMEs understand and

practice CSR.
- Undertake initiatives through existing organizational networks and channels to avoid additional bureaucracy.
- Encourage CSR through public sector procurement processes. This included establishing longer-term contracts in exchange for a stated commitment to CSR from the tendering firm, as well as prioritizing an enforceable commitment to CSR when awarding tenders.
- Remove the word 'corporate' from the language; it makes SMES feel excluded.
- Provide longer-term funding for apprenticeships.
- Link SMEs and businesses in to resources available in educational establishments such as universities.
- WAG itself could be an exemplar for CSR through its own processes, including for example employment practices and environmental work.

Face-to-face interviews

Three of the SME firms that were interviewed suggested that WAG should take the lead on establishing metrics or measurements appropriate to SMEs. One of the firms had attempted to fill in the corporate responsibility (CR) index tool offered by BITC, since it did not want to limit itself to the more environmentally based assessments offered by (for example) the Carbon Trust. It had found the full CR index too resource-intensive for a small firm and wondered if something simpler could usefully be put in place.

Another medium-sized firm approached the same issue from the perspective of tendering for public sector procurement contracts. There had been an increase over the years in demands for health and safety and environmental policies. Now that statements about social impacts were being required, why not come up with what was termed by one interviewee 'some kind of "kite mark" for CSR' that could satisfy the demands of procurement?

A further smaller firm employing around twelve full-time equivalent staff thought that, while existing networks such as chambers of commerce or the Federation of Small Businesses were obviously recognized by WAG, and should be used to disseminate ideas on CSR, it was also important to support local business networks as well. These tend to form around local issues, perhaps at the scale of a town or group of towns, and could often offer opportunities for business ideas to be spread very quickly. This was felt to be pertinent in more rural or semi-rural locations by the respondent.

A number of other suggestions from the face-to-face interviews revolved around either education or procurement, as set out in the following illustrations. For example, one large firm suggested that WAG should invest in education at school level to make children aware of how business could 'fit into society in a symbiotic way'. Children could learn about acting in a socially responsible way from an early stage, according to this respondent. In addition, the same respondent felt that more practical and professional training could be instilled into the curriculum at earlier ages. Later on in that interview the conversation moved to procurement. It was felt that, despite what the interviewee termed 'ecological rhetoric' from WAG, when procurement decisions are made it is always the cheapest price that wins the day. Whatever the truth of the matter, this perception was firmly held by the respondent.

A related point was discussed in a different interview with a firm of consultants based in Wales but with a UK-wide presence. It takes CSR very seriously and has appointed a senior manager in a Welsh office as the UK champion for CSR. The respondent was calling for clear legislation on the matter of community benefit being built into contracts. The perception was that some firms, including the respondent in this case, wanted to differentiate themselves from the competition through their commitment to building in community benefit to their bids. They were frustrated that, while WAG says this is important, it is not something that is officially scored when awarding tenders. The feeling was that 'either it important or it is not' and that WAG should have the courage to legislate if need be.

One interview was with director of a firm that is run as far as possible on the principles of sustainability. He would like to see WAG be bolder in setting targets and making plans for implementation. He sees real opportunity for Wales in this area, as the following quote shows:

> We have already seen two cultural revolutions in business which happened first when quality moved from control to assurance and more recently as equality and respect moved from personnel to the way we do business. The opportunity we have now is to do the same with the principles that underpin the sustainability of our ecosystems, instilling these in the way we do business and ultimately affecting our wellbeing.

He claims there are many examples of businesses doing things differently, going beyond CSR, and moving away from having philanthropy and CSR as a 'bolt on' to what effectively remains 'business as usual'. He alluded to Marks & Spencer as being one very public example of success in this regard, where they can quantify the investment they have made in 'Plan A' and they can say with certainty that it is a profitable investment. He went on to say: 'we as a country need to learn from this and get in front in terms of innovation.' He sees the key challenges as being related to putting in place detailed plans and processes for implementation. It could be that the way this has been approached through light-touch encouragement might have to be mixed with harder-edged measures involving timed targets and even legislation. Some problems might be best left alone, others require 'nudges' and enabling measures, while some issues might require legislation and 'hard target'. However, for most, the notion of using legislation was resisted as likely to lead to 'unnecessary red tape'. Indeed, as one respondent logically pointed out: 'If you have laws for this then it stops being a responsibility and just becomes a legal obligation. Is that still CSR?'

In summary, there was a strong feeling that WAG had a role to play, despite a small minority thinking that government should stay out the of the CSR debate. As can be seen from the preceding sections, a variety of interventions were proposed by respondents. While there was not a general appetite for increased regulation, some were supportive of existing espoused policies on socially and ecologically sustainable procurement being more firmly backed up with sanctions and, if need be, legislation. The general feeling was that WAG could act as a catalyst, promoting knowledge sharing and education through existing structures where possible and using existing expertise. As one respondent put it, WAG could provide some leadership on 'what success looks like'.

DISCUSSION

The contribution to theory
As was discussed in the introduction, this study adds to a growing but still under-represented aspect of the CSR discourse. Arguably the most articulate and reasoned recent challenge to the SME and CSR academy has come from Laura Spence (2007), in a study in which she advocates the 'five Cs' around which future research could cohere. This section will therefore discuss how this study might contribute within these five categories.

The credibility of CSR/SME research
This study has methodological credibility. In the first place, rather than duplicating previous studies into large firms, this was designed with SMEs in mind. The key themes of the study demanded a broadly qualitative approach, although the comparatively large numbers of respondents also allowed some basic frequency data to be presented. In this sense the research adds to the credibility of CSR and SME research in the eyes of both academia and policy-makers.

The engagement of SMEs in contributing to policy should also give the findings credibility for practitioners. As noted by Spence (2007), the issue of language is important, and this research has overtly addressed this with the respondents, going some way to answering the call to engage with SMEs in their terms (see, for example, Jenkins, 2004b).

Comparative work with larger firms and across contexts
This study did not set out to compare SMEs with larger firms, but there is extensive literature on CSR in larger firms against which these findings can be discussed. For example, a dominant strand of the CSR discourse has been concerned with the 'business case' for CSR (see, for example, Barnett, 2007; Brooks, 2010). This has developed as a response to Friedman's rejection of CSR in the early 1970s.

However, the arguments over whether there is a link between CSR and firm performance have been conducted in the realm of the large firm. This research shows that in some senses, although the business case remains important, a significant proportion of SME CSR seems to be conducted without instrumental or strategic motivations. This reinforces the initial claims of Spence and Rutherford (2001), who find that social motivations outweigh profit maximization as drivers of CSR for many owner-managers. One of the findings of this study was the appetite for knowledge on best practice in CSR, which is interesting since the notion of learning about CSR seems to be largely absent from studies on large firms.

Researching the confines of the SME
The Bolton Report (1971) argues that SMEs are closer to their communities. Spence (2007) makes similar arguments, using the term 'embedded' to describe the closeness of the relationship, a term which in this context can be traced to the work of Polanyi (1944). So how does the internal and external environment influence CSR? Looking inside the firm, this study shows how SMEs tend to use the resources, skills and knowledge that they have to hand in executing CSR. This goes some way to explaining the variety of CSR practices to be found. In addition, the influence of staff in the inception of CSR was noted, although decisions to engage remained with top management.

Externally, the local scope of most SME CSR emerged, with demand factors from the local community playing a part. There was evidence that many SMEs responded to requests, sometimes channelled through employees, from local groups and charities. In addition, the values and personal interests of staff resulted in some SMEs aligning themselves with particular causes. Other external stakeholders also influence CSR. For example supply chain pressures, through either private sector supply chains or public sector procurement, resulted in a focus on environmental management and other efforts to document and present social engagement in a positive light.

Spence (2007) suggests that research in this area might also focus on groups such as ethnic and migrant communities. This study did not consider these particular variables, although it is recognized that this remains a potentially fruitful area of research.

Change in CSR in SMEs
SMEs are by their nature flexible, often having the potential to grow or change direction quite quickly. What, then, are the implications for CSR? This research explored how CSR began and developed in SMEs, and there seems to be an emerging pattern of CSR starting as an unplanned, ad hoc activity, and moving to something a little more strategic or instrumental. It is difficult to say if this correlates with, for example, an increase in firm size. However, some evidence suggests that it is often in response to external pressures through the supply chain, or internal pressures to allocate scarce resources effectively.

A number of models of intra-firm CSR development have been proposed, but these have been based on large firm analysis (see, for example, Carlisle and Faulkner, 2004; Mirvis and Googins, 2006). Additionally, these models have not devoted particular attention to the inception of CSR as an emergent phenomenon, which seems to characterize SME CSR.

The character of owner-managers
The characters of the owner-managers and other significant individuals in the firm will have a proportionately greater effect on decision-making than in large firms with many employees (Spence, 2007). While this study did not set out to explore the influence of the owner or owner-manager on CSR, the sections evaluating the drivers of CSR offer a number of indicators

There is some evidence here that the interests and concerns of owner-managers and directors in SMEs influenced the causes on which CSR was focused. A number of SMEs in the study made it clear that the motivations for setting up and growing their business are inextricable from their lifestyle choices and 'view of the world'. This means that the pursuit of profit and growth at all costs is often tempered by more human motivations to 'put something back' into their community or to achieve a work–life balance for themselves and their employees.

Contribution to practice and policy
The findings explored in relation to objective 4 above are concerned with what WAG might do to develop policy to encourage CSR among SMEs. Taking these into account in conjunction with other findings from objectives 1–3, the following tentative recommendations are made for policy.

WAG should do more to promote the 'business case' for CSR, though acknowledging that many SMEs have at least an element of altruism driving their activities. The assembly needs to encourage and emphasize the view that acting ethically and acting effectively are not mutually exclusive concepts. The implementation of this could include an ongoing web-based platform for the sharing of best practice and good ideas, perhaps to include case studies of 'real life' CSR activities in Wales.

WAG needs to ask what kind of skills development is needed to make the most of the opportunities presented through this agenda. This includes skills and knowledge for business people (as touched on above) but might also include 'awareness raising' among public sector employees who interact with business.

Use should be made of current networks to promote the idea of CSR. Do not 're-invent the wheel' or put in place additional structures. Firms of all sizes are generally quite well networked through various organizations such as the Confederation of British Industry, the Federation of Small Businesses, chambers of commerce and various local or regional business clubs.

WAG should explore the creation of a 'light-touch' mechanism by which SMEs can obtain recognition for the contribution they make through their CSR. This recognition may also act as an indicator to other stakeholders, including the local community, current and potential employees, and customers.

Related to the previous recommendation, a light-touch measurement tool might be developed into a 'kite mark' of some kind. This could be designed to help satisfy conditions for public sector procurement bidding as well as acting as an indicator of good practice within private sector supply chain relationships.

WAG itself should be an exemplar for socially responsible behaviour. One visible manifestation could be the inclusion of language on CSR in policy documents across departments and not solely in the policies of DE&T. It might also be a case of being better at publicizing existing CSR-related activities. To this end an audit of such activities within WAG might offer a starting point.

There needs to be recognition that CSR will not look the same from one SME to another or indeed from one large firm to another. Advice on CSR to SMEs should come from existing bodies and through existing channels rather than through specially created sources of advice. This may include existing networks of SMEs and firms, such as peer networks or mentoring relationships between (for example) large firms and other SMEs.

CONCLUSION

This paper began by noting that calls remain for increased understanding of not only the drivers of SME CSR, but also the specific part that governments play as stakeholders in the process (Albareda et al., 2008; Morsing and Perrini, 2009). The research reported on here has made a contribution to this debate by engaging with 114 SMEs through telephone and face-to-face interviews, and the objectives of the study were explicitly aimed at both theoretical and practical aspects of the agenda.

This paper has made a case for intervention in the development of SME CSR by WAG, but with what might broadly be termed a 'light touch'. The use of existing networks and existing expertise would seem to be desirable by SMEs, and there is an appetite for knowledge sharing on good practice and the potential business benefits of CSR. However, the knowledge at our disposal is incomplete, and some suggestions for further research have been made in the discussion section above. For policy-makers and academia to remain relevant to the predominant form and size category of business, namely SMEs, the research agenda needs to be designed specifically with SMEs in mind, whether the research is aimed at building theory or at contributing to practice.

ACKNOWLEDGEMENTS

The authors would like to acknowledge the support of DE&T in the funding and production of this research, as well as Business in the Community (Wales) and the Federation of Small Businesses.

REFERENCES

Albareda, L., Lozano, J. M. and Ysa, T. (2007). 'Public policies on corporate social responsibility: the role of governments in Europe', *Journal of Business Ethics*, 74, 4, 391–407.
Albareda, L., Lozano, J. M., Tencati, A., Midttun, A. and Perrini, F. (2008). 'The changing role of governments in corporate social responsibility: drivers and responses', *Business Ethics: A European Review*, 17, 4, 347–63.
Barnett, M. L. (2007). 'Stakeholder influence capacity and the variability of financial returns to corporate social responsibility', *Academy of Management Review*, 32, 3, 794–816.
Berger, P. and Luckman, T. L. (1967). *The Social Construction of Reality*, London: Penguin.
Besser, T. and Miller, N. (2001). 'Is the good corporation dead? The community social responsibility of small business operators', *Journal of Socio-economics*, 33, 221–41.
Bolton, J. E. (1971). *Report of the Committee of Enquiry on Small Firms*, London: HMSO.
Brooks, S. B. (2004). 'The practice and construction of corporate social responsibility

among small to medium sized enterprises in south Wales', *Contemporary Wales*, 17, 162–77.

Brooks, S. B. (2010). 'CSR and the strait-jacket of economic rationality', *International Journal of Sociology and Social Policy*, 30, 11/12, 604–17.

Brown, D. J. and King, J. B. (1982). 'Small business ethics: influences and perceptions', *Journal of Small Business Management*, 20, 1, 11–18.

Burr, V. (2003). *Social Constructionism*, 2nd edition, London: Routledge.

Business in the Community (2011) 'What is responsible business', http://www.bitc.org. uk/issues/what_is_responsible_business/index.html (accessed 21 January 2011).

Carlisle, Y. M. and Faulkner, D. O. (2004). 'Corporate social responsibility: a stages framework', *European Business Journal*, 16, 4, 143–52.

Carroll, A. B. (1991). 'The pyramid of corporate social responsibility: toward the moral management of organisational stakeholders', *Business Horizons*, July-August, 39–48.

Chrisman, J. J. and Archer, R. W. (1984). 'Small business social responsibility: some perceptions and insights', *American Journal of Small Business*, 9, 2, 46–58.

Chrisman, J. J. and Fry, F. (1982). 'Public versus business expectations: two views on social responsibility for small business', *Journal of Small Business Management*, 20, 1, 19–26.

Curran, J. and Blackburn, R. (1994). *Small Firms and Local Economic Networks: The Death of the Local Economy?*, London: Chapman.

Curran, J., Rutherfoord, R. and Lloyd Smith, S. (2000). ' Is there a local business community? Explaining the non-participation of small business in local economic development', *Local Economy*, 15, 3, 128–43.

Denzin, N. K. and Lincoln, Y. S. (eds) (2003). *Strategies of Qualitative Inquiry*, 2nd edition, London: Sage.

Department of Business Innovation and Skills (BIS) (2009). 'SME statistics for the UK and regions', http://stats.bis.gov.uk/ed/sme (accessed 21 January 2011).

Dunfee, T., Bowie, N., Hennessy, J., Nelson, K. and Robertson, D. (1991). 'Firm size and employees' attitudes about ethics: some preliminary empirical evidence', in B. Harvey, H. van Luijk and G. Corbetta (eds), *Market Morality and Company Size*, London: Kluwer.

Easterby-Smith, M., Thorpe, R. and Lowe, A. (2002). *Management Research: An Introduction*, London: Sage.

European Commission (2006). 'Implementing the partnership for growth and jobs: making Europe a pole of excellence on corporate social responsibility', http://eur-lex. europa.eu/LexUriServ/LexUriServ.do?uri=COM:2006:0136:FIN:en:PDF (accessed 2 February 2011).

Frederick, W. C. (1983). 'Corporate social responsibility in the Reagan era and beyond', *California Management Review*, 25, 3, 145–57.

Friedman, M. (1970). 'The social responsibility of business is to increase its profits', *New York Times Magazine*, 13 September.

Fuller, T. and Tian, Y. (2006). 'Social and symbolic capital and responsible entrepreneurship: an empirical investigation of SME narratives', *Journal of Business Ethics*, 67, 3, 287–304.

Hemingway, C. A. and Maclagan, P. W. (2004). 'Managers' personal values as drivers of corporate social responsibility', *Journal of Business Ethics*, 50, 1, 33–44.

Holliday, R. (1995). *Investigating Small Firms: Nice Work?*, London: Routledge.

Jenkins, H. (2004a). 'A critique of conventional CSR theory: an SME perspective', *Journal of General Management*, 9, 4, 55–75.

Jenkins, H. (2004b). 'Corporate social responsibility: engaging SMEs in the debate', *New Academy Review*, 3, 3, 76–95.

Jenkins, H (2006). 'Small business champions for corporate social responsibility', *Journal of Business Ethics*, 67, 3, 241–56.

Joseph, E. (2000). *A Welcome Engagement: SMEs and Social Inclusion*, London: Institute for Public Policy Research.

Kedia, B. and Kuntz, E. C. (1981). 'The context of social performance: an empirical study of Texas banks', in L. E. Preston (ed.), *Research in Corporate Social Performance and Policy*, Greenwich, CT: JAI Press.

McWilliams, A., Siegel, D. S. and Wright, P. M. (2006). 'Corporate social responsibility: strategic implications', *Journal of Management Studies*, 43, 1, 1–18.

Mirvis, P. and Googins, B. (2006). 'Stages of corporate citizenship', *California Management Review*, 48, 2, 104–26.

Moon, J. (2004). 'Government as a driver of corporate social responsibility: the UK in comparative perspective', *ICCSR Research Paper Series, 20–2004*, ICCSR, University of Nottingham.

Moore, G. and Spence, L. (2006). 'Responsibility and small business', *Journal of Business Ethics*, 67, 3, 219–26.

Morsing, M. and Perrini, F. (2009). 'CSR in SMEs: do SMEs matter for the CSR agenda?', *Business Ethics: A European Review*, 18, 1, 1–6.

North, J., Blackburn, R. and Curran, J. (1998). *The Quality Business: Quality Issues in Smaller Firms*, London: Routledge.

Polanyi, K. (1944/2001). *The Great Transformation: The Political and Economic Origins of Our Time*, Boston: Beacon Press.

Potter, J. (1996). *Representing Reality: Discourse, Rhetoric and Social Construction*, London: Sage.

Robertson, D. (1991). 'Corporate ethics programs: the impact of firm size', in B. Harvey, H. van Luijk and G. Corbetta (eds), *Market Morality and Company Size*, London: Kluwer.

Rubin, H. J. and Rubin, I. S. (2004). *Qualitative Interviewing: The Art of Hearing Data*, 2nd edition, London: Sage.

Rutherfoord, R., Curran, J. and Smith, S. (1997). 'Small business and community: the petite bourgeoisie in urban Britain and some implications for the small business', paper presented at the Institute of Small Business Affairs Conference on Generating Growth, Belfast, 19–21 November.

Shamir, R. (2004). 'The de-radicalization of corporate social responsibility', *Critical Sociology*, 30, 3, 669–89.

Spence, L. J. (1999). 'Does size matter? The state of the art in small business ethics', *Business Ethics*, 8, 3, 163–74.

Spence, L. J. (2007). 'CSR and small business in a European policy context: the five "C"s of CSR and small business research agenda 2007', *Business and Society Review*, 112, 4, 533–52.

Spence, L. J. and Rutherfoord, R. (2001). 'Social responsibility, profit maximisation and the small firm owner-manager', *Journal of Small Business and Enterprise Development*, 8, 2, 126–39.

Spence, L. J. and Rutherfoord, R. (2003). 'Small business and empirical perspectives in business ethics', *Journal of Business Ethics*, 47, 1, 1–5.

Spence, L. J., Schmidpeter, R. and Habisch, A. (2003). 'Assessing social capital: small and medium sized enterprises in Germany and the UK', *Journal of Business Ethics*, 47, 3, 17–30.

Tilley, F. (2000). 'Small firm environmental ethics: how deep do they go?', *Business Ethics: A European Review*, 8, 3, 163–74.

Trevino, L. K. (1986). 'Ethical decision making in organisations', *Academy of Management Review*, 11, 3, 601–17.

Wilson, E. (1980). 'Social responsibility of business: what are the small business perspectives?', *Journal of Small Business Management*, July, 17–24.

8. WALES IN 2010: RECESSION OR RECOVERY?

Jane Bryan and Neil Roche

INTRODUCTION

This article marks the end of a decade of devolution in Wales. It has been a tur-bulent ten years, with the most significant challenges to the local economy being largely beyond the control of the Welsh Assembly Government. The article uses the most up-to-date information available in January 2011 to examine Wales and its economic position within the UK. A series of indicators are used including output; income and expenditure; labour markets (employment, unemployment and earnings); housing markets; and regional competitiveness.

The May General Election is the most likely UK event in 2010 to affect Wales's economic prospects. It failed to deliver a majority to any party, resulting in a coalition between the Conservatives and Liberal Democrats. The jury is still out on the efficacy (and morality) of the current alliance, with many electors finding it difficult to come to terms with the fact that this brand new animal owes rather less than hoped for to the manifestos of its constituent parties and its policies are based on colossal compromise.

Meanwhile, there has always been speculation with regard to how Wales would fare, were Westminster to change political hue. Certainly, the new tensions shed light on the true nature and extent of Wales's devolved powers and provide an impetus to press for greater power (for better or for worse). Indeed, the referendum in March 2011 gave the Welsh electorate an opportunity to vote to extend the Assembly's powers such that it can pass laws on *all* matters in twenty subject areas rather than have to seek agreement fro the UK parliament.[1] These do not include tax, defence or welfare benefits.

Over the last few years the 'real' economy in the UK has been uneasily wait-ing for the inevitable hard hit that must follow the banking crisis and the new measures to reduce the UK's huge and unprecedented level of debt. Up till now, recessionary effects have hit particular groups: obviously the unemployed and those new to the job market, those on fixed and high interest-rate mortgages who may be feeling poorer from the effects of negative equity as their house values have dropped, savers who have seen their money devalued in real terms and individuals on the cusp of retirement who now have to take stock and consider deferring their pensions. For those in secure, well-paid employment and perhaps on tracker mortgages it has been more a case of 'recession, what recession?' Indeed, some of the indicators reported in this piece do show 2010 to have been a year of recovery. However, the picture is more complex.

Up till recently there has been a sense of, if not optimism, then at least hope that Wales's disproportionate share of public sector employment (over 40 per cent of all jobs in north west Wales, mid Wales and south west Wales) would afford some protection against the inevitable economic shrinkage linked to the widespread withdrawal of borrowing opportunities (on the part of both government and business). A different UK political coalition might well have promoted policies which allowed that sense of security to continue, but not so now. The Westminster coalition, from the outset, has determinedly implemented austerity measures which start with reductions in public sector expenditure, a natural consequence of which will be job losses. The coalition has stated clearly its aspiration that these losses will be mitigated by a newly invigorated private sector. If this were to come to pass the likelihood is that it would be concentrated in London and the South East, will be services based, and most likely finance related.

So far, the coalition has made few references to and shown little awareness of current dependencies between private sector companies providing goods and services to the public sector. With the public sector having to cut its coat more carefully, there is bound to be a knock-on effect in the private sector. The most recent business casualties of the recession are discussed in the employment section of this paper.

The Welsh Assembly Government described the budget cuts announced by Westminster's October Comprehensive Spending Review as 'too fast and too deep'. With it, public spending in Wales is set to decline by 12 per cent or £1 billion over four years.[2] The Prime Minister is on record as believing that the private sector will expand to fill the hole left by a shrinking public sector. This cannot be achieved by government policy [successive years of support for small and medium-sized enterprises (SMEs) show this] but rather will depend on the bitter pill of desperation and a radical sea change in the mindset of people living in Wales, whose natural tendency leans towards public service and employment rather than self-employment.

As always, the time lag on the data makes it difficult to link current events and conditions to the numerical measures provided here on Wales's performance relative to the UK and at the local level, with the exception of unemployment and housing data. However, the continuity of data from Government Office

Regions of the UK, unitary authorities and, where appropriate, at the NUTS3 level (output) is an important element. Local-level data are less reliable than aggregate data.

OUTPUT, INCOME AND EXPENDITURE

Provisional data on gross value added (GVA) per head of population for 2009 for the UK regions are given in Table 8.1, while Table 8.2 provides similar information for 2008 for the sub-regions of Wales.

Table 8.1
Regional accounts

	GVA per head 2009[a]		Household disposable income per head 2008		Individual expenditure per head[b] 2007–9	
	£	*% of UK*	£	*% of UK*	£	*% of UK*
London	34,200	171	19,038	128	11,575	113
South East	20,923	105	16,792	113	11,669	114
East	18,591	93	15,509	104	11,201	110
South West	18,211	91	14,680	99	10,650	104
East Midlands	17,349	87	13,611	92	9,438	92
West Midlands	16,788	84	13,337	90	9,391	92
North West	17,263	86	13,386	90	9,246	91
Yorkshire and the Humber	16,569	83	13,115	88	9,136	90
North East	15,621	78	12,543	84	8,533	84
England	20,442	102	15,090	102	10,270	101
Scotland	19,744	99	14,301	96	10,556	103
Northern Ireland	15,795	79	13,260	89	9,532	93
WALES	14,842	74	13,073	88	8,996	88
UNITED KINGDOM	20,357	100	14,872	100	10,213	100

Notes

a   Figures for GVA 2009 are provisional. GVA per head at current prices on residence base.

b   Figures from the ONS Family Spending 2010 edition.

Sources: ONS, http://www.statistics.gov.uk/downloads/theme_economy/RegionalGVA2009. pdf (accessed 19 January 2011); http://www.statistics.gov.uk/pdfdir/gdhi0310.pdf (accessed 19 January 2011); http://www.statistics.gov.uk/downloads/theme_social/family-spending-2009/ familyspending2010.pdf (accessed 19 January 2011).

Table 8.2
Sub-regional accounts

	GVA per head 2008[a]		Household disposable income per head, 2008	
	£	% of UK	£	% of UK
West Wales and the Valleys	*12,860*	*63*	*12,656*	*85*
Isle of Anglesey	11,333	55	12,830	86
Gwynedd	13,664	67	12,745	86
Conwy and Denbighshire	12,218	60	13,438	90
South West Wales	12,382	60	12,544	84
Swansea	15,820	77	12,830	86
Bridgend and Neath Port Talbot	14,246	69	13,024	88
Central Valleys	11,996	58	12,271	83
Gwent Valleys	11,400	56	12,136	82
East Wales	*19,302*	*94*	*13,795*	*93*
Flintshire and Wrexham	17,382	85	13,199	89
Powys	12,952	63	13,209	89
Cardiff and the Vale of Glamorgan	22,234	108	14,019	94
Monmouthshire and Newport	19,504	95	14,431	97
WALES	15,222	74	13,073	88

Note

a   Figures for GVA 2008 (sub-regional areas) are provisional.

Sources: Office for National Statistics/Welsh Assembly Government; http://www.statistics.gov.uk/downloads/theme_economy/RegionalGVA2009.pdf (accessed 13 July 2011); http://www.statistics.gov.uk/pdfdir/gdhi0310.pdf (accessed 13 July 2011).

It has been observed that the UK regions' GVA rankings simply do not change. London is firmly established as the 'hot core' of the UK (a massive 71 per cent higher than the UK average), while the rest of the regions are some way behind. Meanwhile, the 2008 data reported in 2010 showed Wales to be 26 percentage points below the UK average, having dropped a further percentage point away from the UK average to 74 per cent over the year. This position persists in the latest figures. This also means GVA per head in London was around 2.3 times higher than that of Wales in 2009. The North West and Yorkshire and the Humber regions also maintained their relative UK positions (at 86 per cent and 83 per cent below the UK average). London and the North East were the only regions whose positions strengthened (the latter moving from 77 per cent to 78 per cent below the UK average).

The gap between the rich and the poor continues to widen, and it is perhaps why, in anticipation of this problem intensifying, the new Prime Minister has requested research that might be able to decouple well-being from prosperity.[3]

The latest GVA per head figures for the sub-regions of Wales are for 2008. The table shows the position of Wales's sub-regions relative to the UK average as well as providing a within-Wales comparison. Cardiff and the Vale of Glamorgan, and Monmouthshire and Newport, have a track record of leading GVA performance in Wales, and these regions continue to do so. For example, the 2007 figures showed that GVA in the Cardiff and the Vale sub-region was 106 per cent of the UK average, with the latest figures showing that this sub-region is now at 108 per cent of the UK average. Hence, the disparity between the most prosperous part of Wales and the poorest has increased over the period measured, with Cardiff and the Vale achieving nearly double the GVA per head of the Isle of Anglesey.

Bridgend and Neath Port Talbot, and Monmouthshire and Newport, also joined Cardiff in improving their positions against the UK average, whereas south west Wales, Swansea, the Gwent valleys, Flintshire and Wrexham, and Powys suffered declines in their relative position. These adjustments over time reflect where the (best-paid) jobs are and show how difficult it is to avoid the concentration of opportunity in central places.

Table 8.1 also shows household disposable income per head (gross earnings less deductions at source including tax) relating to 2008–9. Our previous article commented that this gap had widened between London and the South West on the one hand and the North East, East and West Midlands and Yorkshire and the Humber on the other, while other regions had been relatively stable. At that time, household disposable income per head in London was 25 per cent higher than the UK average, having widened by one percentage point over the year, along with the South East (up one percentage point). Now this has widened by a further 3 percentage points (now 28 per cent higher than the UK average), while Wales, the South West, the West Midlands, and Yorkshire and the Humber have been stable on this measure. The rest of the English regions have actually dropped against the UK average.

Household disposable income per head in Wales was 12 per cent lower than the UK average in 2007 and this has not improved over the year. Furthermore, a 13 percentage point difference between the highest and lowest in Wales noted two years ago, which closed slightly to 12 percentage points in 2007, has now widened once again to 15 per cent below the UK average.

Table 8.3 gives identifiable government expenditure on services for the period 2009–10. It is interesting in that it shows the extent to which the regions deviate (or not) in terms of their redistributive spending tendencies. For example, health and education expenditure per head in Wales and Scotland is only

Table 8.3
Identifiable general government expenditure on services by function, 2009–10

	£ per head				Index (UK identifiable expenditure = 100)			
	England	*Scotland*	*Wales*	*Northern Ireland*	*England*	*Scotland*	*Wales*	*Northern Ireland*
Domestic general public services	118	231	259	248	85	168	188	180
International services	3	3	4	3	100	98	105	98
Defence	1	2	1	0	98	145	123	2
Public order and safety	517	541	541	749	98	103	103	142
Enterprise and economic development	93	175	167	214	87	163	156	199
Science and technology	44	71	27	39	97	157	60	87
Employment policies	50	48	79	118	94	89	148	221
Agriculture, fisheries and forestry	72	164	146	270	81	184	164	303
Transport	345	581	324	310	95	160	89	86
Environment protection	176	246	179	137	97	136	99	76
Housing and community amenities	237	369	188	674	92	143	73	261
Health	1,896	2,066	1,956	1,881	99	108	102	98
Recreation, culture and religion	121	229	198	224	89	167	145	163
Education and training	1,398	1,511	1,430	1,531	99	107	101	108
Social protection	3,487	3,845	4,097	4,263	98	108	115	119
TOTAL	8,559	10,083	9,597	10,662	97	115	109	121

Sources: Halifax (2011); HM Treasury (2010).

slightly higher than in England. The greatest relative differences in spending patterns relate to the smaller amounts. Note how much more per head is spent in Wales and Scotland on enterprise and economic development than in England. Further note how much more per head is spent on science and technology in Scotland than in Wales. These differences reflect existing sectoral needs but also strategic ambitions.

The Welsh Assembly Government, with the Office for National Statistics (ONS), produces an index of manufacturing output for Wales. The index is often used to gauge the strength of the regional economy. Figure 8.1 shows the Welsh and UK manufacturing performance (indexed to 2006) from 2004 to the second quarter (Q2) of 2010. The recessionary effects on performances are quite clear with rapid falls in output from Q1 2008 to Q2 2009, dropping by around 20 per cent. The food and drink sector fell by some 25 per cent, transport equipment by 29 per cent, metals by 30 per cent and mechanical engineering by 30 per cent. Note that the Welsh index is close to that of the UK. From the Q2 2009 low the index of manufacturing for Wales grew by just under 4 per cent to Q2 2010. Hence, while on the road to recovery, output is still some 9 per cent lower than it was in 2006. The sector has suffered job losses during this period (as many as 20,000–30,000), but still, with 130,000 jobs remaining, and contributing around 17 per cent of Wales's gross value added in 2010, this is a crucial sector.

As manufactured goods are an important contributor to exports it is no surprise that the recession is reflected in Welsh export performance. In 2008 Welsh

Figure 8.1
Gross mortgage lending by the major UK lenders (seasonally adjusted) (£ billions).
Source: Welsh Assembly Government (2010a).

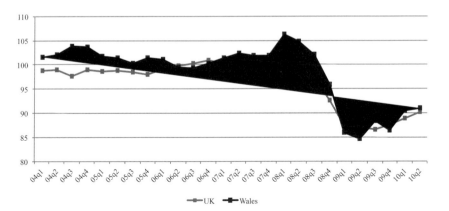

exports were £10.6 billion, falling to just over £9 billion in 2009. Latest data for Q1 2010 suggest that exports are recovering slowly, though still not back to pre-recession levels, at £4.3 billion for the first half of 2010.

There can be no doubt that manufacturing will play an important part in Wales's recovery, and its production capacity is worthy of nurture. It is crucial for Wales to be a good place to do business and make things.

EMPLOYMENT

This section highlights changes in economic data relating to jobs and employment in Wales during 2010, when the economy was emerging from the recession of the previous year but then facing growing concerns over future cuts in public sector spending.

Table 8.4 shows the numbers in employment for UK and regions. The totals are four-quarter averages for the periods July 2008 to June 2009 and July 2009 to June 2010, taken from the Annual Population Survey (seasonally adjusted). The level of employment in the UK fell by 272,000 or 1.0 per cent over the year, to 28.0 million. The largest numerical decreases in employment were found in the South East (where 73,000 jobs were lost) and Scotland (51,000). In Wales employment fell by 0.7 per cent to 1.26 million. Increases in employment were experienced in London (up 1.2 per cent or 44,000 jobs) and Northern Ireland (up 1.2 per cent or 3,000 jobs).

Past editions of the economic profile appearing in *Contemporary Wales* have noted that, compared with the UK as a whole, a lower proportion of people in Wales had been in or searching for work. The measure used to gauge the extent of participation in the labour market is the *employment rate* (calculated by dividing the number of people in employment by the total number of people of working age). A relatively low employment rate has repercussions for the economic output of the region in that less people would then be contributing to overall GVA. Issues such as early retirements resulting from a lack of economic opportunity, and high rates of long-term sickness, have been noted as persistent contributory factors for this participation (or activity) gap in Wales, particularly amongst males.

Table 8.4 shows that the employment rate in Wales for males and females combined decreased from 67.3 per cent to 66.8 per cent over the year to June 2010, a worsening of 0.5 of a percentage point. However, with the employment rate in the UK falling from 71.3 per cent to 70.2 per cent (or 1.1 percentage points), the gap between Wales and the UK as a whole narrowed slightly from 4.0 to 3.4 percentage points. In the four quarters to June 2010, only the North

Table 8.4
Employment numbers and rates: Wales, Great Britain and regions, Annual Population Survey Employment

| | July 2008–June 2009 | | | | | | July 2009–June 2010 | | | | | |
| | Male | | Female | | Total | | Male | | Female | | Total | |
	Thousands	*%[a]*	*Thousands*	*%[a]*	*Thousands*	*%[a]*	*Thousands*	*%[a]*	*Thousands*	*%[a]*	*Thousands*	*%[a]*
London	2,010	76.1	1,592	60.6	3,602	68.3	2,009	74.8	1,637	61.3	3,646	68.1
South East	2,169	82.0	1,888	70.1	4,057	76.0	2,118	79.7	1,866	68.8	3,984	74.2
East	1,467	80.7	1,258	68.9	2,725	74.8	1,450	79.3	1,240	67.7	2,690	73.5
South West	1,299	80.2	1,143	69.8	2,442	75.0	1,270	78.1	1,134	68.9	2,404	73.4
West Midlands	1,274	74.3	1,086	63.1	2,360	68.7	1,252	72.9	1,098	63.8	2,350	68.4
East Midlands	1,123	78.2	966	67.5	2,089	72.9	1,102	76.3	959	66.8	2,061	71.6
Yorkshire and the Humber	1,263	74.9	1,107	65.4	2,371	70.1	1,236	73.0	1,103	64.8	2,339	68.9
North West	1,617	73.4	1,427	64.3	3,044	68.9	1,603	72.7	1,416	63.8	3,019	68.2
North East	592	71.6	535	63.6	1,128	67.5	578	69.6	532	63.0	1,111	66.3
Scotland	1,285	77.5	1,175	68.2	2,459	72.8	1,243	74.8	1,165	67.4	2,408	71.0
Northern Ireland	396	70.2	347	60.5	743	65.3	399	70.3	347	60.1	746	65.1
WALES	667	71.4	606	63.3	1,273	67.3	657	70.2	607	63.4	1,264	66.8
UNITED KINGDOM	15,161	76.8	13,131	65.8	28,292	71.3	14,918	75.1	13,102	65.4	28,020	70.2

a   Denominator is all persons of working age.

Source: Office for National Statistics (2010a).

East and Northern Ireland had employment rates below that in Wales (at 66.3 per cent and 65.1 per cent respectively). By gender, the male employment rate in Wales fell by 1.4 percentage points to 70.2 per cent, but the female rate increased slightly to 63.4 per cent over the year.

Sub-regional differences in male employment rates for Welsh unitary authorities (UAs) are highlighted in Table 8.5. The data here are for the period July 2009 to June 2010. There are a number of areas in Wales where relatively low employment rates persist: Merthyr Tydfil (63.6 per cent), Torfaen (64.3 per cent), Blaenau Gwent (64.6 per cent) and Neath Port Talbot (also 64.6 per cent). Of these four authorities only Merthyr Tydfil displayed an improvement over the year to June 2010 (by 0.5 of a percentage point from 63.1 per cent in the previous year to June 2009).

Table 8.5
Male employment rate (%),[a] Wales unitary authorities, July 2009–June 2010

Anglesey	71.4
Blaenau Gwent	64.6
Bridgend	69.4
Caerphilly	67.4
Cardiff	70.1
Carmarthenshire	72.4
Ceredigion	70.7
Conwy	68.2
Denbighshire	69.1
Flintshire	76.1
Gwynedd	70.9
Merthyr Tydfil	63.6
Monmouthshire	75.9
Neath Port Talbot	64.6
Newport	70.1
Pembrokeshire	71.9
Powys	74.1
Rhondda, Cynon, Taff	67.5
Swansea	70.0
Torfaen	64.3
Vale of Glamorgan	72.5
Wrexham	76.2

a   Denominator is male persons of working age.

Source: Office for National Statistics (2010a).

Employment support overseen by the Assembly Government during this time included the European funded ProAct scheme.[4] Launched to provide training for employees on short-time working, and help to retain skilled staff during the recession, the ProAct scheme had supported over 10,000 individuals in 223 companies in Wales by June 2010. In February the Assembly Government announced the £15 million *Skills Growth Wales*[5] initiative for business, to build on the success of the ProAct programme. The scheme is aimed at companies that have the potential for job creation and growth. It was revealed in May 2010 that Finance Wales, the independent company set up by the Assembly Government in 2001 to provide commercial funding to Welsh small and medium-sized enterprises (SMEs), had invested £37 million in Welsh businesses in the financial year to March 2010. This was an increase of £11 million on the previous financial year, and included 246 equity and debt investments.

Performance figures released for the Assembly Government inward investment arm, International Business Wales, covering the financial year to March 2010, showed that 65 investment projects had been attracted. These safeguarded or created a reported 7,362 jobs. During 2010 there was encouraging news on the inward investment in the automotive sector as Toyoda Gosei announced that the former Valeo facility in Gorseinon, Swansea, was to be the location of its new components factory. Around 600 jobs were expected to be created at the site, with production commencing in 2011. Also, Fillcare, a French manufacturer of hair styling products, revealed plans to recruit around 200 more workers over the next four years in Llantrisant at the site of the former L'Oreal factory. Investment in three new production lines was scheduled to take place.

Unfortunately, despite the economy emerging from recession in the latter stages of 2009, the continued difficult trading conditions were behind the decision of Bosch to announce the closure of its automotive components factory in Miskin with the loss of 900 jobs. The production of alternators was to be transferred to Hungary with the Welsh plant finally closing in 2011. It was revealed in July 2010 that the Linamar car parts factory in Swansea was to close with the loss of 200 jobs. Its Canadian owners were reported as stating that it was no longer possible to retain a competitive position at the site. Also in the automotive sector, over 100 jobs were cut at the Toyota car engine plant in Deeside as part of a UK-wide workforce reduction due to the severe economic climate.

At the end of September, the packaging company Tetra Pak announced plans to stop production at its Wrexham facility with the loss of 150 jobs. Under the proposals, being discussed as part of a ninety-day consultation period, 135 jobs would remain at the site to operate a finished goods warehouse. Falling demand from Russia and the Middle East, which were now becoming self-sufficient in carton manufacture, was given as a major factor in the decision. In October, the Tata Steel subsidiary based in Shotton, Living Solutions, a manufacturer of prefabricated houses, revealed it was to close with 180 jobs being cut. The continuing weak nature of the construction sector and the conclusion of a major contract were blamed for the decision.

Table 8.6 shows the employment breakdown by industry sector in Wales and Great Britain for September 2008 and September 2009, taken from the Office for National Statistics *Business Register and Employment Survey* (BRES). This survey replaced the *Annual Business Inquiry* (ABI) in 2009, but employee estimates for 2008 were produced to allow comparisons between 2008 and 2009 to be identified. This table shows numbers of employees, defined as anyone aged sixteen years or over whom an organization directly pays from its payroll(s) in return for carrying out a full-time or part-time job or being on a training scheme. It excludes voluntary workers, self-employed and working owners who are not paid through PAYE. No female/male split is available through BRES as this information is not collected.

The effects of the 2009 recession are evident in the figures shown in Table 8.6. The total number of employee jobs in Great Britain in September 2009 was 26.2 million, a decrease of 2.9 per cent from the previous September. There was

Table 8.6
Employee jobs (thousands) in Great Britain and Wales, by industry, 2008 and 2009

	Great Britain			Wales		
	2008	2009	%change	2008	2009	%change
Agriculture and fishing (SIC A,B)	278	259	–6.7	18	17	–6.6
Energy and water (SIC D,E)	240	266	10.9	13	15	16.2
Manufacturing (SIC C)	2,534	2,358	–6.9	157	135	–14.2
Construction (SIC F)	1,364	1,261	–7.5	64	58	–9.0
Distribution and restaurants (SIC G,I)	6,243	6,012	–3.7	275	267	–3.0
Transport and communications (SIC H, J)	2,262	2,185	–3.4	64	63	–1.0
Financial and professional services (SIC K,L,M,N)	5,597	5,278	–5.7	161	158	–2.1
Public admin, education and health (SIC O,P,Q)	7,234	7,401	2.3	396	399	0.8
Other services (SIC R,S)	1,237	1,186	–4.1	48	47	–2.3
TOTAL	26,990	26,206	–2.9	1,196	1,158	–3.2
Full time	18,464	17,795	–3.6	787	756	–3.9
Part time	8,526	8,411	–1.3	408	402	–1.7

Source: Office for National Statistics (2010b).

a larger proportionate drop in full-time employee jobs (down 3.6 per cent over the year) than part-time (down 1.3 per cent) in Great Britain between 2008 and 2009. In Wales the number of employee jobs fell by a higher proportion than that of Great Britain as a whole (3.2 per cent as compared with 2.9 per cent) during this time. This equated to a drop of 38,000 employee jobs (from 1.196 million to 1.158 million), mainly in full-time positions, which fell from 787,000 to 756,000. Wales had a higher proportion of part-time jobs (34.7 per cent of all employee jobs) than Great Britain (32.1 per cent), which played a part in the relatively poor GVA per head levels seen above, as these positions are generally lower paid.

The manufacturing sector bore the brunt of the job losses in Wales in 2009. The number of employee jobs fell by 22,000 to 135,000. This represented a drop of over 14 per cent, much larger than the 6.9 per cent fall seen in Great Britain as a whole in manufacturing. Since 2000 there has been a harsh reduction in the number of Welsh manufacturing jobs, largely brought about by the exit of inward investors in electrical and mechanical engineering, clothing and textiles, and metal manufacturing. The sector still makes an important contribution to the Welsh economy, accounting for around 17 per cent of Welsh GVA in 2010, providing relatively well-paid jobs (see 'Earnings' section below) and being an important source of exports from Wales.

Table 8.6 shows a fall of 6,000 construction jobs in Wales between 2008 and 2009 (down 9 per cent), and 7,000 jobs in the distribution and restaurants sector (down 3 per cent). There were gains in energy and water (2,000 more jobs), and in the non-market sector of public administration, education and health (3,000 more) during this time.

The figures in Table 8.6 do not take into account the employment gains and losses that were experienced in 2010. In the public sector it was announced that the Ministry of Defence would be scaling back activities at its Large Aircraft Business Unit in St Athan. Around 200 aircraft maintenance jobs were expected to be cut by the end of 2010, with the remaining 139 likely to go by 2013 following the closure of the facility. It was confirmed by the Identity and Passport Service (IPS) that consultation was to begin on the closure of the Newport passport office. Around 300 staff are employed at the site. The IPS was reported as stating that changes were necessary to increase efficiency and reduce the size of the organization. Public spending cutbacks were also observed at the local government level. Powys Council announced in July 2010 that up to 800 jobs (10 per cent of its total workforce) would go as part of plans to save £16 million over the next four years. In October, Cardiff Council revealed that it was planning to cut 250 jobs over the next year as it addresses a funding shortfall of £90 million over three years.

There were some notable losses in the Welsh food sector. The Welsh Country Foods meat-processing plant in Anglesey revealed in April 2010 that it was to cut 181 jobs. Declining sales of lamb, along with general poor trading conditions, were reported as major contributing factors to the decision. Ethnic Cuisine in Swansea ceased trading with the loss of 220 jobs in August. This followed the loss of a contract to supply the supermarket chain Sainsbury with Chinese-style ready meals.

Elsewhere in the economy, Welsh Water announced that 300 water delivery jobs were to be cut over the next five years as part of a company restructuring aimed at reducing operational costs by 20 per cent. In November, Cardiff-based Glamalco, which fabricated and installed aluminium materials for customers in the construction industry, announced 140 redundancies before going into administration. Cash-flow problems were revealed as the reason for the company's inability to fund ongoing construction contracts.

There were some success stories in the employment market in Wales in 2010. Admiral, the motor insurance company, recruited over 700 workers from the start of 2010 at offices in Cardiff, Newport and Swansea. This took its total workforce in south Wales to around 3,700. The compulsory nature of car insurance was noted as one of the factors helping in the company's strong growth during generally challenging economic conditions. Virgin Atlantic airline announced that more than 200 jobs were to be created over the next two years at a new customer service centre in Swansea. The call centre, to handle customer services and sales, was to be operational in September 2010. UPM revealed that up to 150 jobs were to be created at its paper mill in Shotton, Flintshire, with the construction of a waste recovery facility. A grant of £1.7m was secured from the Welsh Assembly Government to support the investment. Engineering company Mabey Bridge began recruiting workers for its wind turbine tower factory in Chepstow, planned to be operational in February 2011. The site, at Newhouse Farm Distribution Park, will eventually employ 240 workers, and be able to produce around 300 wind turbine towers a year.

One of the areas where Wales has been falling behind other regions in the UK has been in attracting research and development (R&D) activities to the area. R&D tends to be of high value and can lead to opportunities for spin-off developments locally. Research from the UK government's department for Business Innovation and Skills (BIS) comparing investment by the top 1,000 UK R&D-performing companies includes only twenty-two based in Wales and many of these are foreign owned.

The latest available breakdown of total R&D performed in UK businesses is shown by employment and expenditure in Table 8.7. These data are published by the Office for National Statistics and are for 2009. Expenditure on R&D in

Table 8.7
Breakdown of R&D performed in UK businesses: employment and expenditure, 2009

	Employment FTE^a (000s)	Expenditure (£m)	Percentage of total expenditure on R&D
South East	35	3,598	23.0
East of England	30	3,898	24.9
London	10	926	5.9
South West	15	1,267	8.1
West Midlands	12	873	5.6
East Midlands	10	984	6.3
Yorkshire and the Humber	7	452	2.9
North West	14	2,050	13.1
North East	4	313	2.0
Scotland	7	644	4.1
Northern Ireland	4	297	1.9
WALES	4	321	2.1
UNITED KINGDOM	151	15,624	100.0

a   FTE, full-time equivalent employees (i.e. two part-time workers equal one full-time).

Source: Office for National Statistics, *UK Business Enterprise Research and Development 2009*, http://www.statistics.gov.uk/pdfdir/berd1210.pdf (accessed 13 July 2010).

Wales was £321 million in 2009 but, despite this representing an increase from the previous year (2008 = £313 million), still only accounted for 2.1 per cent of the UK total. Of all the UK regions, only Northern Ireland (1.9 per cent) and the North East had smaller overall shares (2.0 per cent). There were an estimated 4,000 R&D jobs (full-time equivalents) in Wales in 2009, or 2.6 per cent of the UK total.

It was announced in November 2010 that six out of the ten *Technium Centres* that provided office space and support services to new companies in Wales were to close. A review of the network, which had been carried out as part of the larger programme to change the provision of economic support in Wales, concluded that a number of Technium Centres were not delivering value for money.

There is growing concern in Wales regarding the cuts in public spending, with the focus turning to how far the private sector can go towards filling the gap left by the reduction in activity in the non-market sector. From this perspective, for a sustainable regional recovery to be achieved, the relatively optimistic prospects evident in the Welsh financial and business services sector would need to be fulfilled and combined with a strong manufacturing sector.

UNEMPLOYMENT

The economic profile appearing in the last edition of *Contemporary Wales* highlighted the relatively large increases in unemployment that had occurred throughout the UK regions as a result of the recession. This section concentrates on the performance of comparative unemployment indicators for 2010, revisiting important issues in Wales such as relatively high levels of economic inactivity and the consequent lower levels of labour market participation.

Regional claimant count unemployment rates over the last decade are shown in Table 8.8. These are calculated by expressing the total number of claimants of unemployment-related benefits in an area as a percentage of workforce jobs plus the claimant count. Table 8.8 highlights that Wales had been able to achieve unemployment rates close to those of the UK as a whole by 2006, but throughout 2008 and particularly then in the recession of 2009 the disparity with the UK average once again appeared. There was an increase in the unemployment rate in Wales of 0.4 of a percentage point in 2008 to 3.2 per cent, and then 2.3 percentage points in 2009 to 5.5 per cent. The rate for the UK in 2009 was 4.7 per cent. This put the Principality amongst the regions having the highest percentage point increase in unemployment during this time, along with the West Midlands (up 2.5 percentage points), Northern Ireland and Yorkshire and the Humber (both up 2.4).

Table 8.8
Annual average unemployment rates: Wales, United Kingdom and regions, all persons, claimant count seasonally adjusted 2000–2009

	2000	2001	2002	2003	2004	2005	2006	2007	2008	2009
South East	1.8	1.5	1.6	1.7	1.6	1.6	1.9	1.6	1.7	3.3
East	2.4	2.0	2.1	2.1	2.0	2.1	2.3	2.1	2.2	4.0
London	3.7	3.3	3.6	3.6	3.5	3.4	3.5	3.0	2.8	4.3
South West	2.5	2.0	1.9	1.9	1.6	1.6	1.8	1.6	1.7	3.4
West Midlands	4.0	3.7	3.5	3.5	3.3	3.4	3.9	3.7	3.8	6.3
East Midlands	3.3	3.1	2.9	2.8	2.5	2.5	2.8	2.6	2.8	4.9
Yorkshire and the Humber	4.3	3.9	3.6	3.3	2.8	2.9	3.3	3.0	3.3	5.7
North West	4.1	3.7	3.5	3.2	2.9	2.9	3.3	3.1	3.4	5.4
North East	6.3	5.6	5.1	4.5	4.0	3.9	4.1	4.0	4.5	6.9
Scotland	4.5	3.9	3.8	3.7	3.4	3.2	3.2	2.8	2.8	4.5
Northern Ireland	5.3	4.9	4.4	4.2	3.6	3.3	3.2	2.8	3.1	5.5
WALES	4.4	3.9	3.5	3.3	3.0	3.0	3.1	2.8	3.2	5.5
UNITED KINGDOM	3.6	3.1	3.1	3.0	2.7	2.7	3.0	2.7	2.8	4.7

Source: Office for National Statistics (2010c).

With the UK economy emerging from recession in 2010 there was an upturn in regional job markets. Table 8.9 reveals that between November 2009 and November 2010 there were decreases in the number of claimants in all of the UK regions except Northern Ireland. In the South East the number of claimants decreased by 27,500 over the year to 127,200 and in the West Midlands there was a fall in those unemployed of 24,500 to 152,200. Wales experienced a decrease of 9,100 claimants to 68,800 representing a decline of 11.7 per cent over the year.

Table 8.9 shows that, by gender, there were contrasting fortunes over the year. Male unemployment in the UK decreased by 156,500 to 986,500 between November 2009 and November 2010, but female unemployment remained fairly static at 426,800. The proportion of females in the total number unemployed increased both in the UK overall (to 30.2 per cent of the total) and in Wales (to 28.2 per cent).

The economic profiles appearing in past editions of *Contemporary Wales* have indicated the success in combating the relatively high proportion of Welsh long-term unemployed (defined as being unemployed for longer than twelve months), particularly amongst males. This had been a problem historically on

Table 8.9

Unemployment: Wales, United Kingdom and regions, claimants, thousands, not seasonally adjusted, November 2009 and November 2010

	November 2009			November 2010		
Area	*Male*	*Female*	*Total*	*Male*	*Female*	*Total*
South East	110.5	44.2	154.7	87.2	40.0	127.2
East	83.7	33.2	116.9	70.3	33.2	103.5
London	147.7	75.0	222.7	135.2	76.5	211.7
South West	66.4	25.2	91.6	54.2	24.3	78.5
West Midlands	130.2	46.5	176.7	107.3	45.0	152.2
East Midlands	80.1	29.8	109.9	64.4	28.1	92.5
Yorkshire and the Humber	115.3	39.0	154.3	99.8	39.3	139.1
North West	146.1	49.7	195.7	124.9	48.4	173.3
North East	64.2	20.4	84.6	56.5	22.0	78.5
Scotland	99.2	32.6	131.9	94.9	36.3	131.3
Northern Ireland	40.9	11.7	52.5	42.3	14.5	56.8
WALES	58.6	19.3	77.9	49.4	19.4	68.8
UNITED KINGDOM	1,143.0	426.4	1,569.4	986.5	426.8	1,413.3

NB: columns may not add up to total because of rounding.

Source: Office for National Statistics (2010c).

account of industrial restructuring in the region. Table 8.10 highlights male unemployment by duration at November 2010 by UK region. In all regions of the UK the proportion of long-term unemployed had increased year on year from November 2009. The highest percentages of claimants who had been out of work for over one year were found in Northern Ireland at 27.2 per cent (up 7.9 percentage points on November 2009), the West Midlands (22.7 per cent) and the East Midlands (20.4 per cent). Wales experienced an increase of 5.3 percent-age points between November 2009 and November 2010 to 19.1 per cent. This was above the all-UK percentage of 18.9 per cent (which had increased 4.7 percentage points over the year).

Table 8.11 shows unemployment rates for Welsh unitary authorities for November 2010. The rates here shown are the claimant count expressed as a percentage of the local resident population of working age (not the workforce population as this may bring in distortions caused by commuting patterns). At this sub-regional level the local authorities with the highest unemployment rates in Wales were Blaenau Gwent, down 1.3 percentage points over the year to 6.3 per cent, Merthyr Tydfil (down 1.3 percentage points to 5.5 per cent) and Newport (down 0.6 of a percentage point to 4.7 per cent). In the rural areas of Wales the rate of unemployment in Gwynedd decreased from 3.0 per cent to 2.9 per cent but it remained at 1.9 per cent in Ceredigion. In Cardiff the rate fell

Table 8.10
Male unemployment by duration: Wales, United Kingdom and regions, November 2010

	Unemployed for over 52 and up to 104 weeks	Unemployed for over 104 weeks	Percentage claiming over 1 year
South East	12,035	3,560	17.9
East	10,145	2,560	18.1
London	19,895	5,340	18.7
South West	5,940	1,150	13.1
West Midlands	16,265	8,015	22.7
East Midlands	9,245	3,880	20.4
Yorkshire and the Humber	14,770	4,220	19.1
North West	16,710	5,370	17.7
North East	7,460	1,760	16.5
Scotland	12,415	3,795	17.2
Northern Ireland	9,175	2,240	27.2
WALES	6,600	2,825	19.1
UNITED KINGDOM	140,670	44,710	18.9

Source: Office for National Statistics (2010c) (from NOMIS).

Table 8.11
Unemployment by unitary authority and Wales, unadjusted, resident-based claimant count with rates, November 2010

	Male		Female		Total	
	Number	*Percentage*	*Number*	*Percentage*	*Number*	*Percentage*
Anglesey	1,200	5.9	471	2.2	1,671	4.0
Blaenau Gwent	1,966	9.2	802	3.6	2,768	6.3
Bridgend	2,335	5.5	895	2.1	3,230	3.8
Caerphilly	3,651	6.7	1,475	2.6	5,126	4.6
Cardiff	6,698	5.8	2,531	2.2	9,229	4.0
Carmarthenshire	2,285	4.2	930	1.6	3,215	2.9
Ceredigion	640	2.6	278	1.1	918	1.9
Conwy	1,686	5.2	587	1.8	2,273	3.5
Denbighshire	1,554	5.4	547	1.8	2,101	3.6
Flintshire	1,992	4.2	880	1.8	2,872	3.0
Gwynedd	1,560	4.3	594	1.6	2,154	2.9
Merthyr Tydfil	1,410	8.1	545	3.0	1,955	5.5
Monmouthshire	693	2.6	320	1.2	1,013	1.9
Neath Port Talbot	1,964	4.6	804	1.8	2,768	3.2
Newport	2,992	6.8	1,178	2.6	4,170	4.7
Pembrokeshire	1,750	5.1	624	1.7	2,374	3.4
Powys	1,118	2.8	525	1.3	1,643	2.1
Rhondda, Cynon, Taff	4,516	6.0	1,817	2.4	6,333	4.2
Swansea	3,474	4.6	1,304	1.7	4,778	3.2
Torfaen	1,706	6.1	677	2.4	2,383	4.2
Vale of Glamorgan	2,075	5.5	764	1.9	2,839	3.6
Wrexham	2,132	5.0	829	1.9	2,961	3.5
WALES	49,397	5.2	19,377	2.0	68,774	3.6

Source: Office for National Statistics (2010c).

from 4.0 per cent to 3.9 per cent, and there were decreases of half a percentage point in both Swansea (from 3.7 per cent to 3.2 per cent) and Wrexham (4.0 per cent to 3.5 per cent).

By gender the highest male unemployment rate was evident in Blaenau Gwent at 9.2 per cent. This authority did have the largest percentage point decrease in the male unemployment rate in Wales, of 2.3 percentage points year on year, but this may be partly explained by its worsening position in terms of economic inactivity (see below). For females, there were increases in unemployment in Anglesey, Cardiff, Carmarthenshire and Gwynedd (all by 0.2 of a percentage point), and Caerphilly, Ceredigion, Pembrokeshire, Rhondda Cynon Taf and Torfaen (all 0.1 of a percentage point).

There are a number of regional responses being taken to speed the process of economic recovery in Wales. In his capacity as Minister for the Economy and Transport, Ieuan Wyn Jones launched the *Economic Renewal Programme* (ERP) in July 2010, outlining the way the Assembly Government will refocus its economic development budget to support a revitalization of the region. Five priorities for delivering the vision were set out in the programme as investing in high-quality and sustainable infrastructure; making Wales a more attractive place to do business; broadening and deepening the skills base; encouraging innovation; and targeting the business support offered.

The ERP notes that the Department for the Economy and Transport (DE&T) will focus its support on work with six sectors: information and communication technology; energy and the environment; advanced materials and manufacturing; creative industries; life sciences; and financial and professional services. The ERP commits the government to move further towards an investment culture, and away from a business grant model. Importantly, International Business Wales, the inward investment division of the Assembly Government, will no longer be a separate function within DE&T.

Relatively high levels of economic inactivity in Wales have been a particular cause for concern for the region; since, with fewer people contributing to producing goods and services within the economy, the levels of economic output are restricted. Table 8.12 highlights the proportion of people who were economically inactive, that is those who were neither in employment or unemployed, such as those who have a long-term sickness. The economic inactivity rate (working age) is the number of people who are economically inactive aged sixteen to fifty-nine or sixty-four expressed as a percentage of all working-age people.

Table 8.12 highlights *Annual Population Survey* data for economic inactivity rates in the regions and Welsh UAs. These data are four quarterly averages for the period July 2009 to June 2010. Wales continued to have one of the highest inactivity rates in the UK for males and females combined. Northern Ireland was the only region experiencing a higher inactivity rate during this time (29.6 per cent). Table 8.12 shows that, at 27.2 per cent, Wales had an inactivity rate 3.4 percentage points over the UK average (23.8 per cent). This represented a further deteriorating picture for Wales from the experience of the previous year (July 2008 to June 2009), when the comparative rates were Wales 24.6 per cent and the UK 21.3 per cent; a gap of 3.3 percentage points. The local authorities in Wales with the highest rates of economic inactivity in the four quarters to June 2010 were Neath Port Talbot (32.5 per cent), Blaenau Gwent (31.7 per cent), Ceredigion (30.5 per cent) and Caerphilly (30.4 per cent).

Table 8.12
Economic inactivity rates: United Kingdom, regions and Wales unitary authorities,
combined males and females, July 2009–June 2010

Government Office Region	Rate	Unitary authority	Rate
South East	20.9	Anglesey	26.3
East	21.2	Blaenau Gwent	31.7
London	25.2	Bridgend	27.4
South West	21.6	Caerphilly	30.4
West Midlands	24.8	Cardiff	25.8
East Midlands	22.8	Carmarthenshire	26.0
Yorkshire and the Humber	24.3	Ceredigion	30.5
North West	25.5	Conwy	26.8
North East	26.3	Denbighshire	27.2
Scotland	23.1	Flintshire	22.5
Northern Ireland	29.6	Gwynedd	26.4
WALES	27.2	Merthyr Tydfil	25.6
UNITED KINGDOM	23.8	Monmouthshire	24.6
		Neath Port Talbot	32.5
		Newport	26.4
		Pembrokeshire	26.4
		Powys	27.1
		Rhondda, Cynon, Taff	29.6
		Swansea	28.8
		Torfaen	29.4
		Vale of Glamorgan	24.2
		Wrexham	23.5

Source: Office for National Statistics (2010a).

EARNINGS

The following section examines earnings data for the UK regions and the sub-regions of Wales. These data are taken from the *Annual Survey of Hours and Earnings* (ASHE) published by the Office for National Statistics.

Since the ASHE was developed in 2004, improving the coverage and weighting of earning samples, Wales has consistently fallen below the UK average in terms of wages. A major reason for this disparity in average earnings is the relative lack of workers in Wales employed in the higher-skilled, and therefore higher-paid, occupational categories, and accordingly a relatively high proportion of workers in the region employed in lower-skilled, lower-paid occupations. However, some encouraging news in the data for 2009 showed that the gap between Wales and the UK average had narrowed, by 2.2 percentage points (the Wales average was now 90.2 per cent of the UK average).

Table 8.13 highlights average (median) gross weekly earnings for full-time workers in Wales and the UK for April 2010. For males and females combined the average wage in the UK was £498.80, while in Wales the comparative figure was £451.10 or 90.4 per cent of the UK average, a slight narrowing of the earning differential. By occupation, earnings in the professional category in Wales (£681.90) remained at 97 per cent of the UK average (£704.10), while in the highest-paid category of managers and senior officials the weekly average wage in Wales of £594.1 was only 82 per cent of the UK average (£721.7), down by over 2 percentage points from that in 2009.

There was also a relative decline for Wales compared with the UK as a whole in a number of other occupational groups. Earnings in personal service occupations in Wales were £314.6 per week, or 94.1 per cent of the national average, down 1.8 percentage points from the previous year. Wages in skilled trade occupations (£450.70) had fallen by 1.5 percentage points to 98.3 per cent of the UK average, and in elementary occupations and for process plant and machine operatives there was a worsening of 0.9 of a percentage point to 95.3 per cent and 95.4 per cent of the UK average respectively. There was better news for Wales in the occupational categories of associate professional and technical (at £549.20) closing the gap to the UK average by 0.7 of a percentage point to 97.6 per cent; administrative and secretarial (also narrowing the discrepancy by 0.7

Table 8.13
Average (median) earnings: Wales and UK, £s, all industries and services, full-time rates for men and women, April 2010

	United Kingdom			Wales		
	All	*Male*	*Female*	*All*	*Male*	*Female*
All	498.8	538.2	439.0	451.1	483.0	401.3
Managers and senior officials	721.7	782.0	609.0	594.1	640.4	523.8
Professional occupations	704.1	744.5	669.2	681.9	684.9	678.8
Associate professional and technical	562.6	592.2	530.1	549.2	574.9	528.5
Administrative and secretarial	381.9	417.8	369.3	360.7	377.5	356.0
Skilled trades occupations	458.4	468.3	319.1	450.7	459.1	317.8
Personal service occupations	334.2	366.5	322.8	314.6	342.0	309.7
Sales and customer service	303.3	318.1	290.0	287.5	306.7	271.9
Process, plant and machine operatives	425.0	442.1	311.3	405.6	426.3	303.8
Elementary occupations	326.6	347.4	278.0	311.3	330.2	261.5

Source: Office for National Statistics (2010d).

of a percentage point to 94 per cent of the UK average); and sales and customer services (94.8 per cent of the UK, up 0.9 percentage points).

Table 8.13 highlights striking differences between UK and Wales at the top of the higher-earning male occupations of managers and senior officials, with those in Wales paid just 81.9 per cent of the UK male average (£640.40 per week compared with an average of £782.00 nationally). Earnings for males working in skilled trade occupations in the Principality (£459.00), which in previous years had held up equal to the UK male average, fell to 98 per cent in 2010.

Average earnings for females in Wales in the professional occupational category (£678.80) remained above the UK average in 2010 (£669.20) but this advantageous gap had narrowed slightly between 2009 and 2010 (by 1.1 percentage points to 1.4 per cent above). Earnings for females in the managers and senior official category in Wales (£523.80) increased enough between 2009 and 2010 to narrow the discrepancy with the UK average (£609.00), but still stood at only 86 per cent of the average national amount. The figures also show the entrenched nature of gender differences in pay within the UK and Wales.

Table 8.14 highlights employment shares in each occupation category using data from the *Annual Population Survey* (four-quarter average July 2009 to June

Table 8.14
Average gross weekly earnings and employment breakdown by occupation, Wales and UK

	United Kingdom		Wales	
	Average gross weekly earnings (£)	*% of all employment*	*Average gross weekly earnings (£)*	*% of all employment*
Managers and senior officials	721.7	15.6	594.1	13.0
Professional occupations	704.1	13.8	681.9	12.5
Associate professional and technical	562.6	14.5	549.2	14.5
Administrative and secretarial	381.9	11.2	360.7	10.8
Skilled trades occupations	458.4	10.5	450.7	12.2
Personal service occupations	334.2	8.8	314.6	9.8
Sales and customer service	303.3	7.4	287.5	7.6
Process, plant and machine operatives	425.0	6.7	405.6	7.3
Elementary occupations	326.6	11.1	311.3	11.8
ALL	498.8	100.0	451.1	100.0

Sources: earnings, Office for National Statistics (2010d); employment, Office for National Statistics (2010a) (from NOMIS).

2010), along with their average weekly earnings (ASHE figures). Only 13.0 per cent of Welsh employees are in the highest-earning occupational category of managers and senior officials, compared with 15.6 per cent in the UK as a whole. A relatively low 12.5 per cent of workers fell into the next highest-paid category, professional occupations, compared with 13.8 per cent in the UK as a whole. Conversely, the workforce in Wales is relatively highly concentrated in the lowest-paid occupations such as sales and customer service (7.6 per cent where the UK average is 7.4 per cent) and personal service occupations (9.8 per cent and 8.8 per cent respectively).

Wales not only has lower average wages than the UK in every occupational category, but has a lower proportion of people employed in the highest-earning categories (such as managers and senior officials). Overall earnings in the region are therefore heavily impacted.

Table 8.15 compares earnings in the UK and Wales for broad industry groups. Wages in Wales for production industries, and in manufacturing, are close to the UK average at 97.8 per cent and 98.6 per cent respectively. However, pay in services industries in Wales was just 88.0 per cent of the UK amount in 2010, with earnings for Welsh males particularly below the UK average (85.1 per cent) compared with females (91.9 per cent). These figures suggest that a large proportion of the service jobs in Wales are low skilled and low paid.

When data on earnings are examined for smaller geographic areas, accuracy and reliability concerns arise. Accordingly, ONS advises against year-on-year earnings comparisons at the local authority level. It is still important, however, to examine differences in earnings within Wales for the reason that funding interventions, such as European Convergence support, might be expected to

Table 8.15
Average (median) gross weekly pay (£) by broad industry groupings, full-time employees,[a]
United Kingdom and Wales, 2010

	Males			Females			All		
	UK	Wales	% UK	UK	Wales	% UK	UK	Wales	% UK
All industries and services	538.3	483.0	89.7	439.2	401.6	91.4	499.1	451.6	90.5
All index of production industries	536.7	530.8	98.9	383.7	361.6	94.2	508.8	497.7	97.8
All manufacturing	527.0	523.3	99.3	377.4	358.3	94.9	499.9	493.1	98.6
All service industries	539.2	458.7	85.1	444.1	408.2	91.9	495.4	436.0	88.0

a   Employees on adult rates whose pay for the survey pay-period was not affected by absence

Source: Office for National Statistics (2010d).

link through to performance on this measure. Table 8.16 shows relative levels of average (median) gross weekly earnings for the latest time period available, April 2010, for local authorities in Wales. The highest average wage levels for males and females combined were found in Neath Port Talbot (£540.30), the Vale of Glamorgan (£525.80), and Cardiff (£486.20). Lowest average earnings were found in Ceredigion and Blaenau Gwent (both £375.20), Powys (£382.30) and Merthyr Tydfil (£406.20). Female earnings were highest in Cardiff at £432.20, which was 8 per cent higher than the Welsh average, while average wages for males in Neath Port Talbot were relatively strong (at £591.90, or 22.5 per cent higher than the average in Wales).

Table 8.16
Average (median) gross weekly earnings (£), Wales and unitary authorities: all, male and female full-time employees, 2010, workplace based[a]

	All	Male	Female
Neath Port Talbot	540.3	591.9	395.8
Vale of Glamorgan	525.8	564.8	388.8
Flintshire	483.9	522.4	386.7
Newport	474.3	517.3	424.3
Bridgend	485.1	510.9	414.0
Cardiff	486.2	503.6	432.2
Torfaen	439.6	491.1	374.3
Wrexham	454.9	488.2	389.0
Caerphilly	451.2	487.8	412.7
Pembrokeshire	454.4	480.8	400.6
Isle of Anglesey	430.8	477.9	329.9
Carmarthenshire	442.0	460.6	411.7
Monmouthshire	414.7	459.9	350.9
Powys	382.3	438.2	338.5
Conwy	418.0	437.4	358.3
Swansea	427.5	436.4	399.1
Denbighshire	434.3	435.2	408.9
Rhondda, Cynon, Taff	425.5	435.2	401.1
Merthyr Tydfil	406.2	413.9	385.8
Gwynedd	414.9	412.4	417.8
Blaenau Gwent	375.2	402.1	354.7
Ceredigion	375.2	375.1	370.7
WALES	451.1	483.0	401.3

a Employees on adult rates whose pay for the survey pay period was not affected by absence.

Source: Office for National Statistics (2010d).

HOUSING MARKETS

2008 marked the beginning of a difficult two years for the housing markets, featuring negative house price inflation which did not turn positive until December 2009, and with much regional variation. Between 2007 and 2009 mortgage approvals halved, although by the summer of 2009 the trend had shown signs of reversing. In March 2009 the Monetary Policy Committee (2010) settled interest rates at 0.5 per cent, where they have remained, despite short-term inflationary pressure in the early part of 2011 linked to rising commodity and energy prices.

The last Review reported that housing affordability had improved to January 2010 but that mortgage lending criteria were still very tight, particularly affecting first-time buyers. Over 2010 the housing markets have not featured strongly in the local or national press, and this reflects the rather moribund nature of housing sales. On the whole, while conditions have been easing over the first three quarters of 2010, it is still difficult to get a mortgage without a big deposit.

Table 8.17 shows UK house prices for Q3 2010, revealing much variation across the regions. Northern Ireland was still struggling with a 13.1 per cent drop in house prices over the year. Other regions suffering house price deflation were Scotland (–3.6 per cent), the North West (–5.0 per cent), the North (–1.2 per cent) and East Anglia (–0.5). With the exception of the East Midlands

Table 8.17
All houses, all buyers (seasonally adjusted), Q3 2010

Region	Index (1983=100)	Q3 2010 standardized average price (£)	Q3 2010 annual change (%)
North East	497.1	125,415	–1.2
Yorkshire and the Humber	537.7	124,152	4.6
North West	477.7	122,181	–5.0
East Midlands	557.4	145,701	8.9
West Midlands	545.4	153,923	2.1
East Anglia	516.5	155,391	–0.5
South West	590.9	195,371	10.6
South East	551.8	223,983	3.1
Greater London	652.3	259,749	4.8
Wales	524.1	135,624	0.1
Northern Ireland	497.3	127,881	–13.1
Scotland	418.9	121,165	–3.6
UK	537.4	166,035	2.6

Source: Halifax House Price Index, http://www.lloydsbankinggroup.com/media/pdfs/research/Q3-2010/UKOverviewQ32010.pdf (accessed 5 January 2011).

(8.9 per cent) and the South West (10.6 per cent) other regional markets were muted but positive. Regional house prices were not available for Q4 2010 at the time of writing, but according to a Halifax press release (10 January 2011)[6] prices in the last three months of 2010 were 0.9 per cent lower than the previous quarter, and with a drop of 1.3 per cent between November and December. The Halifax predicts that interest rates will remain low for some time, which helps affordability. However, there is still much uncertainty about the UK economy, earnings growth is weak and people are facing higher taxes, all of which suppresses demand.

Following the takeover of HBOS by Lloyds TSB there have been some changes to the availability of published sub-regional housing data. For this reason data at the unitary authority level for Wales are sourced from the Land Registry and are not directly comparable with Halifax data. Table 8.18 shows that average house prices in Wales varied considerably. The lowest house prices were found in Merthyr Tydfil (£78,491) with the highest prices to be found in Monmouthshire some 2.3 times higher (£180,693). Demand for housing is typically strong in Monmouthshire, Caerphilly, Cardiff and the Vale, and the annual figures reflect this. Meanwhile, Merthyr Tydfil experienced the highest *annual* price change in November, with a movement of 11.3 per cent, and Blaenau Gwent experienced the strongest *monthly* growth with an increase of 6.1 per cent. Torfaen had the highest *monthly* price fall during November with a movement of –4.1 per cent. On the whole though, house prices are more stable in Wales than reported last year, when the percentage annual change was negative across the board.

REGIONAL COMPETITIVENESS

Table 8.19 provides a summary of indicators to show regional competitiveness. It repeats the GVA and household disposable income data shown in Table 8.1, and then shows the proportion of the population over 16 who are claiming income support, together with manufacturing investment data. In summary, gross disposable household income per head in 2008 in Wales was 88 per cent of the UK average (unchanged on the previous year), and still among the lowest (with Yorkshire and the Humber and the North East). Gross value added per head is 74 per cent of the UK average (no worse than last year) but still much lower than anywhere else.

In terms of claimant support, the highest shares were found in Northern Ireland (a worrying 9.1 per cent), the North West (6.9 per cent), the North East (6.8 per cent) and London (6.7 per cent). Wales is next at 6.6 per cent. These

Table 8.18

Average house price by Welsh unitary authority, twelve months to November 2010

Local authority	Average house price (£) November 2010	Monthly change (%)	Annual change (%)
Blaenau Gwent	74,144	6.1	–6.4
Bridgend	126,241	–0.2	5.1
Caerphilly	106,240	0.9	7.7
Cardiff	146,263	–0.2	3.3
Carmarthenshire	113,384	–0.7	–2.0
Ceredigion	174,432	–1.8	0.2
Conwy	136,998	–0.6	–1.2
Denbighshire	120,651	–1.4	–3.0
Flintshire	130,937	–0.2	0.1
Gwynedd	148,805	0.5	1.7
Isle of Anglesey	135,464	–2	1.9
Merthyr Tydfil	78,491	2.6	11.3
Monmouthshire	180,693	–2.2	1.7
Neath Port Talbot	92,320	1.9	2.5
Newport	121,491	–0.6	1.8
Pembrokeshire	152,967	0.2	2.8
Powys	161,449	0.9	2.3
Rhondda Cynon Taf	80,815	–0.3	1.3
Swansea	115,771	–1.2	–0.2
Vale of Glamorgan	161,828	–0.5	1.5
Torfaen	106,788	–4.1	–1.7
Wrexham	123,646	–2.1	3.4

Source: Land Registry (2010).

figures, lower than the previous report, reflect marginally improved conditions compared with the recessionary months but do not yet pick up the effects of austerity measures on employment.

CONCLUSION

A short-term UK business context is provided by the Institute of Chartered Accountants (ICAEW)/Grant Thornton UK Business Confidence Monitor (2010), which reported that the decline in the Confidence Index accelerated in Q4 2010, reflecting uncertainty about the future of the UK economy. While

Table 8.19
Regional competitiveness

Region	Gross disposable household income per head 2008 (UK = 100)	Gross value added, workplace basis per head 2009 (UK = 100)	Proportion of income support claimants (in population over 16) August 2009	Manufacturing investment by foreign and UK owned companies 2006 (£m)		Manufacturing investment by foreign and UK owned companies 2007 (£m)	
				Foreign	UK	Foreign	UK
London	128	171	6.7	341	310	273	399
South East	113	105	3.8	699	712	438	710
East	104	93	4.1	339	679	338	792
South West	99	91	4.5	441	498	409	578
West Midlands	90	84	5.8	324	678	433	683
East Midlands	92	87	4.8	418	675	369	683
Yorkshire and the Humber	88	83	5.4	305	622	543	780
North West	90	86	6.9	358	1,117	428	1,151
North East	84	78	6.8	346	280	487	287
England	102	102	5.4	3571	5571	3719	6064
Scotland	96	99	6.3	301	648	359	759
Northern Ireland	89	79	9.1	164	287	104	460
WALES	88	74	6.6	475	409	445	441

Note: Northern Ireland proportion of income support claimants in population 16+ is May (not August) 2009 figure

Sources: Regional Economic Performance Indicators, Regional Competitiveness and State of the Regions, BERR, May 2010, http://stats.berr.gov.uk/sd/repi/repi2010.asp (accessed 13 July 2011).

actual business performance rose in Q4, expectations for growth were weaker for 2011. Exports are still being helped by the weak pound but this is offset by poor local demand, rising input prices and squeezed profit margins. Furthermore, the effects of reductions in public spending have yet to work their way through the private sector.

The role of the Welsh Assembly Government in the current climate is a difficult one with less money to spend, hard decisions on where cuts should be made, and with much of the pain still to come. The focus might be on damage limitation, and learning from history. Furthermore, the observation on the stock market (often attributed to Warren Buffett) – 'most people get interested in stocks when everyone else is. The time to get interested is when no one else is' – can be applied more widely. Not only should our policy makers avoid falling pray to policy fashion fads, but they should explore going against the grain. While 'unfashionable' there could still be scope to improve Wales's overseas marketing. Now is also the time to reinforce existing relationships with inward investors. Small and medium-sized enterprises pose a greater challenge. They are a diverse group, and the benefits of supporting them are diffuse and difficult to value. It will be important to listen to businessmen and public-sector support managers who know what works for SMEs and what does not and why, in order that scarce resources find their mark.

NOTES

[1] http://wales.gov.uk/legislation/referendumpowers/?lang=en
[2] http://wales.gov.uk/newsroom/firstminister/2010/101020spending/?lang=en
[3] David Cameron's £20 million 'Happiness Index' research project; http://www.bbc.co.uk/news/uk-politics-11842673
[4] Welsh Assembly Government, *ProAct Project News Release,* http://wales.gov.uk/newsroom/educationandskills/2010/100513proactmil/;jsessionid=TwwRMMYJGL KhJQmLjPvgcMGDVfMcYNvT91S42XYhWJkz5QMCRHpn!-463154188?lang =en
[5] Welsh Assembly Government *ProAct Skills Growth Wales,* http://wales.gov.uk/topics/educationandskills/skillsandtraining/proactskillsgrowthwales/;jsessionid=lh hJM4nhRsnhTnyXxhmppQJ8Ft3vSMNYTwGplxJV0wcjydnWbj4D!-143746665 0?lang=en
[6] http://www.lloydsbankinggroup.com/media1/research/halifax_hpi.asp?WT.ac=015

REFERENCES

Halifax (2011). *House Price Index*, London: Halifax.

HM Treasury (2010). *Public Expenditure Statistical Analysis 2010*, London: HM Treasury, http://www.hm-treasury.gov.uk/pespub_pesa10.htm (accessed 19 January 2011).

ICAEW/Grant Thornton UK Business Confidence Monitor (BCM) (2010). *http://www. icaew.com/index.cfm/route/151990/icaew_ga/en/Members/Business/Business_ Confidence_Monitor/ICAEW_Grant_Thornton_UK_Business_Confidence_Monitor_ BCM* (accessed 19 January 2011).

Land Registry (2010). *House Price Index*, London: Land Registry, http://www1.landregistry.gov.uk/assets/library/documents/HPI_Report_Nov_10_eiplrig78.pdf (accessed 5 January 2011).

Monetary Policy Committee (2010). *Monetary Policy Committee Decisions*, London: Bank of England MPC. *http://www.bankofengland.co.uk/monetarypolicy/decisions/ decisions11.htm* (accessed 19 January 2011).

Office for National Statistics (2010a). *Annual Population Survey*, London: ONS.

Office for National Statistics (2010b). *Business Register and Employment Survey*, London: ONS.

Office for National Statistics (2010c). *Claimant Count*, London: ONS.

Office for National Statistics (2010d). *Annual Survey of Hours and Earnings*, London: ONS.

Welsh Assembly Government (2010a). *Index of Production and Index of Construction for Wales: Quarter 3, 2010*, Cardiff: WAG.

Welsh Assembly Government (2010b). *Economic Renewal Programme*, Cardiff: WAG, *http://wales.gov.uk/topics/businessandeconomy/help/economicrenewal/?lang=en* (accessed 19 January 2011).

9. LEGISLATING FOR WALES 2010–11

Marie Navarro

INTRODUCTION

2011 saw the Welsh electorate vote in favour of further powers to be devolved to the Assembly and the establishment of a new political administration in Cardiff following elections in May. It follows a year in which the General Election saw the end of the political dominance of Labour in Parliament and the emergence of coalition government in Westminster. These changes have had, and will have, a major impact on the laws drafted for Wales and in Wales.

There are three main aspects of the devolved legislation to be considered in this article. First, the devolution of legislative powers from London to Cardiff has slowed down dramatically and changed in its nature. Second, a fair amount of legislation has been generated around the referendum itself. Finally, the article will explore how Wales is preparing for the post-referendum era.

DEVOLUTION OF POWERS

Within the perspective of a referendum in Wales whose outcome would altogether stop the progressive devolution of legislative powers to the Assembly from Legislative Competence Orders (LCOs) (through the addition of Matters in Schedule 5), as they would be replaced by a one-off devolution of all the powers contained in Schedule 7, few legislative powers have been devolved to the Assembly this parliamentary year either through new LCOs or through framework powers in UK Bills.

A record year for LCOs
During the past parliamentary year (July 2009–April 2010), all the LCOs (except one) which were being processed in London as part of the normal LCO process were approved in the 'wash up' period in April 2010. This means that they were all approved (rather quickly) before Parliament was dissolved; otherwise such LCOs would have fallen as did the Affordable Housing LCO.

The following LCOs received Royal approval in April 2010:

- The National Assembly for Wales (Legislative Competence) (Local Government) Order 2010; SI 2010 No. 1211
- The National Assembly for Wales (Legislative Competence) (Culture and Other Fields) Order 2010; SI 2010 No. 1212
- The National Assembly for Wales (Legislative Competence) (Education) Order 2010; SI 2010 No. 1209
- The National Assembly for Wales (Legislative Competence) (Transport) Order 2010; SI 2010 No. 1208

The LCOs had been first introduced in the Assembly between June 2009 and December 2009.

The National Assembly for Wales (Legislative Competence) (Housing and Local Government) Order 2010,[1] also known as the Sustainable Housing LCO, was reintroduced in July 2010 and it was made within a week.

Overall, in the parliamentary year 2009–10, twelve LCOs were made, which is a record in the making of LCOs. These LCOs are:

- The National Assembly for Wales (Legislative Competence) (Social Welfare) Order 2009
- The National Assembly for Wales (Legislative Competence) (Exceptions to Matters) Order 2009
- The National Assembly for Wales (Legislative Competence) (Environment) Order 2010
- The National Assembly for Wales (Legislative Competence) (Health and Health Services and Social Welfare) Order 2010
- The National Assembly for Wales (Legislative Competence) (Welsh Language) Order 2009
- The National Assembly for Wales (Legislative Competence) (Housing) (Fire Safety) Order 2010
- The National Assembly for Wales (Legislative Competence) (Culture and other Fields) Order 2009
- The National Assembly for Wales (Legislative Competence) (Local Government) Order 2009
- The National Assembly for Wales (Legislative Competence) (Education) Order 2010
- The National Assembly for Wales (Legislative Competence) (Transport) (Order) 2010
- Proposed National Assembly for Wales (Legislative Competence) (Housing) Order 2010

- National Assembly for Wales (Legislative Competence) (Housing and Local Government, relating to sustainable homes) Order 2010

This means that twenty-two new Matters were added to Schedule 5[2] between 2009 and 2010 through the use of LCOs.

Currently, in the 2010–11 parliamentary year only one LCO has been made, the Housing LCO [The National Assembly for Wales (Legislative Competence) (Local Government) Order 2010 No. 1211][3] while only one further LCO is still being processed in the Assembly. It is the only LCO proposed by an Assembly Committee, and it started as a petition by Sustrans[4] in 2007. This LCO was introduced in January 2008 and it is in the process of getting clearance by Whitehall, which mean that it is still at the early stages of the pre-legislative scrutiny stage of the LCO and it is unlikely that it will be able to complete its course before the Assembly is dissolved at the end of March 2011.

The Welsh Assembly Government (WAG) has announced for this parliamentary year its intention to only introduce one new LCO, which will relate to Organ Donation in Wales.[5] At the time of writing this article in December 2010, the LCO had not been published, which leaves little chance that such LCO could also be made before the end of the Assembly. In parallel with the halt of Matters being added to Schedule 5 by means of LCOs this year, there is also a slow down in Matters deriving from framework powers contained in UK Bills.

Very few framework powers
In the last parliamentary year only two Acts devolved legislative powers to Wales. These were:

- The Local Democracy, Economic Development and Construction Act 2009 (c. 20)[6]
- The Marine and Coastal Access Act 2009 (c. 23)[7]

They each devolved two Matters in the Fields of Local Government[8] and Sport and Recreation.[9]

Since the 2010 elections and the new Parliament, only one Bill has proposed to devolve further legislative powers to the Assembly in the form of one Matter to be inserted under Field 14 Public Administration. It is the Budget Responsibility and National Audit Bill.[10] The Bill re-establishes the legislative power relating to the Auditor General, which was included at first in the Constitutional Reform and Governance Act 2010 (c. 25)[11] last year but had been removed by amendment to the Bill. In this respect this not a 'new' Matter to be inserted in Schedule 5 but rather a resurrected power from last parliamentary year.

Schedule 5

Overall, there are now 77 Matters in Schedule 5 all inserted between 2008 and 2010.[12] In 2007, when this Assembly started, there were only six Matters contained in the original Government of Wales Act 2006. Twenty-six out of these seventy-seven Matters were devolved last year. This shows that the mechanism of Part 3 and Schedule 5 has worked in that it has allowed a substantial amount of legislative powers to be devolved to Wales.

However, the system, described in the 2005 White Paper (Wales Office, 2005, p. 21) as 'an interim system', has proved difficult to operate and it is lengthy. In that respect it has failed to deliver its purpose of 'finding ways of enabling the Assembly Government to secure its legislative priorities *more quickly and more easily*, within its current areas of responsibility' (p. 3) and of 'enabling the Assembly Government to secure its legislative priorities, and deliver its policy agenda, *more swiftly*' (Para. 3.1, p. 19) than under the Government of Wales Act 1998. It was argued in 2005 that under the 1998 Act the Welsh Assembly Government could not secure the powers it needed to implement its policies.[13] The White Paper states that:

> a particular problem [was] that the Assembly ha[d] to compete alongside Whitehall departments when bidding for legislative time at Westminster. This has meant that on occasion, the Assembly Government has been unable to take *prompt action* in an area of policy where the public expects it to be able to do so, and that can be the case even where the proposed legislation would be non-contentious, such as the inclusion of social landlords in the remit of the Welsh Housing Ombudsman. (Para. 1.21, p. 28)

The UK government then decided to use the Orders in Council mechanism to Wales, which had proved to be a satisfactory device to approve the legislation made in Northern Ireland while the Assembly was suspended.

The UK government then set out in chapter 3 of the White Paper:

> the Government's approach to enhancing the Assembly's legislative powers. Though there has been significant Wales-only legislation at Westminster since devolution, we believe there is a strong case for enabling the Assembly Government to secure its legislative priorities, and deliver its policy agenda, more swiftly. (Para. 3.1, pp. 19–27)

However it is debatable that the three years it took to obtain some of the LCOs means that this was any swifter and allowed for prompt action in Wales. This is without counting the fact that it takes at least another year to get a Measure made under any Matter and for the government policy to be enforced.

The LCO system has worked in that it has given the Assembly many powers to make primary legislation. The number of Matters to be so transferred by LCOs had not been foreseen. No LCO has been rejected, in the end, by Parliament even if some of the LCOs and in particular the Affordable Housing LCO have followed a very bumpy road.

It was also not expected that such a process would take so long. Rumours had it in 2007 that it would take on average only six months for an LCO to be made, which provided a more expeditious way than Acts of Parliament to get powers devolved to Wales. In reality, it took at least ten months to get an LCO through, but the vast majority of LCOs took much longer than that, which raises serious questions about the efficiency of the mechanism. The mechanism has proven repetitive in terms of scrutiny in the Assembly and in London, and it is estimated to cost around £2 million a year (Western Mail, 2010). These arguments have been put forward by the First Minister to explain why a referendum on further powers in Wales is necessary and why a Yes vote would improve the situation in Wales.

A low, too, for executive powers

Finally, powers have continued to be devolved directly to the Welsh Ministers but such powers have also seen their numbers decrease since the UK General Elections.

Last parliamentary year, while only two Acts devolved legislative powers to the Assembly (as well as devolving executive powers to WAG), a further seventeen Acts devolved executive powers directly to WAG. These are:

- Apprenticeships, Skills, Children and Learning Act 2009 (c. 22)
- Business Rate Supplements Act 2009 (c. 7)
- Coroners and Justice Act 2009 (c. 25)
- Corporation Tax Act 2009 (c. 4)
- Health Act 2009 (c. 21)
- Policing and Crime Act 2009 (c. 26)
- Welfare Reform Act 2009 (c. 24)
- Constitutional Reform and Governance Act 2010 (c. 25)
- Children, Schools and Families Act 2010 (c. 26)
- Child Poverty Act 2010 (c. 9)
- Equality Act 2010 (c. 15)
- Flood and Water Management Act 2010 (c. 29)
- Personal Care at Home Act 2010 (c. 18)
- Corporation Tax Act 2010 (c. 4)
- Energy Act 2010 (c. 27)

- Sunbeds (Regulation) Act 2010 (c. 20)
- Autism Act 2009 (c. 15)

This phenomenon is what we have described as a way to 'by-pass the Assembly' in the devolution of powers and in the making of legislation for Wales (Navarro and Lambert, 2009).

Out of the twenty-one Bills announced in the Queen's Speech this year, possibly executive powers could be proposed in the following:

- Public Bodies Bill
- Decentralisation and Localism Bill
- Education and Children's Bill – mainly for England
- Energy Security and Green Economy Bill
- Health Bill
- Pensions and Savings Bill
- Police Reform and Social Responsibility Bill
- Welfare Reform Bill

This year, only one Bill so far devolves executive powers to WAG: the Public Bodies Bill.[14] This makes sense in the general context of this year's UK legislative programme, which relates mainly to reserved Matters to deal with the economic situation. This can also be a consequence of the momentum that is building around the referendum on further powers in Wales; this might considerably limit the transfer of executive or legislative powers by Westminster, which would already be captured in Schedule 7.

In any case, executive powers came forwards in the Public Bodies Bill and as the other Bills get published it will be seen whether further powers are actually devolved to WAG and/or the Assembly.

LAW MAKING IN WALES

While the Assembly is receiving few new legislative powers this year, it is now in a position to legislate on over seventy-seven different Matters and WAG owns more than 7,000 individual executive powers.[15]

Since October 2009 the Assembly has made seven Measures. These are:

- National Assembly for Wales Commissioner for Standards Measure 2009 (nawm 4)
- Education (Wales) Measure 2009 (nawm 5)

- Children and Families (Wales) Measure 2010 (nawm 1)
- Social Care Charges (Wales) Measure 2010 (nawm 2)
- Red Meat Industry (Wales) Measure 2010 (nawm 3)
- National Assembly for Wales (Remuneration) Measure 2010
- Proposed Shipment of Waste for Recovery (Community Involvement Arrangements) (Wales) Measure 2010

This is an increase in the number of Measures passed by the Assembly. In previous calendar years the Assembly made two in 2008 and five in 2009. So far by the end of 2010 it has made five, but a further four have been passed in the Assembly and await Royal Approval. These are:

- Proposed Mental Health (Wales) Measure
- Proposed Waste (Wales) Measure
- Proposed Playing Fields (Community Involvement in Disposal Decisions) Measure
- Proposed Welsh Language (Wales) Measure

The Assembly progressively delivers more and more legislation as its powers expand. In parallel with the decrease in the number of new LCOs that the Assembly scrutinizes, it passed more and more Measures. This is the primary function given to the Assembly under the Government of Wales Act 2006. The focus has at last moved away from the LCOs to concentrate on the Measures. This increase in the law made in Wales is an important element of success of the Government of Wales Act 2006 in that it allows for much more legislation specific to Wales to be made. Before the Act the convention was only to have one Wales-only Act to legislate specifically for Wales. The nine Measures to be made this year is a great improvement for the implementation of the Welsh priorities.

In July 2010, the First Minister announced next year's legislative programme for this last year of the Assembly, which is rather modest, as is any last programme of a parliament or assembly. It is composed of four pieces of legislation: three Measures and one LCO.

2010 Welsh Legislative Programme:

- Proposed Learner Transport Measure
- Proposed Housing Measure
- Proposed Education Measure
- Organ Donation LCO

This means that, before the end of March of this year, the Assembly has to complete the seven different pieces of legislation (one full year's worth of work). The legislation currently under consideration in the Assembly is the following:

- one LCO
    - The National Assembly for Wales (Legislative Competence) (Highways and Transport) Order 2010

- six Measures
    - Proposed Rights of Children and Young Persons (Wales) Measure
    - Proposed Domestic Fire Safety (Wales) Measure
    - Proposed Local Government (Wales) Measure
    - Proposed Safety on Learner Transport (Wales) Measure
    - Proposed Housing (Wales) Measure
    - Education Measure expected to be introduced this month

LEGISLATION PREPARING FOR THE REFERENDUM

This year's referendum was a prominent feature in the legal life in Wales and in London. The referendum had to follow a special procedure established by the Government of Wales Act 2006. Legislation has been generated to provide for the referendum itself, and also to prepare Wales for the possible outcomes of such a referendum in the working of the Assembly.

Procedure for the referendum

Part 4[16] and Schedule 6[17] established the referendum procedure, which is a mixture of the normal referendum procedure and extra steps to involve the main actors in Wales: the Assembly, the Welsh Ministers and the Secretary of State for Wales (SSW). It operates as follows:

Step 1: First Minister or a Welsh Minister to move resolution for adoption of a Proposal for the referendum to be held by a two-thirds majority of the Assembly.

Step 2: First Minister to give notice in writing of the resolution to the Secretary of State for Wales.

Step 3: Secretary of State for Wales to prepare draft Order in Council or refuse to do it within 120 days (if refusal, to give notice in writing to First Minister; to be laid before the Assembly).

- Order in Council *must* specify the question, *can* specify a statement, *must* be bilingual, *must* specify the date (but SSW can change the date by order with consent of Welsh Ministers, negative resolution procedure in Parliament), *must* include provision for funding and audit of accounts, *may* create criminal offences.
- Power to require Electoral Commission to encourage voting; duty of Commission to provide information to voters.

The Secretary of State to commission the Electoral Commission.

- Electoral Commission to produce report stating views on intelligibility of referendum question expressed by SSW.
- Report to be sent to First Minister.
- First Minister to lay report before the Assembly.
- Secretary of State can undertake such other consultation as considered appropriate on draft Order in Council.

Step 4: Secretary of State to lay draft Order in Council to be laid before each House of Parliament for approval and before the Assembly (two-thirds majority in Assembly required).

Step 5: Order in Council to be made by Her Majesty.

Step 6: Referendum to be held – majority of voters; possibility of judicial review.

Step 7: Welsh Ministers to make a commencement order for the relevant sections to commence and can choose the date after approval by the Assembly, if not Order in Council.

Following the procedure, the Electoral Commission reported[18] on the question submitted to it by the Secretary of State for Wales on 9 September and the Commission proposed a redraft of the question to be included in the Order in Council so that it becomes the referendum question.

The questions read as in Table 9.1.

The suggested question was accepted by the Secretary of State for Wales, who included it in the Orders in Council[19] she introduced before Parliament. These Orders made provision on the referendum question and date, arrangements for running the referendum, and limits on campaigners' expenditure.

The Orders in Council were approved by the National Assembly and by both the House of Commons and the House of Lords and they were made by the Queen in mid-December.

Another Order in Council was also brought forward by the Wales Office which related indirectly to the referendum. It amended Schedule 7 to reflect in that Schedule certain changes that were made to Schedule 5 during 2008–10. Indeed, many exceptions to the Matters contained in Schedule 5 did not exist in Schedule 7 and some inconsistencies between the two Schedules had emerged.

Table 9.1
Referendum questions

Original question	Suggested redraft
• At present, the National Assembly for Wales (the Assembly) has powers to make laws for Wales on some subjects within devolved areas. Devolved areas include health, education, social services, local government and environment. The Assembly can gain further powers to make laws in devolved areas with the agreement of the Parliament of the United Kingdom (Parliament) on a subject by subject basis. • If most people vote Yes in this referendum, the Assembly will gain powers to pass laws on all subjects in the devolved areas. If most people vote No, then the present arrangements, which transfer that law-making power bit by bit, with the agreement of Parliament each time, will continue. • Do you agree that the Assembly should now have powers to pass laws on all subjects in the devolved areas without needing the agreement of Parliament first? ☐ Yes, I agree ☐ No, I do not agree	• The National Assembly for Wales: what happens at the moment • The Assembly has powers to make laws on 20 subject areas, such as: – agriculture – the environment – housing – education – health – local government • In each subject area, the Assembly can make laws on some matters, but not others. To make laws on any of these other matters, the Assembly must ask the UK Parliament for its agreement. The UK Parliament then decides each time whether or not the Assembly can make these laws. • The Assembly cannot make laws on subject areas such as defence, tax or welfare benefits, whatever the result of this vote. • If most voters vote 'yes' The Assembly will be able to make laws on all matters in the 20 subject areas it has powers for, without needing the UK Parliament's agreement. • If most voters vote 'no' What happens at the moment will continue. • Question Do you want the Assembly now to be able to make laws on all matters in the 20 subject areas it has powers for? ☐ Yes ☐ No

The draft Schedule 7 Order [National Assembly for Wales (Legislative Competence) (Amendment of Schedule 7 to the Government of Wales Act 2006) Order 2010] was therefore laid before Parliament to update Schedule 7. This is the Schedule that lists the subjects on which the Assembly would legislate in the event of a 'Yes' vote in the referendum.

The Welsh Affairs Select Committee, which scrutinized the draft Order, welcomed it, especially the fact that the changes were proposed before the referendum was held so that it is 'clear to Parliament, the National Assembly and the people of Wales what powers the National Assembly for Wales will be able to exercise if the electorate votes "Yes" in the referendum' (Welsh Affairs Select Committee, 2010, Para. 21)

Not all the restrictions imposed on the legislative powers of the Assembly in Schedule 5 Fields are recorded in the amended Schedule 7. This is particularly the case for the Fields of Environment and of the Welsh Language (ibid. See in particular the evidence from the Wales Governance Centre, EV 12, pp. 35–7). The Committee regretted 'that the Government has *not* used this opportunity to define more clearly the powers of Ministers in relation to the National Assembly for Wales on the grounds of time and cost' (Para. 34). However, it also notes that there would be scope for the National Assembly to legislate on the powers of Ministers of the Crown in certain circumstances, with and sometimes without the consent of the Secretary of State (Para. 34).

The Committee also recognized that additional amendments may be needed in the future, following the outcome of the referendum.

This is because further amendments 'will be likely to be needed to reflect the continuing development of the devolution settlement, and may yet prove necessary to address the issues identified in this report' (Para. 50). In this respect, the

> Committee noted and welcomed the Secretary of State's commitment to engage in early consultation about any further proposals to amend Schedule 7, with Parliament and with the Committee in particular. The Committee intend to continue in their role of maintaining oversight of the operation and development of the settlement, on behalf of the House of Commons. (Para. 50)

This is a very interesting aspect of the question of the legality of the Assembly's action which deserves full attention in the future.

Consequences of the referendum if Part 4 comes into Force

Legally, the only change the referendum made was to decide whether Part 3 or Part 4 of the Act was to apply in Wales. If there had been a No vote then Part 3 would have continued to apply, but in the event of a Yes vote then Part 4 would apply.

Part 3 works with its dedicated Schedule – Schedule 5 – while Part 4 works with Schedule 7. Part 3 provides for the Assembly to make Measures for the Matters listed in Schedule 5 and Part 4 provides for the Assembly to make Acts for the subjects listed under Schedule 7 (which are called not Matters or Fields but 'Subjects').

The two Parts are very similar in their structures and the sections they contain. Part 4 has special provisions dealing with the referendum (see Government of Wales Act 2006 sections 103–6), while Part 3 has special sections relating to the LCOs (see Government of Wales Act 2006 sections 94–6). The main consequence of the change of Schedule applicable is that, while the Assembly would not become a Parliament in name, it would as regards its function, and the laws made by the body would be 'Acts' instead of 'Measures'.

A comparison between the contents of Schedules 5 and 7

Broader competence
In certain areas, the scope of competence of the Assembly will increase quite dramatically. Schedule 7 contains much more broadly expressed powers than Schedule 5. For example, Table 9.2 shows how each schedule reads in relation to Health.

This text of the current provisions which constitute Field 9 (Health) of Schedule 5 is longer than the corresponding Subject 9 in Schedule 7. However, in terms of contents, Schedule 5 Field 9 is much narrower as it includes only two Matters, which are quite narrow themselves. The same result applies when comparing each Schedule 5 and 7 Field/Subject. The Schedule 5 Fields which do contain Matters are usually less extensive in their effect than the comparable Schedule 7 Subjects. Furthermore not all Schedule 5 Fields currently contain Matters.

As the report of the All Wales Convention (2009) noted, broader policies could be implemented under the Schedule 7 provisions than is usually the case with the Schedule 5 Matters, though there are broad provisions in some of the Fields in Schedule 5, notably those relating to social welfare, Field 15.

Greater clarity
As discussed above, Schedule 7 has been amended twice already, to clarify the powers (with the first Order in Council[20]) and to clarify the exceptions (with the second Order in Council[21]). However, both Schedule 5 and Schedule 7 reflect the political agreement at particular times about what London agrees to devolve to Wales; therefore inherent in the legislation is regular change in what is referred to above as 'the continuing development of the devolution settlement' (Welsh Affairs Select Committee, 2010, para. 50). The Government of Wales Act has provided for a mechanism (another Order in Council[22]) to add to the list of Fields/Subjects contained in Schedule 5 or 7.

Less restrictions on legislating in Wales
One issue which will also remain, regardless of the result of the referendum, is that there are or will remain general exceptions to the competence of the Assembly in the devolved Fields/Subjects.

Table 9.2

Contents of health and health services in Schedule 5 and Schedule 7

Schedule 5	Schedule 7
Field 9: Health and health services	**Subject 9: Health and health services**
Matter 9.1 inserted by Conversion Order SI 2007/910 – In force	Promotion of health. Prevention, treatment and alleviation of disease, illness, injury, disability and mental disorder. Control of disease. Family planning. Provision of health services, including medical, dental, ophthalmic, pharmaceutical and ancillary services and facilities. Clinical governance and standards of health care. Organisation and funding of national health service.
Matter 9.1	
Provision for and in connection with the provision of redress without recourse to civil proceedings in circumstances in which, under the law of England and Wales, qualifying liability in tort arises in connection with the provision of services (in Wales or elsewhere) as part of the health service in Wales.	
Matter 9.2 inserted by The National Assembly for Wales (Legislative Competence) (Health and Health Services and Social Welfare) Order 2010 – In Force	
Matter 9.2	*Exceptions –*
Assessment of mental health and treatment of mental disorder.	Abortion.
This matter does not include any of the following – (a) subjecting patients to – (i) compulsory attendance at any place for the purposes of assessment or treatment, (ii) compulsory supervision, or (iii) guardianship; (b) consent to assessment or treatment; (c) restraint; (d) detention.	Human genetics, human fertilisation, human embryology, surrogacy arrangements.
	Xenotransplantation.
For the purposes of this matter, 'treatment of mental disorder' means treatment to alleviate, or prevent a worsening of, a mental disorder or one or more of its symptoms or manifestations; and it includes (but is not limited to) nursing, psychological intervention, habilitation, rehabilitation and care.	Regulation of health professionals (including persons dispensing hearing aids).
	Poisons.
	Misuse of and dealing in drugs.
Interpretation of this field	Human medicines and medicinal products, including authorisations for use and regulation of prices.
In this field –	
'the health service in Wales' means the health service continued under section 1(1) of the National Health Service (Wales) Act 2006; 'illness' has the same meaning as in that Act;	Standards for, and testing of, biological substances (that is, substances the purity or potency of which cannot be adequately tested by chemical means).
'mental disorder' means any disorder or disability of the mind, apart from dependence on alcohol or drugs;	Vaccine damage payments.
'patient' has the same meaning as in that Act;	Welfare foods.
'personal injury' includes any disease and any impairment of a person's physical or mental health;	Health and Safety Commission, Health and Safety Executive and Employment Medical Advisory Service and provision made by health and safety regulations.
'qualifying liability in tort' means liability in tort owed in respect of or consequent upon personal injury or loss arising out of or in connection with breach of a duty of care owed to any person in connection with the diagnosis of illness or the care or treatment of any patient'.	

In contrast to the Scotland Act (1998), which displays 'Reserved Matters' (c. 46, Schedule 5), and the Northern Ireland Act (1998), which has 'Excepted' (c. 47, Schedule 2) and 'Reserved Matters' (c. 47, Schedule 3), in Wales there is no comprehensive legal list of non-devolved matters. In both Part 2 of Schedule 5 and Part 2 of Schedule 7 to the Government of Wales Act 2006, 'general restrictions' to the Assembly's legislative powers are set out. They are indeterminate in that, with provisos, they prevent the Assembly from legislating so as to adversely affect 'any functions possessed by Ministers of the Crown' which (as regards the Part 3 Measure powers) exist at any time without listing those powers and (as regards the Part 4 Act powers) exist at the time that Part 4 comes into force. Ascertaining the scope of such powers has proved to be problematic.

Schedule 7 is different from Schedule 5 in that it allows the Assembly to remove or amend any new function of a Minister of the Crown if it is created after the Assembly gains primary legislative powers.[23] Minister of the Crown functions which exist at the time of the coming into force of Part 4 can be removed or amended either with the consent of the Secretary of State or if such changes are consequential or incidental to an Assembly Act.[24] The All Wales Convention (2009, paragraph 3.10.28, pp. 59–60) describes this as for the 'purpose of proceeding with a Bill which is making provision in a devolved area.' If the Assembly wishes to impose new functions on a Minister of the Crown, the Secretary of State has to agree.

The list of restrictions and exceptions also differ in Schedules 5 and 7.[25] An example of this is the complex prohibitions in the Environment – Field 6, which has recently been the subject of an LCO. Currently in the provisions in Schedule 7, there are no prohibitions in the Environment – Subject 6, yet one can wonder about the extent to which the prohibitions expressly set out in Field 6 of Schedule 5 will apply to the Subject 6 Schedule 7 provisions.

Even if the exceptions to the twenty Fields/Subjects contained in both Schedules are becoming more apparent and are progressively being codified by Orders in Councils (in the LCOs and Orders amending Schedules 5 and 7), the current list of functions set out in Schedules 5 and 7 which are exercised by the Ministers of the Crown and on which the Assembly is consequently restricted from legislating is far from exhaustive. There may still be surprises regarding what the Assembly may not be able to legislate about (as, for example, was the case when the Assembly was unable to legislate on smacking children in 2008. This was considered by the UK government to be a matter relating to criminal law, which is a reserved area that does not appear in either Schedule). Under Schedule 7, the Assembly could remove or amend the function so that it is exercisable in Wales if either the Secretary of State agrees or it is considered to be ancillary to a legislative power possessed by the Assembly.

As a second point, Schedule 7 does not contain the restrictions relating to the criminal penalties a Measure could impose (currently a maximum of two years' imprisonment and a Level 5 fine).[26] Under Schedule 7, the Assembly could attach any criminal penalty to its laws. This is an interesting fact which may bring yet more weight to the arguments that there is a de facto separate jurisdiction in Wales, or that there could be one established shortly.

Greater stability
In relation to the contents of the Schedule 7, Subjects are already on the face of the 2006 Act. The provisions do not have to go through the long and somewhat tortuous LCO procedure that is necessary before new legislative powers can appear in Schedule 5. This is one of the fundamental changes that will occur if Part 4 comes into force. Schedule 5 and its associated LCO process, which often involves protracted prior discussions with Whitehall and Westminster, will disappear.

The result is that, apart from possible future Orders in Council under Part 4 amending the provisions of Schedule 7, the legislative powers of the Assembly will be better ascertained. There will be more legal certainty about the extent of the powers.

Continuing relations with Whitehall and Westminster
Because there is still no definitive list of topics on which the Assembly cannot legislate, there will remain doubts about exactly what is devolved or not devolved. While the Assembly's laws (both the Measures and the Acts) can make the same provisions as are made in Acts of Parliament, their legality can be challenged to a much greater extent than can that of Acts of Parliament. This means that it is very important for the extent of the Assembly's legislative powers to be as clearly agreed as possible. If the Assembly acts outside its powers, the law is then illegal. The Government of Wales Act provides for several safeguards against the Assembly acting beyond its powers:

1   Section 114 of the 2006 Act gives powers to the Secretary of State to intervene and prohibit the Assembly's Clerk from submitting an Assembly Act for Royal assent, if among other matters it is considered that the Act's provisions would have an adverse effect on matter which is not within the Assembly's Schedule 7 legislative powers.

2   Under paragraph 1 of Schedule 9 to the 2006 Act various questions which are defined as 'devolution issues' can be the subject of challenge before a Court or Tribunal. The questions include determining whether an Assembly's Part 3 Measure or Part 4 Act is within the Assembly's legislative competence. Proceedings may be instituted by the UK's Attorney General.

3   As well as proceedings for determining a devolution issue, any person can institute judicial review proceedings to question the legality of the Assembly's laws.

With the potential legal challenges that can be made at any time to legislation made by the Assembly, whether under Schedule 5 or 7, and the power of the Secretary of State to prevent Assembly legislation becoming law, it is probable that consultations will still have to continue with Whitehall if Schedule 7 comes into force to define precisely the scope of the exceptions to the competence of the Assembly. Will this mean a repeat of some of the long drawn-out conversations that have happened, for example with the Environment LCO (which took almost three years to see the light of day)? Only time will tell.

Also, conversations may need to continue with members of both Houses in Westminster on the occasions when Bills are placed before Parliament which affect the legislative and executive competencies of the Assembly and WAG. There is no apparent equivalent of the Sewel Convention[27] between Cardiff and Westminster. This is shown, for example, in the provisions of the Public Bodies Bill 2010[28] currently before Parliament, which shows that such a convention might exist with the Assembly Government but not the Assembly. Among many other matters the Public Bodies Bill seeks to make possible considerable changes to the functions of the Equality and Human Rights Commission under the Equality Act 2006 (Schedule 7). The Commission has a Wales Committee, which reports to the Assembly. There has been no consultation or agreement with the Assembly that the powers of this Committee should be changed. The Bill only provides for the consent of the Assembly Government to be given in the event of proposals to change the 2006 Act without any reference to the Assembly (see Trench, 2008).

PREPARATION FOR THE POST-REFERENDUM ERA IN WALES

As opinion polls in Wales, as well as the All Wales Convention, predicted a Yes vote, the Assembly and Wales started to prepare for the smooth operation of the new system, the amendment of Schedule 7 being only one aspect of this preparation.

Thus, in advance of the referendum, the Assembly Committees began to make preparations for the post-referendum era. The Business Committee prepared new Standing Orders, for example, while the Constitutional Affairs Committee looked at good drafting practice in relation to the Measures. In the run-up to the referendum, the Constitutional Affairs Committee started an inquiry into the drafting of Measures on 24 September 2010.[29] The Committee wanted views and opinions on issues of general significance that have arisen or could arise from the way in which Measures have been drafted. In particular, the Committee wanted to look at whether there were any lessons to be learnt from the experience that might be applied to future drafting of Measures. The Committee received only eight responses before moving on to take oral evidence from witnesses. In our evidence to the Committee, the Wales Governance Centre raised several points of concern which were also echoed by other witnesses: that there is too much legislation and regulation left to the Welsh Assembly Government to decide at a future time in subordinate legislation. Other aspects concern the legal language used in the Measures and their clarity, the improvement of the Assembly Government's explanatory memoranda, the regulatory appraisals carried out in relation to draft legislation and any other issues witnesses might want to raise.[30]

The report, which was published in February 2011, will contribute to the drafting of future Measures and, possibly, of Assembly Acts. It will surely help reach more consistency in the drafting of the Welsh Measures or Acts and help balance provisions to be included on the face of the Measures and those included in subordinate legislation. It will also help to achieve a higher level of scrutiny of legislation.

The Government of Wales Act requires a procedure for the making of Acts which contains at least three stages:

- vote on general principles
- consideration of details of a Bill
- Bill passed or rejected

The Assembly's own Standing Orders can add to these requirements. This has been the case already in relation to the LCO and Measure procedures. The Standing Orders review is being undertaken by the Business Committee, which is chaired by Lord Dafydd Elis-Thomas AM. The Committee issued a call for evidence, which closed on 24 September 2010.

It received twenty-four written responses to the consultation. So far, the Committee has been working on its own internal documents and has not called any witnesses to give oral evidence.[31] The debate in plenary to agree the new Standing Orders is expected to take place just before the dissolution of the Assembly in March.

CONCLUSION

The constitutional and legal framework in Wales has changed considerably in the last four years and this year has seen the winding down of the current devolution settlement. Wales will now see yet another constitutional transformation, which will be fascinating to watch and which will bring further challenges to all those involved in devolution in Wales.

NOTES

[1] SI 2010 No. 1838, http://www.assemblywales.org/bus-home/bus-legislation/bus-legislation-progress-lcos-measures/bus-legislation-progress-lcos-measures-archive.htm#sustainablehousing

[2] http://www.assemblywales.org/bus-home/bus-legislation/bus-legislation-guidance/bus-legislation-guidance-documents/legislation_fields/schedule-5.htm

[3] http://www.assemblywales.org/bus-home/bus-legislation/bus-leg-legislative-competence-orders/bus-legislation-lco-2009-hlg-3.htm

[4] http://www.assemblywales.org/bus-home/bus-committees/bus-committees-scrutiny-committees/bus-committees-third-els-home/bus-committees-third-els-inquiry/bus-committees-third-els-inquiry-lco.htm

[5] http://wales.gov.uk/newsroom/firstminister/2010/100713legislation/;jsessionid=cK3mNHLDn31F381Lpn8WW7ppXXbXFlp0F4JwdcRmkKPrTgWfvm3T!–1787364033?lang=en

[6] http://www.legislation.gov.uk/ukpga/2009/20/contents

[7] http://www.legislation.gov.uk/ukpga/2009/23/contents

[8] Matters 16.2 and 16.3 inserted by section 310 of the Marine and Coastal Access Act 2009.

[9] Matters 12.6 and 12.7 inserted by section 33 of the Local Democracy, Economic Development and Construction Act 2009.

[10] Clause 27and Schedule 6.

[11] http://www.opsi.gov.uk/acts/acts2010/pdf/ukpga_20100025_en.pdf

[12] See, for example, the Assembly's website: http://www.assemblywales.org/bus-home/bus-legislation/bus-legislation-guidance/bus-legislation-guidance-documents/legislation_fields/schedule-5.htm

[13] 'Since its creation, the Assembly has made 23 bids for primary legislation, no fewer than 17 of which have resulted in legislation or proposals for legislation, often in Bills with a significant number of Welsh clauses. However, as the Richard Commission noted 'even with goodwill on both sides, there are practical constraints on the achievement of the Assembly's legislative requirements' (Wales Office, 2005, Para. 1.20).

[14] http://services.parliament.uk/bills/2010–11/publicbodieshl.html

[15] See, for example, the restructured website Wales Legislation Online: http://www.wales-legislation.org.uk

[16] Part 4 Acts of the Assembly *Referendum*; s. 103. Referendum about commencement of Assembly Act provisions; s. 104. Proposal for referendum by Assembly; s. 105.

Commencement of Assembly Act provisions; s. 106. Effect on Measures of commencement of Assembly Act provisions.

[17] Schedule 6 – Referendums on commencement of Assembly Act provisions.
[18] See   http://www.electoralcommission.org.uk/elections/upcoming-elections-and-referendums/wales/referendum
[19] The draft Referendum Order (National Assembly for Wales Referendum (Assembly Act Provisions) (Referendum Question, Date of Referendum, Etc.) Order 2010). The Order was accompanied by a second Order: The draft Expenses Limits Order (National Assembly for Wales Referendum (Assembly Act Provisions) (Limit on Referendum Expenses Etc.) Order 2010).
[20] The National Assembly for Wales (Legislative Competence) (Amendment of Schedule 7 to the Government of Wales Act 2006) Order 2007, SI. 2007/2143.
[21] The National Assembly for Wales (Legislative Competence) (Amendment of Schedule 7 to the Government of Wales Act 2006) Order 2010, SI. 2010 No. 2968.
[22] Government of Wales Act 2006, s. 109; see also s. 95.
[23] Government of Wales Act 2006, Schedule 7, paragraph 1(1).
[24] Government of Wales Act 2006, Schedule 7, paragraph 6(1) and (2).
[25] See in particular the evidence from the Wales Governance Centre, EV 12 (Welsh Affairs Select Committee, 2010, pp. 35–7).
[26] Government of Wales Act 2006, Schedule 5, Part 2, paragraph 2.
[27] 'The UK Government has agreed that there are 3 categories of provision that should not normally be enacted in primary legislation at Westminster unless the Scottish Parliament has given its consent'. See http://www.scotland.gov.uk/About/Sewel/Background
[28] HL Bill 025 2010–11, http://services.parliament.uk/bills/2010–11/publicbodieshl/documents.html
[29] http://www.assemblywales.org/bus-home/bus-committees/bus-committees-perm-leg/bus-committees-legislation-dissolved/bus-committees-third-sleg-home/bus-committes-third-sleg-current_inquiries/bus-leg-ca-inquiry-drafting_of_measures.htm
[30] http://www.assemblywales.org/ca-msres-inqry-cnslt-letter-e.pdf
[31] http://www.assemblywales.org/bus-home/bus-committees/bus-committees-other-committees/bus-committees-third-bc-home/business_committee_-_review_of_standing_orders_page.htm   http://www.assemblywales.org/bus-home/bus-committees/bus-committees-other-committees/bus-committees-third-bc-home.htm

REFERENCES

All Wales Convention (2009). 'Report', http://allwalesconvention.org/getinformed/thereport/thereport/?lang=en (accessed 28 December 2010).
Navarro, M. and Lambert, D. (2009). 'Bypassing the Assembly', *Agenda*, 37, Spring, 34–6.
Trench, A. (2010). *Getting legislation seriously wrong: the Public Bodies bill*, http://devolutionmatters.wordpress.com/2010/11/08/getting-legislation-seriously-wrong-the-public-bodies-bill/ (accessed 28 December 2010).

Wales Office (2005). *Better Governance for Wales*, White Paper (Cm. 6582, June), http://www.official-documents.gov.uk/document/cm65/6582/6582.pdf (accessed 28 December 2010).

Welsh Affairs Select Committee (2010). *2nd Report: The proposed amendment of Schedule 7 to the Government of Wales Act 2006*, HC603, 22 November 2010, http://www.publications.parliament.uk/pa/cm201011/cmselect/cmwelaf/603/60302.htm (accessed 28 December 2010).

Western Mail (2010). 'The facts on what greater Assembly powers could do for Wales', 18 September, p. 20.

BOOK REVIEW

Delyth Morris (ed.) (2010) *Welsh in the Twenty-First*
Century, **Cardiff: University of Wales Press**
ISBN 978-0-7083-2299-4

What difference has a decade made? Glyn Williams and Delyth Morris's
Language Planning and Language Use: Welsh in a Global Age (2000, p. 656)
presented a five-stage model of language survival, in which an initial vision
for the language's future (idealism) leads to activism (protest), acceptance of
the language in certain domains (legitimacy), gradual strategic and official use
(institutionalization) and ultimately extension to an 'optimum range of social
situations' (normalization). Ten years into the twenty-first century, the papers in
this collection suggest that the assertion made then that Welsh is poised between
the fourth and fifth stages remains true. The whole volume has the patient,
unexcitable, optimistic but dutiful tone of a progress report. However, for this
reviewer at least, an Arts academic adjusting his eyes to the light and shade of
Social Sciences methodology, it reads as an implicit commentary on a more
profound cultural shift. What follows, then, is a survey, some analysis and a little
harmless nostalgia.

From a post-Marxian perspective, Glyn Williams tackles the knowledge
economy, arguing that future planning needs to move away from 'static concepts
of language maintenance and language shift', to focus on 'language use as social
practice' (p. 29), abandon 'the preoccupation with Welsh as a minority language'
and reconfigure it as 'as one of several languages confronting the effects of the
new [globalized] economic order' (p. 31). Colin H. Williams meanwhile inves-
tigates Welsh-language provision across the public sector in the wake of the
1993 Welsh Language Act and its attendant schemes. He notes, *inter alia*, that
successful implementation depends on supportive senior management, training and resources to a greater extent than language density, and concludes that
legislation must be supported by the 'socialization processes' of civil society,
especially education, to develop 'an ability and desire to make the most of the
opportunities available' (p. 59).

Colin Baker asks fundamental questions about the nature of bilingual education. His survey of models – from transitional provision, in which pupils
move gradually from using home language to school language, through the

'designated bilingual' pattern widely used in English-speaking areas of Wales, whereby subjects other than English language and literature are taught in Welsh, to dual-language models in which languages are used more equally in parallel contexts – concludes that 'the [common] aim is to separate languages, maintain boundaries, and compartmentalize their use' (p. 64). Against this assumption of diglossia (the use of separate languages in different contexts and for different purposes) he outlines other, integrated, approaches, most especially 'translan-guaging'. In her paper, Delyth Morris confirms, through meticulous quantitative analysis of samples of young people across twelve areas with varying percent-ages of Welsh speakers (from Bala to Ystradgynlais), that an increase in 'situ-ations where the use of Welsh is normative' (p. 98) is essential to successful language planning. Although it presents useful evidence for youth groups seek-ing funding, its conclusion is academically significant, too, for what it says by implication about the relative role of education, peer groups and home language. Enlli Môn Thomas and Robert Mayr offer a lively account of language acquisi-tion with reference to definitive features of Welsh (specifically mutation and gender, although syntax would have been a useful additional category). Its find-ing – that these aspects of the language are cognitive skills which even Welsh speakers need time and opportunity to practise and master – raises interesting questions about learning 'readiness'.

In a longitudinal study of census returns between 1971 and 2001, Hywel M. Jones presents a welter of evidence that out-migration is a more significant factor in the fall in young adult Welsh speakers than the failure to retain the language. His second conclusion – that Welsh speakers are less likely to out-migrate, and that this holds true for those born outside Wales who have learned Welsh and thereby increased their social ties – has clear implications for teach-ing and learning and is an obvious topic for further research.

Out-migration is balanced by in-migration in the closing paper, in which Howard Davis, Graham Day and Angela Dukakis-Smith survey attitudes towards bilingualism among English in-migrants who have settled in three areas in Conwy and Gwynedd. The study confirms previous researchers' findings that attitudes are overwhelmingly positive and that education is a key determinant of integration. It revisits, too, the perennial question of how to take a willing-ness to learn and accessible opportunities to do so 'to the next stage, so that basic [language] skills are embedded in everyday interaction, reinforced and encouraged to develop' (p. 164). The creation of a 'virtuous circle' of teaching learning and integration, the authors conclude, offers the prospect of language regeneration through those who have 'not previously been identified with the Welsh core' (p. 165).

Those who instinctively use the discourse of territoriality to conceptualize the state of the Welsh language will find this collection reassuring. The essays mention heartlands and hinterlands, incursion and preservation, and – yes – the volume contains the familiar distribution graphs and even the obligatory shaded map. However, for this reviewer at least, there are curious absences at its heart.

First, there is no grand narrative of struggle, resistance, loss and gain that informs – see for instance, Clive Betts's *Culture in Crisis* (1976), Meic Stephens's *The Welsh Language Today* (1973, 1979) and Janet Davies's *The Welsh Language* (1993). For protest, read policy; for culture, accommodation; for purity, procedure. The story of Welsh has lost its eschatology. There is no sense that it is in a last-ditch battle for survival.

Second, the fortunes of the language appear divorced from any story of individual effort and collective voluntary activism. The index to this volume contains just one reference to Cymdeithas yr Iaith (the Welsh Language Society), none to *papurau bro*, Nant Gwrtheyrn, Merched y Wawr, Gwynfor Evans or Saunders Lewis.

If Welsh has no champions, it has no enemies here either. The language question, to judge by the evidence presented here, has been answered with an acquiescent nod; the battle has ended in a truce. In this new normative model what could be termed the historiography of resentment has been expunged. From the Acts of Union in 1536 and 1542, via the 1847 Blue Books, the Welsh Not, the occupation of land by central and local government at Epynt and Tryweryn in the mid-twentieth century and the campaigns for the use of Welsh in public life, broadcasting and education towards its end, the language has defined itself as the humane counterweight to a series of indifferent or hostile hegemonies. These have gone. The promotion of Welsh has become a marketing exercise. Its remaining enemy is consumer indifference.

Absent, by association, is the notion of the language as a medium of cultural continuity and transmission. This book contains no hint that maintenance of Welsh represents the defence and restoration of a lost or threatened tradition. In abandoning its eschatology, it has lost its ecology too.

Finally, although the papers reproduced here refer to natural Welsh-speaking areas, they convey no sense that these represent a locus of cultural authenticity, or that there are degrees and gradations of Welshness. They do not suggest to the reader what all Welsh speakers instinctively believe: that there is something more 'echt' about the status of Welsh in Bala, say, than in Bargoed or even Barmouth.

None of the above is a criticism of the book for not being something that it never set out to be. I admit, however, that they are prompted by something close to *nostalgie de boue*. There was an attraction for language campaigners in the 1980s, say, in the paradox of high-minded transgression, conservative revolution, the separateness that made an overwhelmingly (if exclusively) white, middle-class movement identify with the wretched of the earth; but I hope that they raise a more serious question, too. If Welsh loses the otherness that has characterized its understanding of itself since the Renaissance, loses the adrenalin rush of anxiety for its own future, what will it be? Judging by the evidence reported and analysed here, the language that policy directives, targets and positivism seek to save will be a different thing from what was in danger of being lost.

REFERENCES

Betts, C. (1976). *Culture in Crisis*, Wirral: Ffynnon Press.
Davies, J. (1993). *The Welsh Language*, Cardiff: University of Wales Press.
Stephens, M. (1973, 1979). *The Welsh Language Today*, Llandysul: Gwasg Gomer.
Williams, G. and Morris, D. (2000). *Language Planning and Language Use: Welsh in a Global Age*, Cardiff: University of Wales Press.

T. Robin Chapman
Aberystwyth University

GUIDELINES FOR CONTRIBUTORS OF ARTICLES

GENERAL POLICY

Contemporary Wales is an annual review of economic and social developments and trends in Wales. It provides an authoritative analysis drawing upon the most up-to-date research, and represents the only comprehensive source of analysis across the range of economic and social research about Wales. It is a Centre for Advanced Welsh and Celtic Studies journal published once a year, and contains articles selected for their quality and significance to contemporary society in Wales. Submissions are refereed and are accepted for publication on the assumption that they have not been previously published and are not currently being submitted to any other journal. The normal maximum length for articles is about 5,000 words. An abstract of up to 200 words is required.

Contemporary Wales welcomes articles submitted for publication in Welsh. English-language abstracts of articles in Welsh will be included in the journal. In addition, we will endeavour to secure funding for English translations of the articles following hardcopy publication in the journal. Translations will be available on the *Contemporary Wales* pages of the University of Wales Press website.

COPYRIGHT

Copyright in the articles in printed and electronic forms will be retained by the University of Wales, but the right to reproduce their own articles by photocopying is granted to the contributors provided that the copies are not offered for sale. Contributors should obtain the necessary permission to use material already protected by copyright.

PREPARATION OF TYPESCRIPTS

If possible, please email papers as Word attachments to one of the editors:

Paul Chaney: chaneyp@cardiff.ac.uk
Elin Royles: ear@aber.ac.uk
Andrew Thompson: athompso@glam.ac.uk

If email is not possible, please post three copies on single-sided A4 to one of the editors:

Paul Chaney
Cardiff School of Social Sciences
The Glamorgan Building
King Edward VII Avenue
Cardiff CF10 3WT

Elin Royles
Sefydliad Gwleidyddiaeth Cymru
Adran Gwleidyddiaeth Ryngwladol
Prifysgol Aberystwyth
Aberystwyth
Ceredigion SY23 3FE

Andrew Thompson
School of Humanities and Social Sciences
University of Glamorgan
Pontypridd CF37 1DL

The editors can provide further guidance as to the form and style in which contributions should be submitted, but the following gives a brief guide for potential contributors. Additional general information is available on the UWP website, http://www.uwp.co.uk/book_desc/cw.html under the heading 'Guidelines for presentation of texts for publication'. Articles submitted should be typed (Times New Roman, 12 point) using double spacing with wide margins, unjustified on the right. Pages should be numbered throughout consecutively.

PREPARATION OF TYPESCRIPTS ON DISK

Once a paper has been accepted for publication, an electronic version should be sent to the editors by e-mail. Authors should retain a back-up copy of their papers electronically and as a printout. Word versions of the paper are preferred, but other softwares may be acceptable – please contact University of Wales Press for further information. The authors would be grateful if contributors would submit accepted articles in house style according to the guidelines provided here and in line with copies of the journal.

Notes and references
Notes and references should be supplied at the end of the article, also in double spacing. Notes should be numbered consecutively. References should be in alphabetical order of author (see below for style).

Tables, maps and diagrams
These will eventually appear within the printed page but should be provided on separate pages in the typescript and their position indicated by a marginal note in the text. Tables and figures should be provided in separate Excel or tiff files, not embedded in Word. Some other kinds of software may be acceptable – please contact University of Wales Press for further information. All figures, diagrams, maps, charts, etc. must be saved in *black only*, not full colour, and should be saved at 1,200 pixels per inch.

Diagrams and maps may be submitted in the best possible condition on paper if the contributor is unable to supply a disk version. References in the text to illustrative material should take the form 'Table 1', 'Table 2', etc. for tables and 'Figure 1', 'Figure 2', etc. for other illustrations including maps. Do not use references such as 'in the following diagram' since there is no guarantee that pagination will allow this precise positioning. The tables and figures will eventually be labelled 'Table 1.1', 'Figure 2.1' etc. according to the number of the chapter in which they appear.

STYLE OF TEXT

Quotations within running text should be in single quote marks (double for quotes within quotes). Quotations of more than forty-five words should be indented without quotation marks and with a line space before and after.

Underline or type in italic any words which are to appear in italic. In English-language articles, single words or short phrases in any language other than

English should be in italic, but longer quotations in another language should be in roman within single quotation marks.

Dates should be expressed as 1 January 1999; the 1990s; the twentieth century (but 'a twentieth-century record'); 1988–9; 1914–18 (not 1914–8). Numbers up to ninety-nine should be spelt out in full except in a list of statistics or in percentages (e.g. 25 per cent).

Use -ize endings when given as an alternative to -ise, for example, realize, privatize, organize; but note analyse, franchise, advertise.

Capitalization should be kept to a minimum in the text; for titles, initial capitals should only be used when attached to a personal name (thus 'President Clinton', but 'the president of the United States').

Journal style is that 'south' in 'south Wales' should take lower case (also 'north', 'east', 'west' Wales/England etc.), since this is not a specific political, administrative or geographical region. South America or South Africa would take upper case since the term refers to the name of a continent or political entity respectively. When referring to a specific area for economic assessment, e.g. the South West of England, upper case may be used for clarity.

REFERENCES

References in the text should be given in the Harvard system in the following format:

(Dower, 1977), (Welsh Office, 1986), (White and Higgs, 1997), (Gripaios et al., 1995a).

The form of references listed under the heading 'References' at the end of the text should be as follows:

Ambrose, P. (1974). *The Quiet Revolution*, London: Chatto and Windus.

Buller, H. and Hoggart, K. (1994b). 'The social integration of British home owners into French rural communities', *Journal of Rural Studies*, 10, 2, 197–210.

Dower, M. (1977). 'Planning aspects of second homes', in Coppock, J. T. (ed.), *Second Homes: Curse or Blessing?*, Oxford: Pergamon Press.

Note the use of lower case for all initial letters except the first in an article or unpublished thesis title, and capitals for initial letters of all significant words in book and journal titles.

Publications by the same author in the same year should be differentiated by means of a, b, c etc. after the year of publication, both in the text reference and in the list of references.

PROOFS AND COMPLIMENTARY COPIES

Checking of proofs will be done by editors, with contributors expected to reply promptly to queries. Upon publication, contributors will receive one complimentary copy of the issue of the journal in which their article appears and a PDF version of their paper.

In addition, as a contributor to a University of Wales Press publication, after 09/10 authors can purchase any UWP titles, including journals (inc. hardcopies of CW), at 25 per cent discount. The contact for this is Charlotte Austin at UWP department (c.austin@wales.ac.uk)/ or by the web at *http://www.uwp.co.uk.*